T0373731

THE
GRIFFITH
WARS

TOM GILLING AND TERRY JONES

THE
GRIFFITH
WARS

THE POWERFUL TRUE STORY OF
DONALD MACKAY'S MURDER
AND THE TOWN THAT STOOD UP TO THE MAFIA

ALLEN&UNWIN
SYDNEY • MELBOURNE • AUCKLAND • LONDON

First published in 2017
This edition published in 2019
Copyright © Tom Gilling and Terry Jones 2017

All photographs reproduced courtesy of Terry Jones, former editor and
photographer/journalist *The Area News*

All rights reserved. No part of this book may be reproduced or transmitted
in any form or by any means, electronic or mechanical, including
photocopying, recording or by any information storage and retrieval
system, without prior permission in writing from the publisher. The
Australian *Copyright Act 1968* (the Act) allows a maximum of one chapter
or 10 per cent of this book, whichever is the greater, to be photocopied
by any educational institution for its educational purposes provided
that the educational institution (or body that administers it) has given a
remuneration notice to the Copyright Agency (Australia) under the Act.

Allen & Unwin
83 Alexander Street
Crows Nest NSW 2065
Australia
Phone: (61 2) 8425 0100
Email: info@allenandunwin.com
Web: www.allenandunwin.com

Cataloguing-in-Publication details are available
from the National Library of Australia
www.trove.nla.gov.au

ISBN 978 1 76087 503 9

Typeset by Midland Typesetters, Australia
Printed and bound in Australia by Griffin Press

10 9 8 7 6 5 4 3 2

MIX
Paper from
responsible sources
FSC® C009448

The paper in this book is FSC® certified.
FSC® promotes environmentally responsible,
socially beneficial and economically viable
management of the world's forests.

Contents

CHAPTER 1

Aussie Bob takes a punt

Domenico Trimboli was 33 years old when he and his wife, Saveria, bought Farm 869, near Griffith, in the heart of the Murrumbidgee Irrigation Area in far western New South Wales. They were among the thousands of poor Italian migrants who began arriving in Australia in the 1920s.

In the early days, living conditions were primitive, with homes made from hessian bags whitewashed inside and out (they gave the settlement its name, Bagtown) and bare earth floors. Many of the early soldier-settlers walked away broken-hearted, unable to eke an existence from their tiny plots of land, but their places were soon taken by migrants eager to create a new life for themselves in their adopted country. Crops grew in the rust-coloured soil without natural rainfall, watered by the mighty Murrumbidgee River. To those like Domenico and Saveria Trimboli, accustomed to the hardship of life in Calabria, New South Wales appeared a land of hope and opportunity.

The vegetables and fruit trees Domenico planted on his two-acre holding were enough to support Saveria and the three young children they had brought with them from Italy. It didn't take long for Trimboli—now known as Domenic, and a naturalised Australian citizen—to pick up the language as he travelled around Bagtown selling his prize cauliflowers from the back of a horse-drawn cart.

Like their father, the children soon acquired Australian names: Joe (the first born), Josie and Elizabeth. All three were well-behaved children who adapted well to their new country, which was slower to adapt to them. The olive-skinned Calabrian and Sicilian migrants were commonly referred to by Australians as dagoes or wogs, their family traditions and customs viewed with suspicion by the district's Anglo-Saxon pioneers.

In the cane fields of far north Queensland, Calabrian men bound to the old hierarchical ways had formed clans, intimidating and extorting from their fellow countrymen, burning the crops and poisoning the livestock of those who refused to pay. Further resistance was met with bombings, woundings and murder. Although the Queensland cane fields lay thousands of kilometres from the orchards and gardens of the Murrumbidgee Irrigation Area, news of the violence spread quickly among the migrant families in Griffith. They could leave Italy but they could not escape the mafia.

On 26 January 1932 Rocco Trimarchi, who had moved to New South Wales after several years on the cane fields, was shot dead at his farm in Griffith. Trimarchi's son, Samuel, was convicted of the murder, although an autopsy found that two guns of different calibres had been used. Regarded by police as having been 'the head of a branch of the Camorra Society', the elder Trimarchi was Griffith's first godfather.

Several Italian men witnessed the shooting but a police report noted that nearly all of them 'gave different evidence to that in their statements ... which showed that they had been instructed in what to say by some person in the meantime'. Was Rocco Trimarchi's murder the result of a family feud? Was it an honour killing? Those who knew were not saying.

■ ■ ■

Domenic and Saveria Trimboli's second son, Bruno, was born on 19 March 1931. The first of the Trimboli children to be born in Australia, Bruno was a happy-go-lucky boy, average at school and with no obvious talents to set him apart from the other Italian kids in a country town full of Italian kids. His parents worried for his future. Older brother Joe was destined for the army and sisters Josie and Betty were expected, like the daughters of other Italian families, to find good husbands. But where did that leave Bruno?

It was obvious that the Trimbolis' two-acre farm would not be enough to support Bruno as well as his parents. For a young man in a country town, the only financial security seemed to lie in a trade. But Bruno had no desire to spend the rest of his life as a plumber or a painter. Nor did he have much interest in getting a job in a bank or post office.

As a child, Bruno Trimboli had done his share of chipping weeds and picking vegetables, working ten to twelve hours a day from sun-up to sundown. Bruno was not afraid of physical work but hard labour under the hot Australian sun was not his idea of a future. While his schoolmates settled down to work on their family farms, Bruno decided to seek his fortune in the city.

In Sydney wartime memories were still fresh enough for an Italian name to be a handicap, so Bruno Trimboli adopted the name Robert, which became the quintessentially Australian 'Bob'. At the same time he changed his surname, from Trimboli to Trimbole. With the new name came a new job as an apprentice mechanic at Pioneer Tours.

Affable and easy going, Bob Trimbole had no trouble making friends. 'Aussie Bob', as some were already calling him, also started to make a name for himself as a gambler, but for that he needed a steady supply of cash. While his days were spent working on bus engines, nights found Bob playing two-up and baccarat in Sydney's illegal gambling dens. Many of the illegal games were run by starting price (or SP) bookies. Somebody at the game was always good for a tip, a sure thing crying out for a punt, and it wasn't long before Aussie Bob was a fixture at the track.

Bob was not a big drinker. Until the mid-1920s alcohol had been prohibited in the Murrumbidgee Irrigation Area and many of the migrant families had grown used to going without. Bob would drink a beer socially, or have a few glasses of wine with a meal, but he prided himself on his sobriety.

In those days Sydney's pubs and hotels were still governed by the six-o'clock lockout, but some landlords found cunning ways to continue trading out of hours: hoisting blackout blinds on windows after 6pm; serving longneck bottles; setting up kegs of beer in back rooms that could only be entered by patrons who knew a special code-knock. In some places regulars sat around tables with tea cups and saucers in front of them, along with glasses of water and ice and a teapot containing a full bottle of Scotch, just in case the police turned up to check on the curfew.

Their ingenuity was matched by the illegal gambling bosses, who set up games in warehouses, fruit-packing sheds and abattoirs. Their cockatoos would pass the word to taxi drivers about where the game was being played. The organisers—there might be two or three in the bigger towns—had an uncanny knack of knowing when a police raid was imminent. The police were happy enough to turn a blind eye in return for a few quid.

It was an exciting time for young Bob Trimbole, who watched and learned.

When Bob was flush, he had the chance to win serious money. He returned favours by staking mates down on their luck. In the illegal two-up dens Bob would spend hours throwing pennies for a run of heads or tails. When Bob was on a winning streak he was generosity personified: he insisted on paying for everything. But when his luck was out he would not hesitate to beg a loan.

Bob was hooked. Smitten, too, by a young secretary he had met, Joan Quested. 'Joanie' was smart and had a great sense of humour. They had fun together, and for Bob's sake she was prepared to put up with the gambling. They married in Sydney on 18 April 1952. After the wedding, she persuaded him to move back to Griffith. Joan wanted him to have his own business, an automotive workshop. Griffith, she thought, would give them the chance to get ahead. And it would take Bob away from the temptations of Sydney's gambling dens.

Moving to Griffith was what Joan wanted, so Bob was willing to give it a try. But he was less confident than Joan about his ability to run a business. He looked around for something different, thought briefly about taking over his father's farm. But two acres could never be anything more than a hobby-farm and what Bob needed was an income.

The newlyweds lived on the Trimboli farm for seven months before Bob's parents, Domenic and Saveria, decided to sell up and move to the Sydney suburb of Fairfield. Stopping Bob from gambling was not easy, but Joan convinced him that they would have no worldly possessions while he continued to gamble their money away. In 1953 the Trimboles leased premises for an automotive garage in Olympic Street, Griffith, across the road from the town swimming pool. They called it the Pool Garage. Bob and Joan lived next door. The first of their four children, Gayelle Joan, arrived on 17 January 1954. She would be followed by Glenda Julie on 21 May 1955; Robert Kenneth on 7 November 1956; and Craig Grainger on 15 March 1959.

The business started as a repair garage. Later Bob installed petrol bowsers and added a panel beating and spray painting workshop. Joan knew that Bob was taking money from the business to bet. He played cards with men he met at the garage. In April, games of ANZAC Day two-up were played in the fruit packing sheds. The biggest was at Alpen's trucking shed, where hundreds and thousands of pounds changed hands in an all-night game, some of it going to the local Black & Whites Football Club.

Griffith, Joan was finding out, was not the sleepy country town she had imagined, but at least it was keeping her husband away from the sleazy characters he had rubbed shoulders with in the city gambling dens. While living in Griffith meant fewer opportunities for Bob to get near a race track, there was hardly a hotel or club in town that didn't have its own resident SP bookie.

Trimbole would seek out the bookies at the Griffith Hotel, the Victoria Hotel and the Coronation Club, a haunt known almost universally as the 'Coro'. The club never seemed to shut. Popular with journalists, cops and out-of-town lawyers, it had a handful of poker machines and hosted the odd game of cards. Ladies of the night could often be seen loitering in the shadows out the back.

Revelling in the role of successful businessman, Trimbole made plenty of friends among the town's Calabrian community. With his easy command of the 'Australian' language, Aussie Bob quickly gained respect among impressionable members of the Romeo, Sergi, Catanzariti, Agresta, Perre, Zirilli and Barbaro families—clans with strong ties to the southern Italian secret society known as 'La Famiglia'.

There was one man Trimbole was especially keen to befriend: the 'Griffith godfather', Pietro 'Peter' Calipari (also spelt Callipari and Callipare). Calipari owned a shoe shop, Riverina Shoes, in the main street of Griffith, in whose basement he would preside over meetings to sort out business and family disputes among Calabrian families. Since arriving in Griffith in 1951 from the Calabrian town of Platì, Calipari had won esteem while accumulating wealth far beyond what might have been expected from a simple shoe shop. Trimbole and Calipari both belonged to La Famiglia, but the two men moved in different circles, Calipari appearing more interested in cultivating Anglo-Saxon professionals—politicians, lawyers, accountants, real estate agents and property valuers—while Trimbole mixed more with the Calabrians.

Calipari was a confidant of La Famiglia's elders while Trimbole belonged to the second generation. Although charming in person, Calipari was guarded and calculating, a sharp contrast to the impulsive and spendthrift Trimbole, whose gambling was already putting a strain on his marriage. On his way past Riverina Shoes to the Victoria Hotel,

Trimbole would wave a hand and the pair might exchange a few words, but Calipari made sure Trimbole knew his place.

At home, Joan was struggling to get by. The garage was now no more than a front for her husband's gambling. If Trimbole had a win on the horses, there would be money to pay the household bills, but often he didn't win. The phone was cut off. If an important call had to be made, Trimbole would borrow the phone of a neighbouring business. Electricity was going to be next. On 1 November 1968, despite his claims that the garage was successful, Robert Trimbole was declared bankrupt, owing $10,986.63. Within days, the Pool Garage burnt down, the flames destroying Trimbole's commercial assets and all his records. Luckily for Trimbole, the business was insured for a sum of around $10,000. The money would have allowed Trimbole to settle some of his debts but the insurance company smelt a rat—it suspected the fire had been deliberately lit—and refused to pay out.

With her daughters, Glenda and Gayelle, in their teens, Joan felt the family needed somewhere bigger. After the garage fire the family shifted temporarily to Farm 1811, Lake Wyangan before moving to a Housing Commission home on a dog-leg road on Scenic Hill, overlooking Griffith. Money was so tight that Joan had to rely on the generosity of neighbours, borrowing a pint of milk, a half loaf of bread, half pound of butter or few cups of sugar when she needed them. That was how country people lived in those days, neighbours sharing garden produce and passing food staples over a backyard fence, small amounts of money changing hands to tide the recipient over 'until payday'.

It had been a while since Bob Trimbole's last payday. Whatever money he had went on gambling. Joan bowed to the inevitable and started looking for work. It wasn't long before she was helping visitors as Griffith's first part-time tourist officer.

Bob, meanwhile, found himself a new job with a company called Atlantic Amusements that supplied and serviced amusement machines. The machines were often converted to illegal gaming and leased or sold to gambling clubs for a cut of the profits. Bob's 'office' in Griffith seemed to be the Coro Club bar, managed by his mate Archie Molinaro. The Coro's relief barman, Freddy Guglielmini, serviced pinball machines for Atlantic.

The job took Trimbole all over the state but exactly what he did was a mystery to Joan. Bob seemed incapable of giving a straight answer. Family friends put Bob's secretiveness down to his embarrassment at being an undischarged bankrupt. He told Joan the work involved installing and repairing pinball machines but she had her doubts.

The trips away became longer. Bob would return with wads of cash which he attributed to gambling. In years to come Joan would recall Bob walking through the house tossing money in the air, spreading banknotes across the kitchen table and entreating her to 'buy something nice' for herself and the kids.

For all his faults, Bob Trimbole loved his family. All the children were good swimmers and he and Joan enjoyed going to the Olympic pool to watch them race. When Bob promised her that the family's fortunes had turned for the better, Joan wanted to believe him.

CHAPTER 2

Guns and godfathers

Antonio Sergi (born 29 October 1935) met Bob Trimbole soon after arriving in Griffith in October 1952 with his parents, Giuseppe and Maria. Having anglicised his own name, Bob took to calling Antonio 'Tony' and the name stuck. Trimbole was in his early twenties and Tony Sergi in his late teens. (Tony Sergi would later establish a winery at Tharbogang. In future he will be referred to as 'Winery Tony'.)

The Sergis, like the Trimbolis, came from Platì, Calabria, a town renowned for being a stronghold of the Calabrian mafia or 'ndrangheta. Bob always took an interest in new arrivals from Calabria, especially when they came from a large family like the Sergis who commanded serious respect back in Platì.

Giuseppe Sergi and his family lived for a year with Giuseppe's brother Franceso (Frank) on Farm 197, Hanwood, before moving to Farm 970, which was owned by Roy Catanzariti. (When Catanzariti sold the farm, it was bought by another of Giuseppe's brothers, Domenico 'Mick' Sergi.)

Giuseppe's prospects improved when he bought Farm 1305, a 21-acre (eight-hectare) property at Tharbogang, west of Griffith. Planted with orange and apricot trees, the farm promised a stable future far removed from the precariousness of their lives in Calabria. There would be setbacks—a flood drowned many trees—but otherwise Farm 1305 was able to provide a subsistence living for Giuseppe and Maria Sergi and their seven children.

Other Calabrian families bought properties in Tharbogang, Hanwood and Yoogali. These farms typically grew citrus or deciduous fruit, with 'cash' crops of onions, pumpkins or melons grown between rows of trees. A concentration of Calabrian-owned farms near Tharbogang on either side of the Griffith to Hillston railway track would become a regional bastion for La Famiglia.

Simon Mackenzie, a Griffith solicitor who had taught himself to understand the native dialects of his Calabrian clients, showed the migrant farmers how to invest their hard-earned surpluses to get them through the inevitable bad years. The flow of dividends brought a multimillion-dollar cash economy to Griffith. Mackenzie's work on behalf of his Italian clients impressed the godfather, Peter Calipari, who made sure the lion's share of Calabrian business went to Mackenzie's firm. Calipari would later say, 'The Italian people of Griffith should erect a monument to Simon, he is helping to make everyone wealthy.'

■ ■ ■

It wasn't just Italians who built a new future for themselves in Bagtown. Five years before Domenico Trimboli arrived with his wife and children from Platì, a Newcastle fitter and turner named Len Mackay decided to try his luck in the new township on the banks of the Murrumbidgee River. No farmer himself, Mackay knew there was money to be made from selling farmers the things they needed. He opened a furniture store on the southern side of the main irrigation canal, one of thousands of kilometres of water supply channels snaking across the flat landscape. The channels carrying water from the Murrumbidgee had already begun to turn virgin bush into lush orchard, and Len Mackay found a ready market for his pots, pans, kitchenware, household gadgets and furniture. At weekends Mackay turned bus driver, screwing garden seats onto the tray of his delivery truck to carry groups of picnickers down to the shady river.

After a fire burnt down his original shop, Mackay built a larger one on the western side of the expanding township. Three children were born, the youngest, Donald, on 13 September 1933. As Griffith developed into one of the principal towns in the new foodbowl of the Riverina, Len Mackay's furniture store thrived.

The plan had always been for Don and his elder brother, Bill, to take over the family business from their father, and by the mid-1950s both brothers were working in the store. Don was the more outgoing and he became actively involved with local sporting groups and church and community organisations. Public services that were taken for granted in the cities barely existed in Griffith and Don became a driving force behind the establishment of a support group for children with disabilities. It was through his involvement with the church that he met his future wife, Barbara Dearman, a dental nurse who was studying in Sydney to be a physiotherapist. They married in 1957 and soon afterwards Barbara found a job at

Griffith Base Hospital. While Bill Mackay looked after the furniture business, Don's community interests continued to grow: he was instrumental in setting up the future Kalinda School for disabled kids and became foundation president of the Pioneers' Lodge homes for the aged. It was no surprise when Donald Mackay began to be spoken of as a potential political candidate, although nobody could be sure which party he might represent.

■ ■ ■

In the 1965 New South Wales state election the long-serving Labor government was ousted by the Liberal–Country Party coalition and Premier Jack Renshaw was replaced by the Liberals' Robert Askin. With the strong support of Griffith's Italian community, Albert Jamie Grassby—known to almost everyone as 'Al'—bucked the trend by holding the seat of Murrumbidgee for Labor.

Although Peter Calipari's name was not among those listed as members of Grassby's campaign committee, the Griffith godfather had played a significant role in getting Grassby elected by helping deliver the Calabrian vote to Labor. But Calipari's political support came at a price, and it was not long before the newly elected member for Murrum-bidgee was required to pay.

Within a month of Grassby's maiden speech to the New South Wales Parliament, the police raided properties in Griffith, Sydney and Canberra searching for weapons thought to be linked to a series of murders and attempted murders at Melbourne's Queen Victoria produce market. One of the properties searched was the Griffith home of Peter Calipari.

Rumours had been circulating for some time about a cache of weapons said to have been smuggled from Italy to Australia. Some of the weapons recovered by police during the raids had had their serial numbers removed to avoid identification. There was talk of a shadowy Federal Police agent named 'Frank Titzoni' working undercover in Griffith. 'Titzoni' was a mystery man who was said to 'run with the rabbits and hunt with the hounds'. Maybe he was a police agent and maybe he wasn't. Maybe he didn't exist at all.

On 28 September 1965 Peter Calipari appeared before the Griffith Court of Petty Sessions charged with possession of an unlicensed pistol. His was one of four houses searched by police in Griffith and nearby Lake Wyangan, with the chief of the criminal investigation branch saying police had been told that Italians from Calabria were preying on others and had threatened violence and extortion.

The Griffith raids had been organised from Sydney, but local police were called to help. The aim of the operation was to break up groups active in Sydney, police said. Properties were searched for weapons and evidence of extortion or other illegal activities.

A Griffith detective, Senior Constable Jack Ellis, gave evidence against Calipari. He told the magistrate that police had found a .25-calibre Regina automatic pistol and four rounds of ammunition in the locked glove box of Calipari's car. The pistol was wrapped in newspaper inside a plastic container. Calipari denied having any knowledge of the pistol, insisting he hadn't opened the glove box for 'six or seven months'.

Cross-examined by Calipari's solicitor, Simon Mackenzie, Ellis volunteered: 'Mr Calipari is a man of excellent character. Well respected in the Italian and Australian community.' He told the court that Calipari's shoe shop had been burgled three times in twelve months and that Calipari often worked there late.

The new Member for Murrumbidgee, Al Grassby, also gave character evidence for Calipari, claiming to have known him for ten years and praising Calipari for his contribution to the Italian community. According to Grassby, Calipari had been under consideration for a Commonwealth government award for his work.

In his efforts to persuade the magistrate not to record a conviction against his client, Simon Mackenzie listed the names of numerous people who were supposedly willing to give character evidence on Calipari's behalf. They included the Wade Shire president, Nevis Farrell, and the Italian consular agent Frank Testoni.

Mackenzie then made the unusual gesture of offering to take the witness stand himself and testify on oath to the quality of Calipari's character. His explanation for the gun was that as a consequence of the robberies Calipari feared he might be attacked while working alone in the shop.

'The pistol was obtained after the last robbery but Mr Calipari has never fired it,' Mackenzie told the court. 'Mr Calipari is not a man of violence. There is no suggestion the weapon was to be used for illegal purposes.' He asked for the provisions of Section 556A of the Crimes Act to be extended to Calipari, 'to enable him to leave the courthouse free of the stain of conviction'.

Calipari's supporters had done their best to portray the godfather as a simple shopkeeper afraid for his safety, but the magistrate was not convinced. Possession of the gun constituted a 'grave and serious offence', he said, which could not be dealt with by 'dismissing the information and failing to record a conviction'. He fined Calipari a nominal $20 and ordered the pistol to be forfeited to the Crown.

The punishment was less significant than the conviction. By his carelessness with the gun, Calipari had exposed the Griffith families to unwelcome public attention. The godfather's connection to the mafia raids had been 'too close for comfort'.

Al Grassby sprang into action to limit the damage, claiming to have statistics showing that Griffith was 'one of the most law-abiding communities in Australia'.

Within hours of giving evidence for Calipari in court, Grassby stood up in parliament to denounce the police raids and the 'smear of Mafia' that, he claimed, had been cast over his electorate. Ridiculing the idea that there was a 'vicious Mafia Society' in Griffith, Grassby called on the premier to 'clear the good name of Griffith and Murrumbidgee' by a statement repudiating these smears. 'Anyone who believes we have a Mafia in Murrumbidgee is deluding himself,' Grassby declared. 'He has been watching too much late night TV.'

In Griffith, however, many citizens were uncomfortable with the links that were beginning to emerge between their town and the mafia killings in Melbourne. On 4 April 1963, the 47-year-old mafia boss Vincenzo Angilletta had been killed with two blasts of a shotgun outside his home in the Melbourne suburb of Northcote. On 16 January 1964 Vincenzo Muratore was shot dead, in almost identical fashion, while reversing his car from his driveway in the bayside suburb of Hampton. Both were connected to the Calabrian-controlled vegetable wholesale business at Melbourne's Queen Victoria Market. There were suspicions that members of Griffith's La Famiglia had relatives involved in the same business.

CHAPTER 3

A new crop

While Bob Trimbole's gambling habit killed off the Pool
Garage, the Murrumbidgee fruit growers had their own
problems. They would sit around at night and talk, Bob
and his Calabrian mates, about the neverending battle to
make a worthwhile return from growing crops with a short
shelf life on wafer-thin margins; the curse of boom seasons
that produced so much fruit that crops had to be left on the
ground; the exorbitant cost of delivering fresh produce by
road and rail to state capitals. Some were coping better than
others but it was a struggle for every single one of them.

Markets for fruit and vegetables hardly ever returned
much above production costs. Oranges grown in Griffith
might be worth only £150 per packed ton. For fruit going
to the juice factory, it could be as little as £50 to £100 per
ton. Citrus fruit that went to a grading and packing shed
was worth more: £1 to £2 per carton, two to five pence per
orange in pre-decimal currency.

Trimbole had watched his own father and relatives toiling long hours in sweltering summers. Domenic had taught his son the value of growing high value crops. In those early days, it was cauliflowers; by the late 1960s there was a much more lucrative option—cannabis.

No legal agricultural or horticultural crop could generate anything like the returns offered by cannabis. As a processed product, it was largely insulated both from the vagaries of the weather and from the seasonal price fluctuations that bedevilled citrus growers. Having lived through the cropping booms and busts of the Murrumbidgee Irrigation Area, Trimbole could not help noticing the consistently high price of dried cannabis, which seemed to have an unlimited shelf life. When Aussie Bob began to talk about the profits waiting to be made from commercial marijuana trafficking, his friends in La Famiglia listened.

Until the 1960s demand for marijuana in Australia had largely been met by a combination of wild-grown cannabis and plants grown in backyards. As the social use of cannabis began to surge, so did the commercial possibilities for large-scale marijuana cultivation. Those in the know collected seeds from wild cannabis and established plantations in remote national parks.

Trimbole's plan was more ambitious. During his time on the road for Atlantic Amusements Trimbole had identified a network of farmers capable of growing cannabis on a commercial scale. Crops could be grown either close to home or, if necessary, a safe distance away. Trimbole was aware that immediate family and friends owned farms from one end of New South Wales to the other, broad tracts of irrigated country in places where summer crops rarely failed. The properties he was interested in for his marijuana were broadacre farms with irrigation, planted for onions, melons, pumpkins and carrots as well as lettuce, cabbages and cauliflower. The whole operation would be controlled by La Famiglia.

The Calabrians comprised around 70 per cent of Griffith's roughly 12,000 Italians (the Sergi family alone was reputed to number around three hundred people). Trimbole had close friendships among the second and third generations of Calabrian migrant families who owned farms near Griffith. He understood and respected the patriarchal authority that governed Calabrian society, and revered the self-reliance that existed among the Sergis, Barbaros, Romeos and other Calabrian families. While Aussie Bob had married an outsider, his Calabrian friends continued to marry among their own, perpetuating the cult of family and its traditional values of trust, loyalty and Omerta—the mafia code of silence. The Calabrian mistrust of outsiders ensured that illegal activities—however much they might be deplored by some members of La Famiglia—would never be revealed to the police, because doing so would amount to a betrayal of family or clan—an unpardonable sin in a culture that venerated blood ties above everything.

Returns from the early cannabis crops were so good that orange and peach trees were bulldozed to clear paddocks for larger crops. Some orchards were left intact to provide camouflage for cannabis plants growing between the trees. In post–1966 decimal currency growers were receiving $100 to $150 per pound, or around $22,400 to $33,600 per tonne of dried, bagged cannabis leaf from wholesalers buying in bulk.

The person growing a crop might not be a principal in the organisation; in fact, the bosses were rarely found in the paddocks. Farmers (usually La Famiglia 'trustees') who undertook to grow and harvest a marijuana crop were paid a flat fee, with organisers picking up the tab for input costs (seeds, water, fertiliser etc), living expenses and, if they were unlucky enough to be arrested, legal fees.

Trimbole looked after wholesaling with help from his lieutenant and confidant Winery Tony Sergi in New South Wales, and from Gianfranco 'Frank' Tizzoni in Victoria. Trimbole had met and befriended Tizzoni while working for Atlantic Amusements. Like Trimbole, Tizzoni had a job supplying and servicing amusement machines. It did not take the pair long to realise that, while supplying machines to pubs and clubs, they could also cater to the burgeoning cannabis market; it seemed like a logical progression.

La Famiglia established a legitimate fruit and vegetable business, Trimboli, Sergi & Sergi, at Sydney's Haymarket and Flemington markets as a means to transport and distribute cannabis and to funnel cash back to members of the syndicate in Griffith. Huge sums of money would be paid by Trimboli, Sergi & Sergi for phantom 'farm produce' for which no records could be traced.

Bob Trimbole studied the development, harvest, preparation and packaging techniques used in the Riverina's fruit and vegetable industry and applied the same quality controls to the cultivation and trafficking of cannabis.

But growing cannabis was not like growing cauliflowers. Trimbole knew that the police had an eye-in-the-sky searching for cannabis crops. Landsat satellites were used by the agricultural industry to measure areas sown to rice crops and to estimate the volume of irrigation water required each season from the Murrumbidgee and Murray River systems. These satellites could pinpoint and identify legitimate and illicit crops grown throughout the Murrumbidgee, Coleambally and Murray Irrigation Areas.

In order to avoid any disruption to supply in the event of the police stumbling upon a mature crop, it was necessary to have between ten and twenty crops growing every summer. Trimbole supplemented the crops grown in southern New South Wales and Victoria with strategic crops grown in central and northern Queensland. These tropical plants dwarfed those grown in temperate plantations.

Cannabis generated huge profits and the principals started looking beyond the traditional farm investments for ways to launder the cash. In Griffith, locals watched in awe and disbelief as once-humble vegetable farmers began building lavish new homes—the soon-to-be notorious 'grass castles'— from the money they were making out of marijuana.

Australia's marijuana sub-culture was beginning to spread from its roots in coastal towns such as Byron Bay, where the combination of a hippy lifestyle and a sub-tropical climate ideally suited to the cultivation of cannabis attracted both users and entrepreneurs. East coast newspapers such as Wollongong's *Illawarra Mercury*, the *Newcastle Morning Herald* (now the *Newcastle Herald*), the Gosford *Star* and the Wyong *Advocate* regularly reported on the use of cannabis and LSD in 'surfing' communities. In Griffith, Donald Mackay was not the only reader alarmed by reports in his local paper, the *Area News*, about the growing number of local teenagers experimenting with illicit drugs.

CHAPTER 4

Boom town

To the casual visitor, the early 1970s would have seemed like a golden era for Griffith. The town was awash with cash. Farms were being improved and farmers who a few years earlier had been struggling to make ends meet were splashing money on palatial homes. Few would have known that marijuana was behind the boom.

Terry Jones was anything but a casual visitor. A journalist who had spent the previous thirteen years writing for the *Western Advocate* in Bathurst and the *Central Western Daily* in Orange, Jones had arrived in Griffith in 1971 with his wife, Irene, to work for the *Griffith Times*.

Owned by an independent group of commercial printers, the *Times* had been launched as a rival to the Riverina Newspaper Group's *Area News*. Jones took over from the paper's original editor, John Mulcair, who was exhausted after two years of trying to match his better-resourced competitor.

It was not long before Jones bumped into Peter Calipari,

who owned the *Times*'s office on Banna Avenue, Griffith's main street. Greeting Jones each morning with clasp of hands, a hug and kisses, Calipari was never shy about offering advice on stories the paper should be reporting.

Jones's mission was straightforward: to establish the tabloid *Times* as a credible alternative to the *Area News*. Local news would be the battleground. With its more flexible deadlines, the independently owned *Times* could be more nimble at breaking news than the group-owned *Area News*. Jones beefed up the *Times*'s coverage of police matters, court proceedings and the monthly meetings of the local Wade Shire Council. Every letter written to council was a potential news story. Important news that broke after 4pm on production day went straight to page one, a tactic that allowed the *Times* to publish major police and council stories ahead of the *Area News*.

Circulation of the *Times* steadily increased, pulling advertising revenue from the town's supermarkets and machinery businesses away from the *Area News*. But being the established paper gave the latter some advantages. When Jones tried to persuade the local member, Al Grassby, to write a weekly column for the *Times*, Grassby turned him down, citing his ongoing relationship with the *Area News*. He promised, however, to provide the *Times* with regular commentary on political matters—an offer Jones was happy to accept, as long as Grassby understood that the *Times* would also be speaking to his political opponents.

■ ■ ■

As editor of the town's second newspaper, Jones found a warm welcome at the Coro. Among those eager to meet him on his first visit to the club was a short, solidly built man with receding hair that hung lank at the back. Jones had heard a lot about Aussie Bob Trimbole, the skilled motor mechanic who had turned his hand to servicing pinball machines. Jones had already met Trimbole's wife, Joan, at the Griffith tourist centre. The two men shook hands. Trimbole told Jones to let him know if he ever needed any work done on his car.

Their next meeting came several weeks later at the Texan Tavern, a restaurant owned by Trimbole. The interior was a replica of Bernie Houghton's Bourbon & Beefsteak restaurant in Kings Cross, one of Trimbole's favourite haunts during his years in Sydney. The *Times* published a full-page advertising feature ahead of the restaurant's official opening on 11 August 1972. 'Set in the Old West tradition,' it said, 'the Texan Tavern is certain to become one of the most popular informal dining-out centres of the town.'

No sooner had Jones and his colleague Jim Mulcair (John's brother) walked through the door than Trimbole's son Craig lined up a pair of beers on the bar. Trimbole himself was engaged in conversation with two men Jones recognised as Griffith detectives, Jack Ellis and John Robins. When Jones attempted to pay for his beer, Trimbole stopped him. 'These are on me,' Trimbole insisted. 'The *Griffith Times* is always our special guest.'

Without asking, Trimbole placed two large T-bone steaks on the barbecue range and began to ask Jones about his interest in greyhound racing. It struck Jones that for a man he had met only once, Trimbole seemed to be very well informed about him. The conversation moved on to horses and punting, subjects Jones knew a lot about from his days writing form guides for the *Western Advocate* in Bathurst.

Trimbole, Jones quickly discovered, was an obsessive punter who would spend every day at the tracks if he could. 'If you want to have a punt,' Trimbole told him, 'I can get inside information.'

The steaks arrived and once again Trimbole refused to accept payment. 'You're not paying for anything here,' he told the two journalists. 'You're always our guests.'

Before leaving the restaurant, however, Jones and Mulcair witnessed another side of Trimbole's personality, a side that belied his performance as a genial host and family man. Angered by the failure of a drunken patron to leave the restaurant when asked, Trimbole grabbed the man by the hair and dragged him violently up two short flights of stairs before kicking him into the street. Trimbole's wife, Joan, attempted to brush off the incident as just an example of her husband's 'short fuse', but to Jones it looked more sinister, like a warning that Bob Trimbole was not a man to be crossed.

The next day brought another shock for Jones, when he discovered that the opening of the Texan Tavern had not gone as smoothly as it appeared from the gushing prose of the *Times*'s advertising feature. Before opening the restaurant for business, Trimbole was required to place an advertisement in the *Times*, inviting objections to the approval of a liquor licence for the Tavern. As part of his application, Trimbole had to submit a certain number of copies of the newspaper containing the public notice. When the deadline passed with no sign of the advertisement, Trimbole approached the *Times*'s owners, Reg and Frank McCudden, insisting that his wife had 'forgotten' to place the ad. Jones listened in disbelief as Reg McCudden explained: 'I set up the ad on the Lino. Frank put it into the classified page and printed off papers. I think there were about 50 copies. Bob took them all.'

Jones was livid. As the paper's editor, he felt responsible for everything that went in the *Times*, including the ads. 'Jesus, Reg,' he said. 'You mean you ran a special edition of the *Times* just for Trimbole? What happens when someone finds out?'

'No one's going to find out,' said McCudden. 'Terry, we help people out. You don't need to know everything we do. Bob and Joan are good people. All the papers were given to Bob. Joan sent them with the application for the liquor licence. The court approved the licence. Let's get over it.'

Jones could hardly believe what he was hearing. 'What if someone who has a legal licence asks questions?' he demanded. 'What if they object because the Texan Tavern didn't place the advertisement?'

'Stop worrying,' said McCudden. 'Just forget it happened.'

But Jones was right to be worried. Not long after the row with McCudden, he ran into Pat Jones, the managing director of the Irrigana Hotel, who wanted to know how the Trimboles had got their licence without issuing a public notice. Pat hadn't seen an ad in either the *Times* or the *Area News*. If he had, he told Jones, he would have objected. Somehow the issue blew over, but it was close.

Terry Jones was well aware that Frank McCudden and his wife, Marilyn, were among the guests drinking Bob Trimbole's wine at the grand opening of the Texan Tavern. He had only been in town a few months but already Jones was starting to get an uncomfortable feeling about the way business was done in Griffith.

The more Jones thought about that night with Jim Mulcair at the Texan Tavern, the more he wondered about Trimbole's relationship with the two detectives, Jack Ellis and John Robins. It was hard to believe that Ellis hadn't known about the ruse with the newspaper ad. Was it Ellis who put Trimbole up to approaching the McCuddens?

The question was still rolling around in his mind when Jones and Mulcair returned to the Texan Tavern a few weeks later. This time Jones was quick to lay down the ground rules, telling Joan that they were just there for a couple of beers and were not staying for dinner. When Craig put the schooners on the counter, Jones slapped down $10, but once again Trimbole intervened, saying, 'Leave his money on the bar, Craig. They're still our guests.'

The two detectives, Ellis and Robins, were there again.

After a while Trimbole sat down, telling Jones he wanted to 'sound him out'. Jones assumed he wanted to discuss horse racing and gambling, but this time Trimbole wanted to talk about something else. He asked how the *Times* reported court cases.

'It's pretty straightforward,' Jones told him. 'Jim attends court, checks the list and gets access to police charge sheets from the prosecutor. If there's anything he's unsure about, he checks with the clerk of petty sessions.'

Trimbole asked, 'Does every case go in the paper?'

'The community expects to be told about crime and justice,' said Jones. 'We write about every case.'

'Is anyone ever left out?'

'It's one in, all in, Bob. Why are you asking?'

Trimbole launched into a story about a 'young kid' who worked at the Griffith post office and had been charged with stealing. The family was 'very worried' about the case being reported in the paper. 'He's from a good family, one of the biggest families in Griffith,' Trimbole said. 'I was hoping you might be able to leave the report out.'

'We'd have to know his name,' said Jones. 'But there are no promises we'll ever leave anything out. Most of the papers are guided by how the judge or magistrate views the case, what the offence is, how serious it is, if there's a conviction, what kind of sentence the offender gets.'

'His name's Sergi,' said Trimbole.

The next day Jim Mulcair made some inquiries at the court and returned with more information for Jones about the case. He told him, 'It's already been before Children's Court, a young bloke dealt with in a closed hearing. They were Commonwealth offences. Some birth certificate forms disappeared from the Post Office. The forms are missing, the kid's responsible for them, they wouldn't say if he pleaded guilty or not to taking the forms, or what happened to them. The magistrate closed the court, heard evidence, was told the kid had lost his job at the Post Office. Because of his age and good character there was no conviction and the kid's on a good behaviour bond.'

The case was at least a week, if not two weeks, old. Unless there was something more to the theft of the birth certificate forms, the case was hardly worth reporting, Jones thought.

Just to be on the safe side, Jones asked Mulcair to check with Griffith police about a possible follow-up. When the police described it as an isolated incident, Jones gave up on the story. All the same, he couldn't help asking himself, 'What would anyone want with a bundle of birth certificate forms?'

The truth was that the story probably wouldn't have run anyway. Jones was always reluctant to report on children in closed court and in any case he wouldn't have been allowed to mention the kid's name. But Bob Trimbole didn't know that. As far as Trimbole was concerned, Terry Jones had done him and the Sergis a big favour—a favour that needed to be repaid.

The next time Jones visited the Texan Tavern, Trimbole insisted on introducing him to a group of Calabrian men Jones recognised as La Famiglia elders. Jones shifted awkwardly as Trimbole announced him, in English, as the editor of the *Griffith Times*.

The Calabrians seemed no more comfortable in his company than he was in theirs. They muttered quietly, exchanging looks among themselves, until Trimbole spoke a few words in Italian. Suddenly the atmosphere changed. The men nodded and smiled. One by one they stood up to shake Jones's hand.

One of the men, whom Jones recognised as Antonio Sergi, insisted on buying him a drink, which Jones declined, saying he had to get home for dinner.

'We understand,' said Sergi, grasping both of Jones's hands.

A smiling Trimbole told Jones, 'What you did means a lot to me, Terry. If you ever need anything, anything, come to me. If you need a quid, come and see me, any amount, just tell me what you need.'

Jones came away from the encounter with Winery Tony convinced there must be more to the story of the missing birth certificates than the police were saying.

■ ■ ■

It wasn't just La Famiglia that was keen to embrace Jones. When, on the eve of the 1972 federal election, Jones refused to publish anti-immigration advertisements placed by White Australia supporters, he won himself an enthusiastic new friend: Al Grassby. The advertisements, which aimed to derail Grassby's campaign for the federal seat of Riverina, had already appeared in the rival *Area News*, but Jones rejected them as being highly offensive to the *Times*'s Italian readers.

Minutes after polling booths closed at 6pm on 2 December, with Labor poised for victory, Grassby called Jones at home. 'Terry, Terry,' he said, almost hyperventilating. 'Thank you for your help. Gough Whitlam has won a famous victory. Please join our celebrations at the Griffith Hotel. You must be here with us. You, Irene and little Ann-Catherine, we want all of you with us, please come.'

In the end Jones decided to make the trip alone, leaving Irene and their daughter at home. A down-to-earth journalist, he had no inkling of the reception that awaited him. A round of applause greeted Jones as he walked into the ALP celebrations. 'Listen everyone,' said Grassby, 'Let's welcome our friend Terry Jones. You all know him and what he has done in this campaign. Griffith's many Italian families owe Terry a debt of gratitude. They were the targets of a scurrilous campaign by white extremists. They tried to buy space in the *Times*, but Terry refused to take their dirty money.'

Conveniently forgetting that he had once turned down Jones's request to run his weekly column, Grassby now urged his supporters to read his column in future editions of the *Times*. 'Terry's newspaper will have my column,' he crowed. 'Buy the *Times*!'

Jones had not set out to be a friend of La Famiglia or of Al Grassby but, as far as they were concerned, he was now an ally of both. It was a reminder of the power of a newspaper editor in a country town—a power that Jones would use to the full in the years to come.

Time was running out, however, for the *Griffith Times*. Under Jones's editorship the *Times* had cut deeply into the circulation of the *Area News*. If the McCuddens decided to expand, the *Times* would pose a significant threat to other small papers in the region. The Riverina Newspaper Group, owners of the *Area News*, had invested heavily in new presses and could not risk losing more readers. The only way for the group to protect its assets was to buy the *Times*. After two years in the editor's chair, Terry Jones suddenly found himself without a paper.

CHAPTER 5

Shame

On 16 October 1973 Donald Mackay was formally announced as the Liberal candidate for the state seat of Murrumbidgee. The political landscape in the Riverina was changing. Capitalising on Grassby's profile as an advocate for multiculturalism, Gough Whitlam had made 'Flash' Al his Minister for Immigration. Lin Gordon, Grassby's successor as the Member for Murrumbidgee in the NSW lower house, was desperate to hold onto the block Italian vote that had always gone to Grassby. While it was hard to see Liberal–Country Party votes ousting Gordon from a seat the ALP had held since 1941, pre-election polls suggested that Labor was losing its grip on the seat.

Although Gordon won in Murrumbidgee, the result of the November 1973 state election was closer than Mackay had dared hope. Next time he would need only a swing of just over 2 per cent to unseat Gordon. A similar swing against Labor would also bring down Al Grassby in the federal seat of Riverina. Mackay had good reason to be optimistic about his own prospects, either in state or federal politics.

It was no surprise to anyone that Al Grassby made Italy the destination of his first official overseas trip as Australia's Minister for Immigration. Grassby arrived in Rome on 24 January 1974 to be met at the airport by none other than the Griffith godfather, Peter Calipari.

As usual, Grassby had his media machine working frantically behind the scenes. The *Area News* in Griffith ran a steady stream of stories about the minister's 'international goodwill visit'. An audience with the Pope was followed by a reception from the mayor of Rome and another at the Australian Embassy. In Vincenza, Grassby claimed to have been 'surrounded by 200 guests, all of them invited relatives of families who had migrated to make new lives in Australia'. He and Calipari also visited the mafia stronghold of Platì, where the mayor presented Grassby with a 'golden key' to the town. Everywhere he went, Grassby was mobbed, as photographs and letters were thrust into his hands addressed to Italian migrants in the Riverina.

■ ■ ■

In Griffith, it was business as usual for Bob Trimbole, whose faith in the skills of his cannabis farmers had been well rewarded. Using their own signature techniques—such as the rigorous culling of male plants to improve the yield of the remaining female plants —and refining techniques learnt from others, La Famiglia was achieving yields of 3000 to 5000 pounds (1350 to 2300 kilograms) per acre of female plants.

Trimbole's growers preferred trafficking in cannabis leaf rather than the more highly prized (but significantly more labour-intensive) 'Buddha' or 'Thai sticks', which often contained a higher proportion of THC (tetrahydrocannabinol), the main psychoactive ingredient. The Calabrians were confident they had perfected the art of conserving THC in cannabis leaf by hanging the branches head-down to dry, sometimes using racks previously used for onions or pumpkins.

The same preference for the easy option—hanging, drying and bagging the cannabis leaf—deterred Trimbole's farmers from venturing into hashish, another time-consuming, labour-intensive product that involved beating or rubbing cannabis leaves against leather or sacking, or squeezing leaves between cloth to extract resin. Although hashish fetched a higher price, it could take between 30 and 50 kilograms of cannabis leaf to produce one kilogram of hashish, which made it a non-starter for farmers in the business of growing, harvesting and transporting their product to market as quickly as possible to avoid detection.

The need to conceal the proceeds of his marijuana operation was an ongoing problem for Trimbole, who was rumoured to be laundering large sums of money through the Nugan Hand merchant bank, co-founded by the Griffith-born lawyer Frank Nugan and his American partner Michael Hand, a former Green Beret who had been decorated for bravery in Vietnam. Frank Nugan's elder brother, Ken, had turned his father's firm, the Griffith-based Nugan Group, into one of Australia's biggest fruit and vegetable distributors. Frank's line of business was altogether shadier, as Nugan Hand began setting up offices in Singapore and Hong Kong and, eventually, in the Thai drug capital, Chiang Mai.

While cannabis production boomed, so did the number of arrests for cannabis cultivation, supply and use. There were suspicions that the huge cashflow generated by commercial cannabis production was inducing some police to turn a blind eye, yet the number of arrests across New South Wales for cultivation and trafficking exploded between 1967 and 1974.

■ ■ ■

In February 1974, while local member Al Grassby was being feted in Italy, detectives acting on a tip-off raided a property at Tharbogang, eight kilometres north-west of Griffith, and discovered a five-acre cannabis crop worth an estimated $250,000. The marijuana plants, ranging in height from one metre to nearly two, were thought to have been planted the previous September or October. Detective Sergeant Jack Ellis, a regular visitor to Aussie Bob's Texan Tavern restaurant, was photographed by the *Area News* posing with a large marijuana plant. According to the paper, 'About 20 people, including a number of local farmers, spent the weekend assisting detectives to cut and burn the plants . . . All of the plants have now been destroyed with the exception of a few which detectives have taken for analysis.'

Within a week of the discovery of the first big marijuana crop in the Griffith district, Sergeant Jack Ellis was back on the front page of the *Area News*, receiving the Queen's Medal for Long Service and Good Conduct from the officer-in-charge of the Riverina Police District. Ellis, who joined the New South Wales Police Force in 1956, had been stationed in Griffith since 1962.

There were some in Griffith who doubted Jack Ellis's good conduct. The way Ellis had spoken up for Peter Calipari in court, and his attempt to trivialise the charge of possession of an illegal weapon, had raised many eyebrows.

A number of citizens—the core of a group that would come to be known as the Concerned Citizens of Griffith—were becoming suspicious of the money pouring into the town, and of relations between members of the Griffith police and La Famiglia. Prominent among the emerging group was the manager of the *Area News*, June Webster, a shrewd newspaper executive as well as a mother of three. It was obvious to the citizens that a number of trial crops had already been grown while local detectives looked the other way. In order to take on the growers, the citizens would need to organise themselves and to learn everything they could about marijuana: how it was grown, its addictiveness, its legal status in other countries and the psychiatric effects of long-term use.

After reading an article in *Time* magazine, a member of the group, David Ledgerwood, wrote to the United Nations in Geneva, asking for information about drugs and enclosing a $20 donation towards the UN's Fund for Drug Abuse Control, whose stated aim was to 'eliminate illicit drug traffic and . . . prevent and reduce drug abuse worldwide'. As a result of this and other letters to police, doctors and politicians, the Griffith citizens gradually built up a store of knowledge about the marijuana industry in Australia and overseas.

It was widely felt that the power behind local law enforcement lay in the hands of three Griffith detectives, led by Jack Ellis, and that these three were in the pockets of La Famiglia. The true story behind the events at Tharbogang would prove their suspicions accurate.

■ ■ ■

In July 1973 Rocco 'Roy' Barbaro (born Platì, Italy on 23 September 1949) had contracted to buy the 22-acre (nine-hectare) Farm 1774 at Tharbogang from Francesco Romeo. Barbaro had previously worked as a gardener for the Commonwealth government. Soon after buying the farm Barbaro declared his intention to remove more than three acres of peach trees and about one and a half acres of apricot trees in a tree-pull scheme. By September the peach and apricot trees had been removed and pushed against two boundaries of the property. Rocco Barbaro then set about planting a commercial crop of marijuana.

While driving on nearby roads a Griffith man, William Holden, noticed how Barbaro had bulldozed his old peach trees to form a hedge to conceal what Holden described as an unidentifiable 'green crop'. During a conversation at the Griffith Police Citizens' Club, Holden had casually told two uniformed senior constables, Warren Jeffers and Graham Jarrold, about the mysterious crop.

On Friday 1 February 1974 Constables Jeffers and Jarrold, whose duties mainly involved working with youth at the club, examined the crop through binoculars from a nearby property. The thriving crop didn't look like anything the pair had seen before but bore a strong resemblance to photographs of cannabis plants they had seen on a poster at Griffith police station. Jeffers and Jarrold watched for a quarter of an hour as two men worked on the crop before reporting their findings to the officer-in-charge, Inspector Bill Tarrant, who immediately referred the policemen to Detective Sergeant Jack Ellis, the senior of three plain clothes CIB officers stationed in the town.

After pointing out the location of the cannabis crop to Ellis and Senior Constable John Robins, Constable Jeffers asked whether he and Jarrold could be of any further assistance.

'No,' said Ellis. 'Leave it to us. We're going out to have a look.'

Ellis did not ask Jeffers and Jarrold for either a written report or a formal statement. He did, however, immediately call Winery Tony Sergi.

Rather than using a police car, Ellis and Robins drove out to Tharbogang the next day in Robins's car. They were met by Sergi and a group of Italian men. Shortly before their arrival, a Water Resources Commission employee, Desmond Coates, had called at the homestead to speak to Rocco Barbaro about delivery of irrigation water. While Coates was talking to Barbaro a white stationwagon arrived at the farm; inside were Detectives Ellis and Robins. As Coates drove away the detectives gave him a cheery wave.

Meanwhile, Constable Jeffers' curiosity had got the better of him and he drove to Tharbogang to see the marijuana for himself. As he approached the farm from Griffith, Jeffers saw a dark plume of smoke curling skyward. After parking his car, he went to investigate the source of the fire. When he reached the farm, Jeffers was astonished to see a group of eight to ten men, all of Mediterranean appearance, burning what looked like cannabis plants. Ellis had arranged with Winery Tony for Italians to harvest the marijuana. Jeffers approached Ellis and asked: 'What are these fellows doing here?'

Ellis replied: 'They're ashamed at what Barbaro has done. They want to help get rid of it.'

Constable Robins told the same story to Inspector Tarrant, who had also come to see the crop. 'The Italians were so ashamed that one of their countrymen would grow marijuana in Australia that they volunteered to harvest the crop,' he told Tarrant.

The inspector considered it highly unusual that Ellis had not asked uniformed police to help the detectives destroy the marijuana.

Not all the cannabis plants were being thrown on the fire. Tarrant saw another group of men throwing plants into the corner of a shed. Among the group he recognised Winery Tony and Aussie Bob Trimbole.

After returning to Griffith police station, Sergeant Ellis asked Inspector Tarrant to read a written statement to Rocco Barbaro, who he said could not read English.

The statement outlined the charges of growing, possessing and selling marijuana. According to Barbaro, he had been given marijuana seeds by a Greek man, Michael Poulos, whom he had met at a club in Canberra. Poulos offered Barbaro $5 to $10 for every plant grown from the seeds. Barbaro said he believed the plants might have been illegal as Poulos asked him not to tell anyone about them. He admitted, nevertheless, to growing 15,000 marijuana plants intermingled with corn, climbing beans and squash plants.

Interviewed later by a reporter from the *Area News*, Ellis insisted that none of the cannabis plants had reached maturity or been harvested at the time police raided the property. (Looking at the photograph of the tall, burly detective dwarfed by two-metre high cannabis bushes, some readers might have found this hard to believe.) According to Ellis, all of the plants, with the exception of a few taken for analysis, were burnt along with peach trees stacked on the property. Barbaro faced a maximum of two years' jail plus a fine for possession of marijuana; the penalty for selling the drug was ten years' jail and a fine of $2000.

Simon Mackenzie appeared for Barbaro at Griffith Court, where the charges were mentioned briefly before a magistrate. Barbaro was remanded to appear again on 25 March.

■ ■ ■

The Tharbogang crop turned out to be just the beginning. Less than three weeks after the discovery of Rocco Barbaro's crop, a Department of Agriculture fruit inspector, Patrick 'Paddy' Keenan, stumbled onto a second large cannabis plantation on Farm 20, Hanwood, about ten kilometres south of Griffith.

The farm belonged to 56-year-old Giuseppe 'Old Joe' Scarfo (born 3 February 1918 in Calabria), who had migrated to Australia with his wife, Rosa, in 1952. On arriving in Australia Scarfo had moved to Griffith to grow vegetables on leased land. The Scarfos had raised seven children. One of their daughters, Angelina, was married to Winery Tony.

On 18 February Paddy Keenan was undertaking a routine inspection of fruit trees on Giuseppe Scarfo's property when he stopped to speak to a woman. She did not understand English and Keenan did not speak Italian. As Keenan began walking towards a fruit packing shed close to the homestead, the woman rushed to a car and sounded the horn, obviously as a warning to whoever was inside the shed. As he approached the shed, Keenan noticed fifteen to twenty bushy green plants lying outside, drying in the sun. Inside, he saw Giuseppe Scarfo and one of his sons, together with Winery Tony, a small boy and two women. A large number of marijuana plants were hanging on wires in the process of being dried. The people in the shed appeared to be packing dried marijuana into plastic bags.

Catching sight of a rifle leaning against a wall of the shed, Keenan prudently decided not to comment on what he had seen, but simply asked for someone to accompany him to inspect the fruit trees on the farm.

As Keenan walked away from the shed he saw Winery Tony and the boy drive off in a light-coloured sedan. Keenan would remember it as a Holden Monaro with a dark stripe over the top running from front to back.

After inspecting the fruit trees Keenan drove straight to Griffith police station where he told Detective Jack Ellis, in the presence of Constable John Robins, what he had seen. He told the detectives that one of the people he had seen in the shed was Winery Tony. Later he made entries in his diary recording the visit to Giuseppe Scarfo's farm and noting that he had seen cannabis plants.

At about 8am the next day, a young man known as Antonio 'Young Tony' Sergi knocked on Paddy Keenan's door. Young Tony was a nephew of Winery Tony.

Young Tony Sergi said, 'You know yesterday you told the police that you saw Tony Sergi at Scarfo's farm yesterday. Pat, I think you are making a mistake. The person you saw was not Tony Sergi from the winery.'

When Keenan insisted that the man he had seen at Scarfo's farm was Winery Tony, Young Tony said, 'Pat, I'm not trying to make you tell lies or change your mind, but I think you might have seen someone who looked like him.'

Keenan repeated that he knew who he had seen at Scarfo's farm. Young Tony then appealed to Keenan to change his evidence because the allegation 'could ruin Tony Sergi'. Before leaving, he told Keenan that police had 'gone to the winery and given Sergi a hard time'. Young Tony would later deny the approach ever took place, but in his report Justice Woodward stated that he accepted the version given by Keenan and rejected Young Tony's denial.

Later that day Keenan told several of his colleagues, including Eric Price, about his visit to Scarfo's farm. Price was with Keenan when Keenan received a telephone call from Detective Sergeant Ellis saying that Sergi had witnesses who would swear he was at the winery all day on 18 February. Keenan immediately smelt a rat.

His suspicions were confirmed when Ellis asked him to come to the police station. Ellis told Keenan he had spent a fair bit of time with Winery Tony, who said there were three people at the winery who would confirm he was there at the time Keenan claimed he was at Scarfo's farm. Ellis told him, 'It's your word against Mr Sergi and his three witnesses. Police can do nothing about it.'

When Keenan mentioned the surprise home visit from Young Tony, which he interpreted as a blatant attempt to intimidate him, Ellis showed no interest.

Again, neither Ellis nor any of his detectives made any effort to take notes or a formal statement from Keenan about what he had seen at Scarfo's farm.

To Keenan, it seemed that Ellis's only concern was to protect Winery Tony.

Speaking to the *Area News*, Ellis appealed to members of the public to 'assist police in any way possible to apprehend such offenders', telling potential informants that 'even if it turns out to be a mistake, no-one will be embarrassed'. He said police were 'always on the lookout' for such crops but that they were often well camouflaged. 'Any information given to police is always treated in the strictest confidence,' Ellis assured the paper's readers—a promise that would soon prove hollow.

Within a few days of Paddy Keenan making his report of the Scarfo crop, the body of a man named Joseph Patrick Keenan was found floating in an irrigation canal near Griffith. Sergeant Ellis, who led the investigation, told the inquest that Joseph Patrick Keenan was an alcoholic and that his death was not suspicious. To the Concerned Citizens of Griffith, however, the similarity of names between the dead man and the witness was more than coincidental. They were convinced that a murder had occurred.

Thanks to Ellis, the *Area News* could now reveal that police had arrested 'Old Joe' Scarfo and charged him with possessing and selling a commercial amount of cannabis estimated to be worth $150,000 (around $100,000 less than the Tharbogang crop). Ellis failed to mention that Scarfo had been taken into custody as the result of a phone call. Old Joe had as good as surrendered himself to police outside Tony Sergi's winery at Tharbogang on 19 February.

After allowing several days for Scarfo's marijuana plants to dry out, the crop was burnt. The *Area News* was again on hand to report the operation, conducted by twenty police from Griffith, Leeton, Darlington Point, Goolgowi and Carrathool. Work started at 7am and plants were loaded into a bulk fruit bin before being piled into heaps and incinerated. The paper also reported that police had found 'a large number' of green plastic bags containing dried cannabis ready for distribution and sale.

Sergeant Ellis confirmed that the marijuana crops grown by Barbaro and Scarfo were among several discovered in police raids across New South Wales which had netted a total of $1 million worth of drugs. Ellis himself could sometimes be spotted flying over Griffith with members of the Narcotics Bureau on aerial searches of local properties. Armed with search warrants, police also raided a number of farms, homes and sheds within an eight-mile (thirteen-kilometre) radius of the Griffith post office, but no arrests were made. Despite growing evidence to the contrary, Ellis assured readers of the *Area News* that there was little likelihood of an organised network of farmers supplying cannabis to markets in the capital cities.

In the coming weeks the town buzzed with talk of the Barbaro and Scarfo cases. Few believed Ellis's claim that 'shame' had motivated men like Aussie Bob Trimbole and Winery Tony to harvest and burn Barbaro's cannabis crop.

When the cases came to court, it was Sergeant Ellis who swore all the evidence against the two defendants, failing to mention that Constables Jeffers and Jarrold were the first to identify the Barbaro crop, or that Paddy Keenan had seen Winery Tony packing marijuana in 'Old Joe' Scarfo's shed. According to Ellis, both crops had been discovered as a result of 'raids' led by him. The truth, however, was that in both cases Ellis had been forced to act as a result of discoveries made by others. Rocco Barbaro and Giuseppe Scarfo quickly admitted their guilt. But by quoting 'farm gate' values of $250,000 and $150,000, rather than street values of between $2 million and $5 million, Ellis underplayed the scale of the cannabis operation by a factor of at least ten.

Cross-examined Ellis portrayed Barbaro and Scarfo as largely illiterate Italian farmers who could not understand English or grasp the seriousness of what they had done. Both men freely accepted marijuana seeds 'from persons they'd never known for any length of time', agreeing to grow crops only because of the money offered to them. It was doubtful, Ellis suggested, that they even knew what type of seeds they were. Barbaro had made nothing from his cannabis crop, he said, as none of the plants had been harvested.

While the court accepted the police version of events given by Detective Sergeant Ellis, others did not. The failure to seek evidence on oath from Constables Jarrold and Jeffers or from Paddy Keenan left a question mark over the prosecution case, which now appeared to have been cooked up by Ellis alone. Neighbours of Giuseppe Scarfo, well aware that it was his son Michael who ran the Hanwood farm, suspected that Old Joe might not be as guilty as he claimed.

■ ■ ■

Despite Ellis's efforts to play down the crime and mitigate the roles of both defendants, on 26 March 1974 Barbaro and Scarfo were committed for trial.

The pattern for the trial had already been set. Detective Sergeant Ellis would effectively run the prosecution case by himself, in a way that was highly favourable to the defendants. Simon Mackenzie would be able to run his case without any fear of awkward surprises or uncongenial witnesses. Neither Jarrold, Jeffers nor Keenan would be allowed to give evidence. Inconvenient facts, such as the presence of women and children in the packing shed, would be omitted. The roles of Bob Trimbole and Winery Tony would be covered up. Barbaro and Scarfo, depicted by Ellis as honest, hardworking farmers, would plead guilty to growing crops they knew little about and had not profited from. Ellis would point out their previously unblemished records and give his opinion that neither was likely to re-offend.

It was little wonder Barbaro and Scarfo were sentenced to imprisonment, suspended upon both entering into good behaviour bonds, and ordered to pay fines of $250 and $500 respectively—sentences significantly lighter than some that had recently been imposed for the much less serious crime of possession. The Concerned Citizens were outraged. Barbara Mackay wrote an angry letter to the *Area News*, noting that, 'Last Friday the Griffith *Area News* reported a Leeton trial where three youths received jail sentences and fines of $900, $600 and $300 for smoking the end product of the growers. The contrast between these two judgements is alarming.'

Rocco Barbaro and Giuseppe Scarfo might have been denied the chance to sell their cannabis crops, but both would be well rewarded for their efforts. Details of the financial arrangements behind the crops would be revealed several years later during Justice Woodward's Royal Commission of Inquiry into Drug Trafficking. In September and October 1974 Barbaro received two cheques for $4250 and $4750 respectively, both cheques drawn on the account of Trimboli, Sergi & Sergi, Fairfield, a total of $9000 allegedly as payment for the sale of produce at Farm 1774. In May 1975 Barbaro received another cheque for $6000 from Trimboli, Sergi & Sergi. In June 1975, he deposited two further cheques for $4998.69 and $5001.31, both drawn on Trimboli, Sergi & Sergi and together adding up to exactly $10,000.

Another cheque for $8000 and two for $3000, also from Trimboli, Sergi & Sergi, were paid to Barbaro between September and November 1975. In all, Rocco Barbaro had received $39,000 in payment for fruit and vegetables, allegedly harvested from Farm 1774, where Barbaro had pulled out his peach and apricot trees to grow marijuana. It was an obvious pay-off from La Famiglia.

On 12 August and 2 September 1974 two cheques for $5439.50 and $6060.50 drawn on Trimboli, Sergi & Sergi were deposited into 'Old Joe' Scarfo's trading bank accounts, allegedly for the sale of farm produce. The combined total of $11,500 was enough to cover Scarfo's $500 fine; reimbursement of $1000 in legal costs and a $10,000 pay-off from La Famiglia for having fulfilled his 'contract' as a front-man.

June Webster began urging reporters at the *Area News* to find out all they could about Griffith's marijuana trade. She noted how a group of supposedly uneducated Calabrian farmers had been able to defy the cycle of booms and busts in the fruit and vegetable industry to acquire miraculous wealth. So far all Webster and the Concerned Citizens had to go on were rumour and speculation, but the pressure to discover facts was growing. One thing was certain: the investigation of the marijuana trade could not be left to the Griffith police.

■ ■ ■

By the middle of 1975 Don Mackay was receiving a trickle of information that appeared more reliable than the familiar rumours. While it did not include names, it mentioned places. Some of Mackay's information was included in a three-page typed document written by June Webster that was handed to two officers of the New South Wales Drug Squad on 26 August 1975. The document contained a litany of allegations and insinuations against Bob Trimbole and Winery Tony, as well as against the judge who sentenced Rocco Barbaro.

The dossier was headlined 'Drug problem in Griffith NSW' and stated at the outset, 'For ease of expression the following information is supplied as though it were proven fact. No proof is available to substantiate any of these claims at present, though I know that a group of concerned citizens have been compiling evidence for some 18 months.' The first item alleged that 'the headquarters for the growing of "grass" in this area is Sergi's Winery, a new installation completed in March 1975, estimated to be worth $1 million. The Sergi family involved regularly had their cheques dishonoured 3 years ago.' The third item stated, 'The outlet for grass grown in this area is either a wine shop [or] warehouse somewhere in Sydney operated by a fellow called Bob Trimbole.' Another item noted that several of the local police 'are on a roster system to escort Mr Trimbole in and out of Griffith. He arrives at night and leaves at night with his special cargo.'

While the dossier fell far short of being admissible evidence, it signalled the emergence of an increasingly fearless citizens' group dedicated to tackling the marijuana growers and traffickers head-on. Convinced that the local police could not be trusted to investigate, let alone prosecute, the drug bosses, the Concerned Citizens decided to take matters into their own hands. While some of the allegations seemed like little more than gossip, the range of information contained in the dossier suggested a large number of informants. It was clear that the Concerned Citizens of Griffith had plenty of community support for their battle against the marijuana industry.

So long as the allegations remained unsubstantiated, La Famiglia had little to fear. But Mackay possessed information that was far more dangerous, both to La Famiglia and to himself. It concerned a remote property at a place called Coleambally.

CHAPTER 6

Coleambally drug bust

In 1941 the annual value of market gardening in the Murrumbidgee Irrigation Area had been about $4 million. By the mid-1970s it was around $100 million—a figure that did not included any of the cannabis that alone was worth up to $200 million, double the value of legitimate fruit and vegetable produce.

The Trimboli, Sergi & Sergi warehouse at Flemington Markets was the major clearing house for commercial cannabis crops grown by La Famiglia at locations around New South Wales. Bob Trimbole had trucks travelling between Sydney and Griffith almost around the clock.

Trimbole's marriage was over. He had sold the Texan Tavern and was now living in Sydney's western suburbs. Friends in Griffith heard that Bob had moved in with another woman, a single mother.

Living in Sydney made it easy for Trimbole to control the distribution side of the business. He had no trouble finding drivers. Mixing easily with the workers at the markets, Trimbole offered generous money to men willing to drive from Sydney to Griffith and back two or three times a week.

Trimboli, Sergi & Sergi had been known to work closely with legitimate trucking businesses out of Griffith as well as national haulage companies such as TNT and Lindsay Fox's Linfox. Trucks would depart from Griffith fully laden with fruit and vegetables after doing the rounds of local packing sheds collecting pallets of boxed and graded oranges or bins of onions, melons or pumpkins. On the whole, they were legitimate businesses shifting legal loads.

Bob Trimbole's personal trucking fleet, usually no more than a solitary semi-trailer and trusted driver, would leave Sydney most afternoons to arrive in Griffith late, often driving down empty. The driver would park in Banna Lane, just behind the main street, Banna Avenue, and check in to a pre-booked room at the Area Hotel. While the truckie slept, Trimbole's semi-trailer would be taken to pre-arranged locations to be loaded with hessian bags or drums of marijuana, dried, prepared and bagged as cannabis leaf. Most was grown near Griffith but some came from as far away as Hay and Hillston.

The next morning the semi-trailer would be found exactly where it had been left the night before. Sometimes a truck would be covered in red dust from driving out to Hillston or some other isolated area; Trimbole's drivers knew better than to ask. The truck would then be driven back to the Trimboli, Sergi & Sergi packing area at Flemington, where the cannabis would be unloaded.

Few ever complained about working for Bob Trimbole. He paid his drivers their full entitlements and picked up the cost of hotels, meals and drinks. All they had to do was ask no questions and drive.

■ ■ ■

The cannabis trade was flourishing but Trimbole was still an undischarged bankrupt, making it difficult for him to manage a legal business. In particular, Trimbole's bankruptcy complicated the operations of a shelf company, Duskjur Pty Limited, used by Trimbole, Winery Tony and Pasquale 'Pat' Sergi (born 1 January 1946 in Platì) as an investment vehicle to buy properties worth hundreds of thousands of dollars. Through Tony Sergi, Trimbole was introduced to the Sydney accountants who did the books for Sergi's winery. Trimbole needed around $21,000 to settle debts that dated back to 1968 when the Pool Garage burnt down. Aware that Australian Taxation Office inspectors had begun to take an interest in the cannabis-generated cash splash, Trimbole disguised the source of the money by asking seven of his La Famiglia friends in Griffith to contribute cheques of between $2000 and $5000 to pay the Official Receiver. On 5 July 1975 Bob Trimbole was officially discharged from bankruptcy.

At the same time Trimbole, possibly using an alias, was involved in preparations for a huge cannabis crop at Coleambally, 60 kilometres south of Griffith, on a property owned by Leonardo Gambacorta.

Born on 5 October 1924, Gambacorta had arrived in Australia in May 1953. Three years later he bought a small farm in Sandgate, Queensland. Gambacorta was typical of many Italian immigrants who went to work in the cane fields or the mines. After selling his farm, he moved to the Griffith area with his wife, Grazia, to work as a farm labourer. It was not until 1973 that Gambacorta was able to buy his own farm, a meagre two acres just outside Griffith.

It was a frugal life, with Gambacorta receiving Department of Social Security assistance to supplement the money he was earning from the farm and from working as a casual labourer. A taxable income of only $979 in 1974 made Gambacorta an obvious target for La Famiglia, who made him an offer he could not refuse—to grow marijuana.

In early 1974 Gambacorta approached a real estate agent, Francesco Cavallaro, seeking to buy a farm with 'an abundance of water'. Within a few months Gambacorta was negotiating the purchase of a 1200-acre (486-hectare) farm at Coleambally. In the previous two years the owners had lost $3982 and $1438 on their agricultural business but this didn't appear to worry Gambacorta, who agreed to buy the Coleambally property for $70,000.

On 25 June 1974 Gambacorta paid $3670 cash into his wife's savings account and another $5002 into their joint account. Those who knew the couple did not believe Len's story that the money came from the two-acre farm. A month later they were able to deposit $45,000 into their Griffith bank account, including three cheques totalling $25,000 from the Bank of New South Wales account of Trimboli, Sergi & Sergi at Fairfield. Another cheque for $25,000 from the Rural Bank followed. The cheques—amounting to $70,000 in all— had all the hallmarks of payments from an agent to a grower, yet the Gambacortas only owned a two-acre farm.

The cheques continued to arrive. Gambacorta began spending money on farm equipment such as a Same Saturno tractor from D. & D. Machinery, Griffith. Francesco 'Frank' Sergi of Tharbogang (born 24 January 1935 at Platì) commissioned a welder to build a prefabricated steel shed and later paid for timber and galvanised sheets for the roof.

Large sums of 'black' money were now passing through the hands of legitimate business owners in Griffith, with real estate agents and solicitors handling lucrative property transfers.

In July 1975 Gambacorta entered into a leasing agreement with a man named Antonio Katarzis (possibly an alias for Trimbole), who agreed to rent an area of 1000 acres on the Coleambally farm for $6000, payable in advance. The site boasted a water bore, a six-berth caravan, various tractors, a Massey Ferguson seed drill and other agricultural equipment.

A Ford tractor was bought from J.S. Vagg & Co, Griffith, another legitimate business that had no reason to suspect that the equipment it was selling would be used to cultivate marijuana.

On 19 August $700.20 was paid for 100 bags of urea fertiliser.

Len Gambacorta was spending like a drunken sailor, frequenting clubs and punting on the races. At the end of the month he exchanged contracts to buy a town block in Grimison Avenue, Griffith for $2800, with plans for a two-storey house to be built by Nunzio 'Norm' Greco. But while Gambacorta, Trimbole and their La Famiglia friends dreamt of a bumper payday, the police were preparing to strike.

■ ■ ■

On 10 November 1975 three Sydney detectives and a senior constable from the small Riverina town of Whitton raided a remote property still known in the district as Stevenson's (after the previous owner) but now owned by Len and Grazia

Gambacorta. They found a marijuana plantation spread across 31.5 acres (thirteen hectares)—the largest crop yet discovered in New South Wales. While the drug bust made headlines in the Riverina, the rest of Australia would be preoccupied with even more sensational news: the dismissal the following day of Gough Whitlam's Labor government and its flamboyant Minister for Immigration, Al Grassby.

The Coleambally drug swoop was the result of a tip-off by Donald Mackay, who had discreetly handed information to the Drug Squad in Sydney, bypassing corrupt detectives in Griffith. Hastily planned by Detective Senior Constable Ron Jenkins from an office in Mackay's furniture shop, the raid would come as a nasty shock to Sergeant Ellis and his Griffith colleagues, who were deliberately kept in the dark.

The initial plan was for Jenkins to enter the property with two Sydney colleagues, Detectives Ross and Drury. At the last minute, Jenkins asked Senior Constable Howatson, who had a four-wheel-drive vehicle, to make himself available at the Darlington Point–Whitton Road junction in his Toyota LandCruiser. Constable Jenkins would accompany Howatson in the 4WD while Constable Ross followed in a drug squad vehicle and Constable Drury rode a trail bike.

From the rendezvous on the Whitton Road the party travelled 21 kilometres along a dirt track to the Gambacortas' farm, passing through eleven gates, all of which were locked. They broke through the final gate at around 12.30pm. Beyond the gate was a caravan as well as various vehicles, tractors and farm implements. In the distance, obscured by trees, a large steel shed stood on the edge of an irrigated plantation containing rows of cannabis plants. The growers appeared to have made no attempt to hide the marijuana crop, but to have relied on the remoteness of the property to safeguard against discovery. Some trouble had been taken, however, to plant a large crop of parsnips along the approach road to conceal the true purpose of the farm.

As the police approached the caravan, they saw six or seven men run away. Amid the chaos they managed to arrest Griffith man Giuseppe 'Joe' Agresta (born 25 December 1939 in Platì) and his brother, Pasquale Agresta (born 18 January 1938 in Platì), who was carrying a shotgun that Giuseppe claimed was used for shooting snakes. A third man, Luigi Pochi (born 7 January 1937 in Platì), was later flushed out of the marijuana crop. It was unclear whether Pochi was among the six or seven who had tried to escape. The three men told police they had gone to the property to chip weeds in a crop of parsnips.

From a police point of view, the Coleambally raid was a disaster. The four police were completely unprepared for the arrest of twice their number. Constable Drury on the trail bike had to choose which of several men to chase through the cannabis plantation; when some escaped by scrambling over the fence, Drury was unable to follow on the bike. In the circumstances, it was a miracle that three were arrested.

In an annex to the caravan, the detectives found a portable generator supplying electricity for air-conditioning and refrigeration. They also found several two-way radios. It was clear to Jenkins that crop workers had been living onsite.

The arrests were just the beginning. Jenkins had to establish a crime scene and think about what to do with literally tonnes of marijuana. Pasquale Agresta told Jenkins that he lived on the farm, and that only he, his brother Joe and Luigi Pochi were looking after the place.

When they searched the caravan, the detectives found a .25-calibre automatic pistol and cartridges, as well as bottles of marijuana seed and a parcel of marijuana foliage. According to Joe Agresta, the farm was owned by Leonardo Gambacorta and the seeds were supplied by Antonio Katarzis, who promised to pay $50,000 for the crop. There was evidence of a previous crop having been harvested and packed inside the shed.

After being arrested, the three men were taken to Darlington Point police station and then on to Griffith. As gossip spread about the Coleambally drug bust, rifts began to emerge within the town's usually harmonious multicultural population. It was a nervous time for the Italian community, who were already feeling the loss of their champion, Al Grassby, in the wreckage of the sacked Labor government. Accusing fingers were now being pointed at the Calabrian cannabis growers for giving Griffith a 'bad name'.

Coming so soon after the busts at Tharbogang and Hanwood, the discovery of the much larger Coleambally crop represented a financial catastrophe for La Famiglia, whose marketing operation stood to lose tens of millions of dollars' worth of business.

In an attempt to limit the damage to the organisation, Giuseppe Agresta took the blame for the whole Coleambally transaction, insisting that his brother Pasquale and Pochi were there for the first time and knew nothing about the cannabis crop.

Quizzed by police about the involvement of Tharbogang farmer Francesco 'Frank' Sergi, who had paid for materials used to build the shed where the cannabis crop was to be dried and packed, Giuseppe Agresta said he had not seen Sergi since he started growing the marijuana. (Agresta claimed he could not buy the materials himself because he was bankrupt and could not get credit.) Although he admitted to taking a tractor to Frank Sergi's place for repairs, Agresta insisted that Sergi knew nothing about the marijuana crop, did not grow, sell or supply the drug, and was not guilty of anything.

CHAPTER 7

Mackay has to go

The families of Pasquale and Giuseppe Agresta and Luigi Pochi now had a problem on their hands: raising money for bail. The brothers' wives quickly got in touch with Frank Sergi's brother, Domenico 'Mick' Sergi, of 52 Wood Road, Griffith. Due to the seriousness of the alleged crimes, bail was likely to be substantial. Members of La Famiglia were accustomed to keeping sizeable amounts of cash under the floorboards for bail and other emergencies. At short notice, Mick Sergi reckoned he would be able to raise $20,000, which he delivered to Mackenzie's office the day after the Coleambally arrests, only to be told that it would not be enough. Bail was eventually set at $30,000 for Giuseppe Agresta; $10,000 for Pasquale and $10,000 for Pochi.

Mick Sergi immediately set about raising the cash, with 61-year-old 'Uncle Rocco' Agresta, of Farm 1399, Yoogali kicking in $2500 and another relative around $4000. Brother-in-law Giuseppe Pasquale Staltare, who worked part

time repairing wooden pallets used to haul fruit and vegetables, put up another $3500 after receiving a call from Mick
Sergi at around midnight on 10 November 1975. Another
brother, 24-year-old Roy Peter Agresta (also known as
'Rooster' Agresta), who was also a brother-in-law of Mick
Sergi, was lucky enough to have $6500 in savings and wins
from backing horses that he was able to hand over after a
late-night visit from Mick.

In just five years Mick's brother Frank Sergi had increased
the annual trading profit of his fruit packing business from
around $6000 to more than $132,000. Such profits were
far beyond what could normally be expected from selling
oranges, lemons and peaches, even in a bumper year. Like
several other members of the Sergi family, Frank made use of
his wealth to build an ostentatious new home. On the streets
of Griffith it was widely assumed that such riches could only
derive from one crop: marijuana or 'Calabrese corn'.

During the mid-1970s Frank Sergi was conspicuous not
only for his newfound prosperity but also for his expenditure
on tractors and bagged urea, items usually required for broadacre cropping rather than horticultural farming.

It was no surprise when, a fortnight after the discovery
of the Coleambally marijuana crop, detectives arrested Frank
Sergi for conspiracy. Questioned by detectives Jenkins and
Ross, Sergi was at first cooperative, admitting to having
financed a shed, provided a tractor and bought fertiliser, but
it wasn't long before he changed his mind and stopped talking.

A month earlier, Frank Sergi had been negotiating with
real estate agents Elder Smith Goldsbrough Mort Limited to
invest $250,000 in a valuable property near Griffith owned
by the sheep and cattle drover Lionel Joseph Crump. Frank
inspected the farm on 27 October and again a few days

later, this time accompanied by Giuseppe 'Joe' Sergi, father of Winery Tony. A deal, evidently approved by the elder Joe Sergi, was imminent when police found the Coleambally crop. As a result of the seizure Frank Sergi could no longer count on the cash and the property deal fell through.

The size of the Coleambally plantation—and the value of the confiscated crop—caused some to worry that the criminals behind the multimillion-dollar business might turn to violence to protect their profits. Indeed, there were fears that this might already have happened. On 31 October, less than a fortnight before the Coleambally bust, a young Griffith woman named Linda Humphries had disappeared. The recently married 21-year-old had last been seen driving her car in Griffith. There was speculation Linda had stumbled across a drug crop while driving to farms around Griffith in search of casual work as a fruit picker. Her car was found at Fitzroy Falls near Moss Vale but there was no trace of Linda. It was feared that she might have been murdered.

Meanwhile, police and citizens now confronted the problem of how to dispose of $50 million worth of cannabis. A proposal to use heavy machinery to bury the crop was rejected because most of the marijuana had already seeded and would germinate if buried. After discussions with the Department of Agriculture, police appeared to lean towards poisoning the crop.

When the Member for Murrumbidgee, Lin Gordon, asked the New South Wales government for $8000 to pay for the crop's destruction, Don Mackay countered by demanding that equipment found at the farm—including an air-conditioned caravan, two cars and four tractors—be sold off to meet the cost. At the same time, he reminded readers of the *Area News* that $50,000 in cash had been produced for bail at short notice, indicating the 'massive funds' available to those behind the crop. In the end the government paid for the operation, with police reportedly on 24-hour guard 'until all trace of the crop has been eliminated'.

Mackay's anti-drugs stance was already well known, but there were some who wondered whether the aspiring politician was taking a big personal risk by making such outspoken statements against La Famiglia. Nobody was aware that it was Mackay who had told the Drug Squad about the Coleambally crop.

It was more than a year before the men accused in the Coleambally drug case went to trial in the Griffith District Court. In the interim, a series of marijuana busts across New South Wales increased public concerns about the alleged existence of a secretive Calabrian criminal organisation known variously as the 'ndrangheta, L'Onorata Societa or La Famiglia.

Interest in the case extended far beyond Griffith and the Riverina. Newspaper reporters and photographers from Sydney and Melbourne congregated in the editorial office of the *Area News*, which had hired its former nemesis Terry Jones as editor. Aware of the importance of the trial and of the interest it was likely to generate across Australia, Jones made the *Area News*'s telephone lines and darkroom freely available to out-of-town journalists.

Money was no object for the five accused, all of whom had high-profile barristers on their side. Griffith solicitor Simon Mackenzie had engaged barristers John Foley and Alec Shand, QC, to represent Frank Sergi. Another top-flight barrister, Roger Gyles, was appearing for Len Gambacorta, while Giuseppe Agresta, his brother Pasquale and Luigi Pochi were represented by Linton Morris.

Under fierce cross-examination by the defence barristers, Detective Jenkins and his colleagues denied allegations that they had concocted confessions and planted marijuana seeds on the accused men. There was talk among reporters that the trial was at risk of being aborted because one of the jurors might be related to one of the accused.

More worrying to the Concerned Citizens and the group's unofficial secretary, June Webster, were rumours identifying Don Mackay as the source of the information that led the Drug Squad to Coleambally. As general manager of the *Area News*, Webster was privy to some of the talk among journalists covering the case. She was concerned that Mackay had made enemies with his call for farm machinery to be sold off to pay the cost of destroying the Coleambally crop. Rumours of Mackay being a police informer made her even more worried. She and Jones agreed to keep Mackay's name out of any conversations they had with reporters from Sydney and Melbourne.

Five days after the start of the Coleambally trial, news broke of another big drug bust in New South Wales, at Euston, a small town on the banks of the Murray River, where police had found a fifteen-acre (six-hectare) cannabis plantation. Police were said to have found a utility on the Euston property registered in the name of a business in Griffith.

The *Area News* office was still buzzing with speculation on whether the trial would be aborted when the paper's veteran court reporter, Harry Fenwick, returned from the trial with chilling news: Detective Jenkins had been instructed by the judge to show his police notebook to the defence barristers. Knowing what information it contained, Jenkins had protested but was overruled by Judge Jack Newton. Harry Fenwick had watched while the lawyers, with the accused men sitting behind them, leafed through its pages. One piece of information would have been of special interest to the defendants: the name of the informer, Donald Mackay.

'Sweet Jesus,' Fenwick murmured, after he had finished recounting the story, 'they've as good as signed the man's death warrant.'

June Webster was the first to speak. 'Don has to be told,' she said. 'He needs to know his life is in danger. They already know he's the source of the Coleambally tip-off. Now they'll be blaming him for Euston, whether he said anything about it or not.'

Nobody at the *Area News* would have been foolish enough to publish what they knew about Don Mackay's informing, but a reporter from out of town just might.

Meanwhile, the Coleambally trial was turning into an ordeal for the police. The amateurish organisation of the raid had been laid bare and the defence barristers had succeeded in casting serious doubt on the verbal admissions of guilt. There was disbelief that the Sydney detectives had imagined they could handle the raid without help from local police. Had the detectives from the Drug Squad trusted police from Leeton and Narrandera, it would have been possible to put up road blocks, organise back-up and maintain effective radio communications. As it was, the Coleambally raid was looking more and more like the kind of gigantic police cock-up that would result in guilty defendants walking free. Even the corrupt Griffith detectives who raided crops at Tharbogang and Hanwood had done a better job.

Notwithstanding doubts over the men's confessions, and in spite of their unsworn protestations of innocence from the dock, Gambacorta, Pochi and the Agresta brothers were all found guilty of supplying Indian hemp and given sentences of between two and five years. The jury was unable to reach a verdict on Frank Sergi.

Outside the court, many were convinced that the guilty four had taken the rap for the men behind this crop and at least one other.

■ ■ ■

Attention now turned to Euston. Of the fifteen-acre cannabis plantation, nine acres (four hectares) had already been harvested. Some of this was found drying in a shed hidden among nearby trees. Four men were arrested on or near the property, while at least six more fled. All four taken into custody had been born in the province of Calabria in southern Italy.

Before the raid, police in the outer western Sydney suburb of Fairfield had spent six days watching the homes of two brothers, Antonio and Domenico Velardi, born in Platì, Calabria. Both were living on invalid pensions. When detectives went to both homes they discovered nearly two tonnes of marijuana—until then the largest single seizure of prepared cannabis leaf found in New South Wales.

Some of the cannabis was stored in hessian bags weighing approximately 50 pounds, the rest in green garbage bags containing either ten pounds of cannabis in bulk or ten separate one-pound packages. Police also found kitchen scales, string and unused green garbage bags similar to bags found at Coleambally.

At about 2pm on 5 March 1977, Drug Squad detectives from Sydney, assisted by local and interstate police, went to Willra Station at Euston, the property of Vincenzo Ciccarello, and found six acres remaining of a fifteen-acre marijuana crop. (Soil samples taken from the marijuana found at the home of Antonio Velardi proved that it had been grown at Willra Station.) Among other items found at the property was a pair of trousers with a laundry mark inside bearing the name 'Sergi' and a packing case branded F. & S. Sergi, Tharbogang. Inside the glove box of a Holden panel van police found papers belonging to another vehicle registered to a business called Pant Ranch, a Griffith clothing store owned by Bob Trimbole's two daughters, Gayelle Bignold and Glenda Trimbole.

Examination of the sleeping quarters indicated that nine people lived onsite but, as had happened at Coleambally, the majority escaped arrest.

Police investigations revealed that Vincenzo Ciccarello had bought Willra Station on 1 April 1976 for $92,000 with the help of a $42,000 loan from the Rural Bank, Dareton.

Ciccarello claimed to have been given $83,000 cash—comprising five separate amounts of $18,000, $25,000, $22,000, $13,000 and $5000—by an Italian man he only knew as 'Bruno', whom he had met in a hotel at Redcliff. After listening to Ciccarello's account of his financial struggles, 'Bruno' had offered to help him buy a bigger property. Of the $83,000, $65,000 was supposed to have been a ten-year loan to be repaid at 10 per cent interest (unfortunately 'Bruno' had the only copy of the contract), while the rest was to be spent on irrigation equipment and a bulldozer.

The Concerned Citizens, who had been carefully monitoring evidence emerging from the Euston raid, had no doubt that 'Bruno' was Aussie Bob Trimbole.

In Sydney and Melbourne, newspaper reports linking the Euston cannabis crop to Griffith were seized upon as further evidence that the town owed the bulk of its wealth to the cannabis trade. Claims by tax officials in Sydney that profits from marijuana accounted for 54 per cent of all taxable income passing through the town's trading banks were scorned by the president of the Griffith Chamber of Commerce, while the president of Wade Shire Council assured readers of the *Area News* that Griffith was 'not dependent on drugs for survival'. Everyone could see, however, that vast amounts of marijuana money were sloshing through the local economy.

Several items found at Euston were easily traced back to the Mitre 10 store in Griffith, owned by Jock and Bill Donaldson, friends of June Webster and of Donald Mackay. Tradesmen in Griffith had more work than they could handle: builders, bricklayers, plumbers, plasterers and painters were all taking on extra staff. Building supply companies were facing unprecedented demand for house bricks. Contractors employed by La Famiglia were being pressured to doctor invoices and receipts and to accept huge payments in cash for work on 'grass castles'.

It was boomtime in the Riverina but slurs about the source of its wealth were beginning to tell. Shop owners in Griffith found it increasingly difficult to deal with outside suppliers, some of whom were terminating long-term contracts for fear they might be inadvertently implicated in La Famiglia business. Members of the Chamber of Commerce complained of being shunned by wholesalers in New South Wales and Victoria with whom they had done business for years. Many citizens felt the whole community was being tarred by the actions of a few.

After defence counsel in the Coleambally trial argued that it was not an offence to grow marijuana in New South Wales, the Liberal Upper House member Tom Erskine, who had been born and raised in Griffith, called for the law to be changed to make it a crime to grow or cultivate cannabis in the state. 'With the Act as it is,' Erskine commented, 'we could all have a few marijuana plants growing in our gardens.'

■ ■ ■

In March 1977 the *Bulletin* magazine sent a reporter, Malcolm Turnbull, from Sydney to investigate the story behind the Griffith drug trials. Like other visiting journalists, the future prime minister went straight to the office of the *Area News*.

In his crisp white short-sleeve shirt, well-cut casual trousers and polished shoes, the urbane and friendly Turnbull made quite an impression as he walked around Griffith, gathering material for his story.

The cover of the *Bulletin* on 9 April 1977 featured a graph showing a hypodermic needle, a spoon containing white powder and an assortment of pills and tablets, but much of Turnbull's story was about Griffith and its 'Calabrese corn'. The *Bulletin* was not usually a big seller in Griffith but this edition quickly sold out. Turnbull had researched his story well and showed himself to be more perceptive than many of the journalists who made the trip from Sydney and Melbourne. 'Any Calabrian with newly acquired possessions, a big car or a new house is accused of having a little patch of Calabresi corn,' he wrote. 'The citizens of Griffith who aren't Calabrian are strongly opposed to the growing of marijuana, but their resentment is heavily tainted with racism.'

Noting that cannabis worth nearly $20 million on the street had been harvested from the farm at Euston and that a crop worth around $80 million had been awaiting harvest at Coleambally, Turnbull commented: 'The illegal industry could be worth more than the local production of the entire Murrumbidgee Irrigation Area, which is over $60 million.'

Among the people interviewed for the story was Brother Desmond, the principal of the Catholic high school, who told Turnbull that students could earn money harvesting marijuana. The teenagers were picked up late at night by the growers, blindfolded and then driven out to the farms where they sometimes worked until 5am. Experienced pickers were able to earn up to $400 a night. While none of this was news to local journalists, the alleged involvement of young people in the marijuana business—as pickers, users and dealers—was a critical issue for Donald Mackay and the Concerned Citizens.

Nobody except Mackay knew where he had got his information about the Coleambally crop, but his belligerent attitude to the marijuana growers was making him some dangerous enemies. While Mackay was not the source of the Euston tip-off, several newspaper reports had linked him to the raid. The combined loss to La Famiglia from the Coleambally and Euston seizures was anywhere between $50 million and $100 million and the finger of blame was pointed squarely at Donald Mackay.

After hearing that Mackay had made 'accusations' and 'nasty insinuations' about the Trimbole family, Bob Trimbole burst into Griffith police station and complained to Detective Sergeant Jim Bindon: 'If Mackay doesn't stop denigrating my wife and kids in Griffith, I'll kill the bastard.'

In early July 1977 Mackay revealed to Terry Jones that he had received a phone call from a man who threatened to burn his furniture shop down if he did not quit his anti-drugs campaign. Jones wanted to report the threatening phone call in the *Area News* but Mackay refused, convinced that the publication of anonymous threats was counter-productive and would result in copycat calls.

There was another reason: Mackay was planning to run again for state parliament and he didn't want to be accused of trying to make political capital out of the threatening phone call. The next election was more than a year away and Mackay did not want drugs to be the main issue. In Griffith, however, the subject was never far from the news. In the second week of July marijuana was back in the headlines when the state's attorney-general, Frank Walker, decided Frank Sergi would not have to stand trial again for his role in the Coleambally crop.

Many in Griffith were not surprised by the attorney-general's intervention. They had seen how Sergi avoided conviction in the first Coleambally trial and were aware of the strong links that existed between the Labor Party and the Italian community in the Riverina. They knew that La Famiglia's power went beyond the ability to buy expensive lawyers.

The decision to 'No Bill' Frank Sergi (in other words, to take no further proceedings against him) put Griffith back in the national spotlight. On Sunday 10 July a TV reporter and camera crew from Melbourne turned up outside Donald Mackay's home, wanting to talk about the town's drug problem and about allegations of schoolchildren being paid to pick cannabis. They were following up a series of stories by Richard Willis and Antony Cheeswright that had appeared in the Melbourne *Herald* about 'a syndicate in [the] Griffith district . . . reaping multi-million dollar harvests' of marijuana. Don Mackay had been widely quoted in the *Herald*'s articles.

Mackay rang Terry Jones at home. He wanted Jones, as editor of the *Area News*, to speak to the reporter. While Jones was always happy to provide background information to fellow journalists, he was uncomfortable about being a spokesman. He felt that was the role of community leaders, not newspaper editors. Jones suggested asking the Wade Shire Council president, Bob Irvin, or the Liberal Upper House member Tom Erskine.

Mackay told Jones he would sort something out.

Reports of Griffith teenagers picking cannabis had raised the political stakes and the state Liberal opposition was quick to capitalise, with a group of Liberal parliamentarians visiting the Riverina for two days to investigate for themselves. Don Mackay was, as always, a key source of information.

Members of La Famiglia were rumoured to have uttered warnings that 'something' would happen to Mackay if he didn't stop talking. In fact, the decision to murder Donald Mackay had already been taken.

■ ■ ■

The previous month, Bob Trimbole had convened a secret meeting of at least six members of La Famiglia's hierarchy in Griffith at which it was decided that Mackay 'had to go'. Details about the meeting were not revealed until nearly a decade later, when parts of a formal statement by Trimbole's trusted Melbourne partner-in-crime, Gianfranco Tizzoni, were finally released.

In the statement, given in June 1983, Tizzoni claimed that by May 1977 'the threat by Mackay to our operations was considered so important that the problem was discussed at a meeting between . . . Bob Trimbole and myself . . . in Griffith. [Tizzoni named two other people as having attended the meeting. The names are omitted because Tizzoni later withdrew the allegation.] During the meeting we discussed three alternatives designed to overcome the problem. One was to buy off Mackay at any price; another was to compromise him by getting him involved with a woman. The third alternative and the last resort was execution.' Two days after making the statement, Tizzoni retracted his claims. Few doubted that Tizzoni's retraction was to save his own skin.

Senior members of La Famiglia were told to ensure they had alibis on the day the murder was to be committed, either by leaving town for the weekend or by having plenty of witnesses to confirm their whereabouts.

In the week leading up to Friday 15 July 1977, several of Trimbole's most prominent associates, as well as members of his own family, made arrangements to be out of Griffith.

■ ■ ■

On Wednesday or Thursday of the previous week Don Mackay had received a phone call from a man calling himself 'Ray Adams', who claimed to have recently won the lottery and wanted to furnish a house near Jerilderie for his son-in-law and daughter, or son and daughter-in-law. He asked Mackay to meet him outside the Flag Inn at Jerilderie at 10.30am on Tuesday 12 July. Mackay agreed to come and gave Adams a description of his car and its registration number. Mackay told one of his employees, Bruce Pursehouse, about the call.

But the day before the meeting, Mackay realised he had to speak at a funeral on the Tuesday and asked Pursehouse to make the trip to Jerilderie in his place. Since Adams already had a description of the car, Mackay told Pursehouse to use the same vehicle.

The next morning Pursehouse drove to Jerilderie, 140 kilometres south of Griffith, accompanied by his father-in-law, Patrick Gaynor, 83, who was staying with him. After arriving at Jerilderie at about 10.20am he pulled up outside the Flag Inn to wait for Mr Adams.

While he waited, he happened to notice a white Ford Falcon sedan parked opposite some public toilets in the nearby park. At a few minutes after eleven, Pursehouse rang Mackay to say that Adams had not arrived. Mackay asked him to wait for another half an hour and if nobody had arrived by then to drive back to Griffith. When Pursehouse returned to the car he saw the white Falcon sedan pull away from the kerb and cruise past the motel before stopping outside the Jerilderie post office, just a few metres from where Pursehouse was parked.

After sitting for a short time in the car, the driver got out and walked into the post office, before driving away from Jerilderie on the Griffith–Narrandera road. While the Falcon was parked outside the post office, Pursehouse and his father-in-law had a good look at the driver and discussed his appearance. In a subsequent statement given to crown prosecutor Barry Newport, Pursehouse recalled:

> [H]e was the only one that we saw there who appeared as though he may have won the lottery . . . He had a blue pin-striped suit on and he had heavily-oiled down black hair, combed straight back, and he had a dark moustache going down past the side of his mouth. He also was wearing dark wrap-around sunglasses, and my father-in-law made comment to me when this gentleman got out and we had a good look at him. We called him Al Grassby . . . I would describe him as of flash appearance or a flash dresser . . .

Whilst we were sitting in the car . . . my father-in-law was staring at this gentleman and I said to him, 'Don't look at him.' I said, 'I'll turn the mirror round and look at him through that and if he wants to contact us, he will come to us, he knows what we look like, we don't know what he looks like, so don't stare at him.' . . . I could see him sitting in the car and I had a good look at him and he could not see me looking at him at the same time.

Pursehouse's evidence about the abortive meeting in Jerilderie would prove crucial to unravelling the chain of events that followed.

■ ■ ■

On the same day that Bruce Pursehouse waited in vain for the mysterious Mr Adams, a reporter and photographer from Sydney's *Daily Telegraph* arrived in Griffith to look for one of the alleged teenage marijuana pickers. Heading straight for the office of the *Area News*, Colin McKay and Phil Merchant introduced themselves to Terry Jones, who confirmed rumours of the teenage pickers but admitted that none of his reporters had managed to interview one. Undeterred, McKay insisted he would find and interview a picker.

By mid-afternoon McKay and Merchant were back at the *Area News* with an interview and photographs of a youth who claimed to have harvested cannabis. Jones asked whether the *Telegraph* intended to publish the boy's picture. 'We've got him in the shadows,' said McKay. 'It'll be a silhouette. Nobody will be able to identify him.'

Jones was sceptical. 'You need to be bloody careful, Col. This isn't Sydney. There are only a few hundred boys of any given age in and around Griffith. If the facial outline is clear, it won't be too hard to identify the lad.'

'You worry too much, Terence,' said McKay.

After a few minutes in the darkroom, Merchant emerged with dripping wet photographs of the boy who claimed to be a drug picker.

'Strewth, Col,' said Jones, 'I reckon I'd be able to identify the kid from that, even though you can't see his full outline. There's no way I'd be running that picture.'

'Maybe you're right,' said McKay. 'We'll make it a bit darker.'

On the same day, 12 July, Tony Wright from the *Border Mail* in Albury came to Griffith to interview Donald Mackay. It was a typically forthright interview, with Mackay renewing his attack on the marijuana growers and even voicing his suspicions of the former Griffith detectives Jack Ellis and Brian Borthwick. Wright's story referred to 'grass castles' and also mentioned the 'overnight success' of Robert Trimbole and Antonio Sergi.

Colin McKay's story, published on 15 July in the *Daily Telegraph*, caused a sensation in Griffith. The talk in the town's shopping centre was all about the teenage marijuana pickers: Who were they? Where was the marijuana being grown? Who was behind it?

■ ■ ■

Meanwhile, members of La Famiglia were keeping a much bigger secret—the secret of Donald Mackay's impending execution.

The secret was almost blurted out during a conversation between customers in Polegato's butcher shop on Griffith's main street, Banna Avenue. Joe Polegato was serving a group of customers when a copy of the *Daily Telegraph* was spotted lying on the counter. At the mention of Donald Mackay's name, a bystander commented, 'He won't be around long.'

That day Don and Barbara Mackay, together with their sons Paul and James, went to lunch at the Irrigana Hotel. Also dining in the Irrigana that day were solicitor Simon Mackenzie and two former local detectives, Brian Borthwick and Arthur O'Sullivan, both of whom had flown down that morning from Sydney. The detectives left for the Victoria Hotel, where they met friends and had a few drinks before going to Sergi's winery, where they made arrangements with Tony and Mick Sergi to meet later at the Area Hotel.

It was at the Area Hotel that Terry Jones saw Borthwick and O'Sullivan. Besides saying 'G'day' and asking after Borthwick's wife, Pam, Jones did not say much to Borthwick, who seemed keen to avoid a longer conversation. Soon afterwards, the former detectives were joined by Winery Tony and Mick Sergi, neither of whom was a regular at the Area Hotel. As the Sergis ordered a round another local detective, Graham Keech, joined the group for a drink.

Thursday was the night Jones and his colleagues from the newspaper usually had a few beers at the Area Hotel, but it was rare to see police there. Detectives and uniformed police tended to favour the Irrigana across the road, where they mixed with local tradesmen and builders who were often happy to offer casual work to police on their days off. To Jones, it seemed that the two Sergis were deliberately making themselves conspicuous, laughing and joking and shouting rounds of beer.

Between 5.30pm and 6pm Jones left to drive home to Hanwood, about ten kilometres from Griffith. As he headed for the door, he waved to Borthwick. At almost the same time Don Mackay closed up his furniture store in Ulong Street, just behind Banna Avenue, and asked his staff where they were going for a beer. Mackay's usual watering holes were the Jondaryan Club, a few blocks from his home, and the Griffith Hotel, just up the road from his shop. 'If you go to the Griff, I'll have a couple with you,' Mackay told his staff. 'I've got to be home at 6.30 to babysit James.'

On his way out, Bruce Pursehouse reminded Mackay that he needed the furniture truck to move house on Saturday morning, meaning Mackay would have to drive the Mini Minor van with its distinctive logo on the side: MACKAY'S OF GRIFFITH FLOORCOVERINGS BLINDS FURNI-TURE FREE MEASURE & QUOTE.

One of Mackay's salesmen, Robert Farrell, got to the bar at 5.45pm, just ahead of Mackay, who bought a round of drinks with his friend Gerry Fitzgerald, a radiologist. Mackay was in a jovial mood, chatting and exchanging greetings with the regulars gathered for the weekly football club raffles. Around the bar there was a bit of talk about Frank Sergi's 'No Bill' and about the kids picking cannabis. Encouraged by a local quarry worker, Lionel Burns, to 'get up the marijuana bastards', Mackay replied, 'There's only one I'm after.'

Patricia Betts, who was running the raffles, saw Mackay arrive in his Mini Minor van and then leave before the prizes were drawn. Betts had known Mackay for eighteen years; the two would always exchange a few words, but this time Mackay left the hotel without speaking. Betts had the feeling that he was worried about something.

As Mackay walked out, Betts noticed another man leave. She remembered him being of Italian appearance, well-groomed, five foot one or two inches (1.5 metres) tall, with black collar-length hair and wearing light blue trousers and a royal blue jumper.

Two hotel waitresses, Marion Cunial and Edna Horrigan, arrived for work just after 6.15pm, noting Mackay's van parked behind the hotel. The car park lighting, which would normally have been turned on at exactly 6.15pm, was not working. Later Horrigan discovered that lights that would have been shining on Mackay's mini-van had been smashed.

Donald Kelly, who was employed as a barman but was working that night at the drive-in bottle shop, sold Mackay a cask of Coolabah wine at about 6.30pm. Mackay gave him $6.20 and was given four cents change. Before leaving the bottle shop, he exchanged a few words with another customer, Peter Marcus.

Kelly heard nothing out of the ordinary as Don Mackay walked alone into the darkened car park, but others did. Working late in an office that adjoined the hotel car park, accountant Roy Binks heard something that sounded like a whip cracking, and 'human noises'—a groan and the sound of someone vomiting. Binks heard the noises twice, two or three seconds apart, but did not investigate.

One man who made sure he was nowhere near the Griffith Hotel that night was Aussie Bob Trimbole, who was nearly 600 kilometres away having dinner at a restaurant with Ronald Dawson, a stables manager at Randwick Racecourse. Introduced to Trimbole in 1977 by a jockey named Alf Matthews, Dawson had been told 'it would be worth my while to tip him some winners'. At dinner Trimbole complained about the quality of a bottle of wine he had ordered, yet tipped the waitress, Ann Carlan, eight dollars. It was a generous tip, but a small price to pay for a watertight alibi.

CHAPTER 8

They've killed Don

Just after 7am on Saturday 16 July 1977 the phone rang at Terry Jones's home in Hanwood. The caller was Patrick O'Neill, a reporter for *This Day Tonight*, who had flown down to research a program on Griffith. O'Neill had shocking news. Don Mackay's furniture van had been found in the car park of the Griffith Hotel. There was a pool of dried blood and several .22-calibre bullet casings on the ground next to the van. It looked like murder.

Jones listened in dumb horror and disbelief. It was just days since Don Mackay had told him about the anonymous threat to burn down his shop. Everybody in Griffith knew that Mackay was taking a risk by speaking out against the marijuana growers but few imagined it could cost him his life.

After arranging to meet O'Neill at the *Area News* office, Jones drove into Griffith. He went straight to the Griffith Hotel car park and saw for himself Mackay's distinctive van and local police guarding the crime scene. One of the police pointed out the blood on the side of the van and showed him the bullet casings scattered on the tarmac. It had all the hallmarks of a mafia hit.

■ ■ ■

Patrick O'Neill was waiting for Jones at the *Area News* office. He had already spoken to the police. Together he and Jones went over everything they had been told. Mackay had been expected home by seven o'clock the previous evening but no one had seen him. He had not called his wife, Barbara, or anyone else.

As a journalist, Jones understood the urgency of getting the news to colleagues on the metro papers in Sydney and Melbourne—no easy task early on a Saturday morning. After failing to get an answer from any of the Sydney papers, Jones called Richard Willis at the Melbourne *Herald*. It was Willis and Antony Cheeswright who had broken the story about Griffith's teenage marijuana pickers. As Mackay campaigned for changes to the state's drug laws, Willis had become a confidant and friend. Some of the most damning quotes in Willis's drug stories came from Mackay.

The sergeant in charge of the Riverina, Kevin Horne, was on his way to Griffith from Wagga Wagga and had promised Jones an interview. Jones knew Horne from his days as a police roundsman on the *Newcastle Herald* and was confident that Horne wouldn't hold back. If it was true that the mafia had killed Mackay, the police would need all the help they could get. Obviously the story could not wait for the *Area News*, whose next edition was three days away. Jones offered to ring Willis straight after the interview and give him all the quotes he needed to be first with the story.

Surprisingly, Willis did not sound enthusiastic about being first to report what looked like a classic mafia-style political assassination, but as the significance of the story began to sink in, he changed his mind. 'I'm going to have to move pretty quickly to get anything into print,' he told Jones. 'I'll ring the paper and tip them off there's a big story coming through.' Then he added, 'What about pictures?'

The *Area News* had files full of pictures of Don Mackay, but the *Herald* would want photographs of the crime scene. One of Jones's photographers, Max Roberts, had been up early and had seen Jones's car parked outside the *Area News* office. Roberts was already at the Griffith Hotel getting pictures of the car park and of Mackay's Mini Minor van.

'There's only one problem,' Jones told Willis. 'How the hell do I get the pictures out of Griffith on a Saturday morning? What about a charter flight? Do you reckon the *Herald* would foot the bill?'

'They might,' said Willis. 'What can you tell me now that I can give them straight away?'

Jones was used to dictating news reports over the telephone. He quickly gave Willis as much of the story as he knew. After telling Willis about the bloodstains and shell casings in the hotel car park, he told Willis, 'It looks like whoever was waiting for Don had a struggle to subdue him, or to remove his body, because of the drag marks on the ground. The blood smear on the side of the car gives the impression a hand reached out to grab at the side door of the car, then slid down the side of the car.'

As to who was behind Mackay's murder, it was obviously too risky for the *Herald* to print names, but Terry Jones had no doubts. 'I'll bet anything Bob Trimbole's involved,' he told Willis. 'If Don's been killed, Trimbole is the one who would have organised it.'

News of the killing travelled fast. When O'Neill telephoned the local Upper House member, Tom Erskine, to arrange an interview he found the politician so upset he could hardly speak. 'I could hardly understand him, he was so agitated,' O'Neill told Jones later. 'He just kept saying over and over: "It's murder . . . it's murder . . . they've killed Don!"'

June Webster, the manager of the *Area News*, was equally distraught when Jones rang to tell her that Don Mackay was missing, feared murdered. She and Mackay had been at the forefront of the Concerned Citizens' campaign against the marijuana growers, gathering information and collaborating with the police. 'Oh, my God, the bastards,' she cried. 'Poor Don . . . Barbara . . . the kids.'

By late on Saturday morning Jones had managed to contact the news desk of the *Daily Telegraph* in Sydney. The Melbourne *Herald* had decided to charter a plane to fly a reporter down to Griffith. The plane would then return to Melbourne with Max Roberts's photographs of the crime scene, which would be made available to any newspaper that wanted them.

A lot had happened since midnight when Griffith police and the Riverina regional police had been mobilised after the grim discoveries in the car park of the Griffith Hotel.

It was around 10.30am when Terry Jones and Patrick O'Neill crossed the road from the office of the *Area News* to the Griffith police station. They were met by Sergeant Kevin Horne, who offered a firm handshake: 'You're early,' Horne said, 'but don't worry. I'll be with you in a moment.'

Jones introduced himself, reminding Horne that they had met in Newcastle, and then introduced O'Neill.

'You fellows move fast,' said Horne. 'I'll see if the boss is ready to go.'

While O'Neill and Jones waited in the foyer Norm Murphy burst in, panting. Murphy worked for Radio 2RG and the MTN–9 broadcasting centre in Griffith. 'Terry, is it true? Has Don Mackay been murdered?'

'It looks that way, Norm,' Jones replied. 'What have you heard?'

'The same as everyone else. Don's car is down at the Griff . . . they've found bullets on the ground . . . there's blood all over the place.'

Sergeant Horne, the most senior detective in the Riverina region, took the three to meet the newly appointed officer-in-charge of Griffith Police, Inspector Viv Lockhart, who announced, 'I'm just going to listen. I won't be making any comments.'

Lockhart had only been in the job a week and he had spent most of it leading a search for five missing hikers in the Cocoparra Range north of Griffith. There might have been another reason for his reticence: Lockhart had dined the previous night at La Scala restaurant with a group of former Griffith and Wagga police and members of the Sergi family. He had every reason to feel badly compromised.

With Lockhart unwilling to speak, Horne took over, laying out what the police knew about the Mackay 'missing person mystery'. Horne finished his briefing with the familiar pronouncement, 'Police hold fears for the safety of Mr Mackay.'

When asked bluntly by Jones, 'Was it murder?', Horne conceded, 'It's suspicious. We have every reason to fear Mr Mackay was the victim of a mafia-style murder.'

'Can we say that?' Jones asked.

Horne nodded. 'Mr Mackay's involvement in exposing those involved in drugs was well known,' he said.

Pressed further, Horne noted the significance of the spent .22 cartridges found at the scene, describing them as a calling card left behind by the killer or killers.

In less than ten minutes the conference was over. 'Terry, we're going to need a lot of public help here,' Horne said as Jones got up to leave. 'I'll be in touch tomorrow.'

Back at the office, Max Roberts had assembled photographs from every facet of Don Mackay's life, a testament to his tireless contributions to the community across two decades.

Before Jones could sit down, Richard Willis was on the phone from Melbourne. 'We're calling it a mafia killing,' Willis said. 'It's all over page one. The paper should already be on the way to Griffith.'

The Sydney papers were soon calling, checking facts, wanting pictures. Jones told Kevin Perkins at the *Telegraph* to refer to Don Mackay as 'an anti-drugs campaigner'— a description that would come to define Mackay for ever after, overshadowing all his other achievements.

In the excitement Jones had forgotten to ring his wife, Irene, who had been trying frantically to call him. 'Is it true?' she asked. 'Has Don been killed?'

Jones confirmed what Irene had heard on the radio news. 'It looks bad, Rene. There's not much hope for him.'

Irene was worried. 'What about you and June? Don was talking a lot about drugs and so were both of you. How many people are they going to kill?'

'I've spoken to June,' said Jones. 'She's frightened. She and Don worked really closely on this.'

Jones tried to play down the suggestion that there might be other names on the hit list, but it was a possibility none of them could ignore.

'Will you speak to Katie?' Irene asked. 'She's asking where you are. When she woke this morning you were gone. She wants to know when you'll be home.'

Six-year-old Ann-Catherine, known as Katie, was the eldest of Terry's and Irene's three children.

'Has someone hurt Mr Mackay?' she asked. 'Is he killed? The man on the radio said there was blood on his car and they found bullets. Why is Mr Mackay killed, Daddy?'

Jones hadn't expected Katie to be aware of what had happened to Don Mackay. It felt wrong to be hearing those facts again from the mouth of a six-year-old.

'You talk to Mummy, love,' he told her. 'She knows what happened to Mr Mackay. She'll tell you about it.'

But Katie was not to be put off. 'Why did people want to kill Mr Mackay?'

As Jones wondered how to answer his daughter, Irene took the phone. 'Try and be home before dark, won't you?' she said. 'And be careful.'

Jones promised to try, but it was long after dark when he finally left the office. The usual bustling Saturday night traffic in Griffith was nowhere to be seen. There was hardly a soul walking the streets. The news of Don Mackay's murder seemed to have filled the town with a sense of dread. Jones felt it himself as he stopped outside the post office to post a letter. Nobody knew who might be next.

By Monday the police had more information about what had happened on Friday night. At midnight Barbara Mackay had called a close family friend, the solicitor Ian Salmon, to say that Don had not come home and to ask him to make a quick search around town. It was Salmon who had found the Mackay Furniture Store mini-van in the car park of the Griffith Hotel and discovered the blood and bullet casings on the ground. Straight after giving his information to the police, Salmon had called a distraught Barbara, home alone with her children.

The *Area News* came out on Tuesday. Avoiding the mafia headlines used by the Sydney and Melbourne newspapers, Jones took a deliberately low-key approach, not wanting to inflame feelings against the town's large Italian community. Senior reporter George Gay interviewed Barbara Mackay, who said she believed her husband was dead but insisted he 'had no enemies' and told Gay that she 'did not know who would have wanted to kill him'.

Asked about his campaign against the marijuana growers, Barbara said, 'If everybody held back from pursuing what was right because of possible consequences, evil would reign unchecked.'

While confirming that threats—including a bomb threat—had been made against her husband 'over a period of time', Barbara Mackay said she particularly hoped her husband's death 'would not cause division with the community'.

In parliament, a call by the acting leader of the opposition, John Maddison, for a royal commission into drugs was slapped down by a spokesmen for the premier, Neville Wran, who said that the government was 'not likely' to order a royal commission into drugs until the parliamentary select committee had made its report. He also ruled out a visit by the Labor premier to Griffith on the grounds that there was 'nothing practical he could do'.

Rather than publish a photograph of the crime scene at the Griffith Hotel, Jones chose to use pictures of Neville Wran and John Maddison, the two men who would have the biggest say over whether or not to establish a royal commission of inquiry into drug trafficking in New South Wales. The *Area*

News did, however, carry a photo of Barbara Mackay holding her youngest son, James, who had hardly let his mother out of his sight since his father failed to return home on Friday.

Jones was not the only one worried about setting elements of the community against each other. The Wade Shire president, Bob Irvin, called for Griffith to 'keep it cool' in the wake of Mackay's disappearance. Acknowledging that 'a cloud is over our community', Irvin urged readers to 'keep our great area together and not jump to conclusions'.

The Member for Riverina, the Nationals' John Sullivan, who had defeated Al Grassby with the help of Don Mackay's preference votes, was not so diplomatic. In a prepared statement given to the *Area News* he wrote: 'The people of the Riverina will not react kindly to this type of intimidation. The mongrels who were responsible must be brought to book as quickly as possible.'

In the absence of clues, reporters from the capital city newspapers continued to speculate on what had happened to Mackay. The *Sydney Morning Herald*'s Peter Smark mentioned reports of a mystery plane landing in the early hours of Saturday morning to pick up Mackay's body and dump it at sea. There were stories of a Mafia hitman having come from the United States to kill Mackay and rumours of Mackay's body having been disposed of in Lake Wyangan or Barren Box Swamp; buried in the concrete footings of a new shop in Banna Avenue; or put through a mincer at the Bartter Enterprises blood and bone rendering works at Hanwood.

■ ■ ■

It did not go unnoticed that several suspected members of La Famiglia from Tharbogang had very impressive alibis for the afternoon and night of 15 July: they were carousing with police. The company dining at La Scala restaurant with Tony and Mick Sergi included not only former detectives Brian Borthwick and Arthur O'Sullivan, both suspected of corruption, but serving detective Graham Keech, who was supposed to have been on duty at the Griffith police station. Innocent bystanders were the newly appointed officer-in-charge of Griffith Police Command, Viv Lockhart, and his minder, Sergeant Peter Johansen.

Among the first out-of-town journalists to contact Terry Jones at the *Area News* was Bob Bottom, whose reporting for the *Bulletin* and later for the *Sunday Telegraph* had been credited with forcing the Askin government to establish the Moffitt Royal Commission into Organised Crime in 1973. Bottom asked, 'What are you hearing about the dodgy police alibis?'

Jones told Bottom he'd seen Borthwick and O'Sullivan drinking with the Sergis in the public bar of the Area Hotel around 5pm on Friday.

'It looks bloody suspicious,' said Bottom.

Led by Senior Sergeant Joe Parrington of the Sydney Homicide Squad, the Mackay investigation team included two other Sydney detectives, Fred Shaw and Rick Campbell.

It didn't take long for Parrington to be warned: 'Don't trust local police.' Soon after his arrival he was reported to have 'changed the locks' at Griffith police station.

Not everyone was suspect. Sergeant Jim Bindon had distanced himself from any hint of corruption ever since his arrival in Griffith in 1974. As soon as he discovered that Constable Keech had been among the party at La Scala, he alerted Parrington.

Sydney reporters Jim Madden of the *Sun* and John Wells of the *Daily Mirror* both heard that a notorious retired policeman, Fred Krahe, had been in Griffith the week Donald Mackay went missing. Krahe was on the payroll of the Nugan Group, which was involved in a messy power struggle involving company auditors and shareholders. When he wasn't leaning on 'uncooperative' Nugan Group shareholders, Krahe had been running around Griffith telling reporters that he had 'inside information' that Donald Mackay was having an affair with a woman and had run off with her.

Four days after Mackay's disappearance, Sergeant Horne told reporters that 50 officers and inspectors from the Water Resources Commission had begun a search of the canal system in the Griffith district. It was expected that properly searching the roughly 1300 kilometres of canals in the area would take a week. Police were also looking for a green 1963 EJ Holden sedan with a white roof, which had been seen by about ten people in the vicinity of the Griffith Hotel car park on the night Mackay disappeared.

The *Area News* also reported that Italian families had received abusive or threatening phone calls since Mackay's disappearance. The Italian consular agent in Griffith, Mr Stan Pellizzer, said several people had contacted him about the calls.

While inspectors from the Water Resources Commission searched the canals, police and rescue squad members began dragging Lake Wyangan. Weeds hampered the searchers and near-freezing temperatures meant that police divers could spend no more than twenty minutes in the water. They found no trace of the missing businessman's body.

With tension growing among Griffith's Italian community, the minister appointed by the Wran government as Liaison Officer for Ethnic Affairs, George Paciullo, made the decision to visit the town. The harmony of Griffith's mixed ethnic community had been 'put under a strain' by the disappearance of Don Mackay, Paciullo told the *Area News*, but would 'come out on top' in the long run.

■ ■ ■

On Thursday 21 July, six days after Mackay's disappearance, the premier, Neville Wran, announced the setting up of a royal commission into drugs, although it would only be finished once the joint parliamentary select committee had finished its report on the illegal drug trade. The following week the New South Wales government offered a $25,000 reward for information in the Mackay case.

On 26 July 6000 people attended a thanksgiving service for Don Mackay on the lawns of the Griffith Base Hospital, close to the proposed site of a nursing home that Mackay had helped found. Shops and businesses throughout the town closed between 1pm and 2pm and schoolchildren were ferried to the service on free buses. Barbara Mackay was there with three of their children (the youngest, three-year-old James, was unwell) to hear speakers pay tribute to her husband's fundraising and community work and his contribution to the Pioneer Lodge nursing home project.

It was an ecumenical service attended by representatives of the Uniting, Anglican, Catholic, Baptist and Seventh Day Adventist churches and there were hopes that such an event would help heal the divisions that were opening up in the wake of the presumed murder.

Soon afterwards workmen with jackhammers were instructed to demolish a concrete slab under Giuseppe 'Fish Shop Joe' Sergi's new fish shop on Banna Avenue. The slab had been poured on 16 July, the day after Mackay went missing. No body was found.

Meanwhile there was pressure on the government to increase the reward for information to $1 million—nobody in Griffith believed that $25,000 would be enough to tempt an informant to breach the mafia code of silence.

■ ■ ■

It was not only Australian reporters who were converging on Griffith. On 31 July the English broadcaster David Frost came to town with a camera crew to film an interview with Barbara Mackay. Four months earlier Frost had filmed a series of explosive television interviews with the disgraced former US President Richard Nixon. His arrival in Griffith stirred up a media frenzy.

The interview at the Yoogali Club, the region's major function centre, was open to the public, with the cameras to begin rolling at 5.30pm. Every seat in the auditorium had been taken by 3pm. By the time David Frost walked out on stage nearly 2000 people were crammed into the auditorium. Sitting with Barbara Mackay and June Webster in the front row were the Upper House member, Tom Erskine; the former Member for Murrumbidgee and Riverina, Al Grassby, and current Member for Murrumbidgee, Lin Gordon; the Catholic priest Father Raphael Beltrame; and the Wade Shire president, Bob Irvin.

Frost began by inviting Barbara Mackay to join him on the stage to describe what it felt like for an ordinary wife and mother living in an Australian country town to be thrust into the public spotlight under such horrifying circumstances. With characteristic frankness and courtesy, Barbara talked about her married life with Don in a vibrant rural community where everybody knew everybody else, and how they both worried that the futures of young people in Griffith were being threatened by the availability of illicit drugs. She told Frost what most of the people in Griffith already knew, that teenagers caught smoking pot were paying bigger fines in court than growers and suppliers of cannabis. On the question of her husband's disappearance, Barbara admitted that she and her children had all but given up hope of Don being found alive.

Frost then invited Al Grassby to join him on the stage. Waving to the audience and calling out to people he knew, Flash Al stepped up as though it was his show, not Frost's. Asked for his impressions of Griffith, Grassby declared, 'This is the most multicultural town in Australia. I can honestly say, I know nothing of drugs and Griffith. Personally, I can say I am not aware of drugs in this town or the Riverina.'

The previous week Grassby's wife, Ellnor, had told an interviewer the same thing. Hearing Flash Al repeat his wife's whitewash, the audience erupted in a chorus of boos and cat-calls.

Someone shouted, 'Hey Al, what about Hanwood, Tharbogang and Coleambally?'

Another called out, 'Al, are you covering up for someone?'

Someone else yelled out, 'You and your wife are pathetic. She was in town defending the drug growers last week. This week it's you!'

After Grassby was booed from the stage, Giuseppe 'Fish Shop Joe' Sergi stood up to identify himself. 'I'm the one who had to dig up the foundations of my new fish and chip shop on main street,' Joe Sergi told Frost. 'I was happy to do it. And I don't hide the fact I'm a Calabrese, southern Italian living in Griffith.'

There was loud applause for Joe Sergi, in contrast to the boos that hounded Al Grassby from the stage. To many in the Yoogali Club that night, it looked as if Grassby's once stellar career was over.

As filming came to an end, Frost issued a stark challenge to the audience: 'How many of you will be willing to come forward and tell what you know to the royal commission into drug trafficking? The cameras will not be rolling. Can we have a show of hands?'

Everyone in the Yoogali Club looked around as just five people raised their hands.

Frost thanked his audience but nobody was ready to leave. A chastened Al Grassby cornered Terry Jones. 'I'm not happy, Terence,' Grassby mumbled. 'This isn't good for Griffith, it's not good at all.'

Lin Gordon seemed to sympathise. 'Al was set up,' he told Jones. 'It was dreadful.'

But Gordon was out of touch with the mood of the audience, many of whom felt that Grassby had made an idiot of himself by claiming that there were no drugs in Griffith.

As for the five who had publicly volunteered to come forward and give evidence to the royal commission, nobody could decide whether they were brave or naïve or foolhardy.

■ ■ ■

It was not until the first week of August that the Wran government released details of what became formally known as the Royal Commission of Inquiry into Drug Trafficking. The person chosen to head the commission was Justice Philip Woodward of the New South Wales Supreme Court. The terms of reference, Neville Wran said, had been drafted to allow the fullest investigation into the cultivation, production, manufacture, distribution, supply, possession and use of prohibited and addictive drugs. The royal commissioner would also have the power to recommend changes in state laws pertaining to drugs.

In light of Donald Mackay's disappearance, arguably the most significant of the terms of reference was the requirement for Justice Woodward to inquire into:

> The identity of persons involved in: (a) the cultivation, production, manufacture, distribution or supply where contrary to the laws of this state, of drugs of the kinds referred to in paragraph one, or in the possession or use by others, when contrary to those laws, of those drugs; or (b) illegal or improper activities in connection with the matters referred to in sub paragraphs.

The prospect of growers and traffickers being named and investigated by the royal commission gave hope to those who felt that the police investigation into the probable murder of Donald Mackay was going nowhere.

Although Sergeant Horne rejected suggestions that the inquiry had become 'bogged down', Parrington's team of 30 detectives appeared to have discovered little that was not known within hours of Mackay's disappearance. While the police had managed to identify almost every car in the car park of the Griffith Hotel at around 6.30pm on 15 July, they were no closer to tracing the mystery Holden sedan. By early August Parrington had returned to Sydney.

In fact, the investigation was making progress, but some useful developments were not being made public. The police knew about Bruce Pursehouse's trip to Jerilderie to meet

'Mr Adams' and were exploring the possibility that it had been a failed attempt to lure Mackay to his death.

Meanwhile a public appeal for donations to boost the government's $25,000 reward raised a disappointing $8525. It was reported that 'some people of Italian origin' who were keen to contribute to the fund were 'frightened' of their donations being revealed.

CHAPTER 9

Follow the money

While the New South Wales Parliament debated new legislation to criminalise the growing of marijuana, petty users and
dealers continued to come before the Griffith District Court.
In mid-September 1977 a nineteen-year-old nurseryman
appeared before Judge Jim Staunton on a charge of supplying
marijuana. The nurseryman—hardly a Mr Big of the drug
trade—pleaded guilty after having been arrested with ten deals
of cannabis, weighing 72 grams, in his haversack. He claimed
to have bought the drug in Sydney to sell in Griffith.

The case was notable because police evidence was given
by Detective Senior Constable Graham Keech, one of the few
detectives in Griffith not under suspicion of being corruptly
involved with drug traffickers. According to Keech, the
nineteen-year-old had made the mistake of trying to sell
some of the cannabis to an off-duty policeman.

Judge Staunton sentenced the young nurseryman to nine
months' jail, describing his excuse of having bought $200

worth of cannabis in the hope of making a profit of $40 as 'hardly better than none'.

As well as being jailed for supplying marijuana, the man was remanded in custody to be sentenced for smoking marijuana.

The court's decision angered many readers of the *Area News* who remembered only too well the New South Wales attorney-general's decision to 'No Bill' Francesco Sergi over his involvement in a $50 million marijuana crop at Coleambally.

In parliament, the Poisons (Further Amendment) Bill—the so-called Mackay Bill, which prohibited the cultivation of plants that were a source of illegal drugs and significantly increased the penalties for trafficking—was inching closer to being passed. But under cover of parliamentary privilege, the reputations of Griffith and the Riverina were being savaged, with the leader of the Country Party, Leon Punch, describing Griffith as the 'pot capital of Australia'.

Local member Lin Gordon responded by comparing drug arrests in Griffith with those in five other regional centres of New South Wales: 'Over the period of three years from 1974 to 1976, there were a total of nineteen convictions for drug offences in Griffith . . . In that same period Taree had 86 convictions, Orange 40, Eurobodalla 62, Lismore 73 and Wollongong 517 . . . As a member for the Griffith area I will never accept the description of Griffith as the pot capital of NSW.'

It was Gordon at his simplistic best, loyal to a fault but betraying a hopeless lack of 'street savvy'. If you believed Gordon, the town's cannabis problem consisted mainly of smalltime street dealing in amounts of a few ounces or grams, rather than crops valued at tens of millions of dollars.

Everybody in Griffith knew that Gordon's statistics were a travesty of the facts, because the major drug growers and suppliers—the men at the top of Griffith's multimillion-dollar marijuana business—enjoyed police protection.

Not every parliamentarian was as naïve about the performance of the police as Gordon. In the Upper House, Tom Erskine acknowledged that police 'had been prepared to turn a blind eye to men involved with the marijuana crops'.

The corruption went much deeper, however, than the Griffith detectives. On 13 September Leon Punch told the house that part of a $500,000 Italian kidnap ransom had been brought to Australia by Domenico Barbaro and used to finance cannabis crops around Griffith. A report by the Calabrian anti-mafia police described the purpose of Barbaro's visit to Australia in 1974 as being to 'take money from kidnappings to that country to . . . invest in Indian hemp plantations' and to launder the proceeds. The Minister for Immigration who signed an entry permit for Domenico Barbaro was none other than Al Grassby. It was one of three permits issued to men, all named Barbaro, who had previously been denied entry to Australia on character grounds.

Rushing to Grassby's defence, the premier, Neville Wran, who was also Minister for Police, mocked the idea that Barbaro was a major criminal, suggesting that Barbaro was guilty of nothing more serious than 'larceny of a goat' and insisting he had been allowed into Australia 'to see his dying mother for the last time before she met her maker'.

Domenico Barbaro was now back in Italy serving a fifteen-year sentence for his role in the kidnapping, but the mafia money trail was of great interest to the Woodward Royal Commission, which had just begun preliminary hearings in Griffith.

As investigators began to round up members of La Famiglia for interview as potential witnesses for the Woodward Royal Commission, Al Grassby and his wife, Ellnor, took every opportunity to play down the involvement of Italians in the marijuana trade.

La Famiglia's favourite Italian-speaking solicitor, Simon Mackenzie, was rarely out of the royal commission. It seemed that every second witness called by Judge Philip Woodward was one of Mackenzie's clients.

Justice Woodward had been given access to bank records and a number of professional firms in Griffith, including accountants, had been subpoenaed to tender private files that would reveal a convoluted trail of murky deals, money-shuffling and suspicious investments in property.

Warrants had been obtained for investigators to enter many of Griffith's 'grass castles' to search for evidence of drug transactions and large-scale money-laundering. As a result, the Australian Taxation Office began to take a close interest in many of the witnesses before the commission, with investigations launched into the affairs of 'Aussie Bob' Trimbole and 'Winery Tony' Sergi, among others.

The hearings of the Woodward Royal Commission, which opened in Griffith in August 1977 before moving to Sydney, would keep the town in the spotlight for months, providing the metropolitan dailies with a stream of sensational stories.

The royal commission's chief investigator, Detective John Whelan, was running his inquiries in tandem with Joe Parrington's homicide investigation into the presumed murder of Donald Mackay. From their temporary headquarters in the Wade Shire Council local government chambers in Griffith, Whelan's team systematically reinterviewed witnesses identified by Parrington's detectives. Notable among them were southern Italians associated with Robert Trimbole.

At the preliminary hearings in Griffith, Justice Woodward summonsed 25 prominent citizens—nearly all of whom gave permission for their names to be published—to supply information on the marijuana growers. While the information they gave 'lacked precision in terms of evidentiary value', it pointed Woodward's investigators towards 'an identifiable group of persons involved in large scale cultivation of marijuana'.

Woodward would later be more specific about the identities of the men whose 'grass castles' and 'expensive farms' he suspected of being bought with the proceeds of marijuana. He named them in his final report as 'Robert Trimbole; Antonio Sergi Farm 1305; Leonardo Gambacorta; Pasquale Agresta; Francesco Sergi; Rocco Barbaro; Antonio Sergi Farm 1774 ['Young Tony' Sergi bought Farm 1774 from Rocco Barbaro in October 1974]; Giuseppe Sergi; Francesco Barbaro; and Giovanni Sergi.'

While acknowledging the help he received from some citizens, Woodward regretted that 'no information whatever came from any section of the Calabrian community', although he was shrewd enough to suspect that 'fear played a part in promoting such reticence'.

■ ■ ■

It was not only La Famiglia that was starting to feel the heat. By the end of September former detectives Jack Ellis, Brian Borthwick and John Robins were in the sights of both the Woodward Royal Commission and Police Internal Affairs investigators for their roles in giving alibis to members of the Sergi family on the night Don Mackay went missing.

Ellis was interviewed on 26 September. Not for the first time, he faced questions over his dubious investigative methods, especially his failure to take notes or collect statements from witnesses—in particular Patrick Keenan—after the 1974 discovery of a commercial marijuana crop on Giuseppe Scarfo's farm at Hanwood.

In an interview at police headquarters in Sydney, Ellis claimed that Keenan had appeared 'nervous and frightened' when giving information about what he had seen at Scarfo's farm, and that Keenan, by his own account, had not gone inside the shed but had only gone to the door and 'did not stay very long'. According to Ellis, 'Keenan said that Scarfo had invited him into the shed to have a beer, but he had refused to go into the shed.' Ellis also denied approaching Winery Tony about the matter, telling investigators, 'Before I had any opportunity to interview Antonio Sergi I was approached by Patrick Keenan and he told me that he had been to the winery at Tharbogang and that the bloke he saw at Farm 20 at Hanwood with Giuseppe Scarfo was not the bloke who had the winery at Tharbogang.'

Asked about his failure to take a statement from Keenan, Ellis said that Keenan had pleaded with him 'not to take him to court'. There was no record of this conversation ever taking place.

In his interview Constable Brian Borthwick supported aspects of Ellis's evidence, although his recollection of events at Scarfo's farm sometimes contradicted the contemporaneous notes in his diary.

The inconsistencies in Borthwick's evidence would have come as no surprise to the Concerned Citizens of Griffith, who were convinced that a deal had been made by 'Old Joe' Scarfo to plead guilty, with no mention being made that Winery Tony had been in his shed packing marijuana into bags. As far as they were concerned, the whole thing smacked of a conspiracy between the three detectives to cover up Sergi's involvement in the Hanwood crop.

A more worrying insight into Detective Sergeant Ellis's investigative methods came in the second week of October, when Winery Tony appeared before the royal commission.

Sergi gave evidence that Ellis had told him about Patrick Keenan's description of having seen an off-white car at Scarfo's farm, possibly a Holden Monaro or GT, with a blue or dark-coloured stripe over the hood and boot. Sergi denied ever having owned or driven such a car. His statement to the commission went on: 'Jack Ellis . . . told me that a fruit inspector had told them that he had seen me on my father-in-law's farm at Hanwood and work[ing] where the marijuana was.' According to Sergi, after Keenan had allegedly gone to the winery (to make sure of his identification) the police came to the winery and told him that Keenan now admitted he had made a mistake and it was not Sergi he had seen at Hanwood.

The story Winery Tony told the royal commission was not new—most of the details had been aired at the trial of Rocco Barbaro and Giuseppe Scarfo—but it confirmed that Ellis had been willing to put Keenan at risk by identifying him as an informant.

A copy of the statement made by Winery Tony Sergi was tabled before the Woodward Royal Commission and immediately made available to the media.

Asked how he had found the money to build his winery, Sergi told the investigators: 'I still owe a lot of money, not everything is paid, a lot of money come from the vegetables, some money come from my mother and father; from Italy I got about $25,000 from my mother's mother, when my mother get it she give it to me; my father got $40,000 from Italy and gave $10,000 to each of my children and I been using that.' In addition, Sergi claimed to have 'borrowed money from everywhere, I borrowed from the bank they have the first and second mortgage, the Commonwealth Development Bank and the Commonwealth Bank and I borrowed from friends; at the present time I owe about one million dollars'.

> Investigator Schloeffel: Did you ever borrow money from a man named Bob Trimbole?
>
> Sergi: I borrow money from him a fair bit too.
>
> Schloeffel: How long have you known Bob Trimbole?
>
> Sergi: I know him since I arrive in Griffith, he had a garage, everybody know him.
>
> Schloeffel: Did you know him as a man who had a lot of wealth?
>
> Sergi: I don't think so, I see him working all the time in his garage. He was a gambler.
>
> Schloeffel: Our information is that he was a declared bankrupt prior to May 1975. Do you know if this is correct?
>
> Sergi: I never asked him, but I heard that he was bankrupt.
>
> Schloeffel: Our information is that between June 1975 and July 1977 you received unsecured loans from Bob Trimbole to the sum of $277,350. Would this be correct?
>
> Sergi: Yes, bits and pieces.
>
> . . .

> Schloeffel: Are you able to tell us if you are aware how Bob
> Trimbole went from being a bankrupt in 1975 to being
> in a position where he was able to lend you large sums
> of money?
>
> Sergi: I haven't got a clue.

In his report Justice Woodward noted, 'The last $100,000 borrowed from Trimbole was to pay for grapes. He asked for the money and Trimboli gave him a cheque for $100,000. It turned out that none of these loans, or other loans given by Frank Barbaro, Frank Sergi (Tony's uncle) and others had been made on an interest basis. In Tony Sergi's words, 'they were done on a friendly basis'.

Asked whether he had offered to pay cash for the winery shed in return for a cheaper price, Sergi replied angrily, 'No, that's bullshit. I didn't say anything about paying him part cash. I told him that I would pay him cash when it was finished, I meant that I would pay him for the job, when it was done, he must have mistaken what I said.'

Investigator Schloeffel was also interested in Sergi's involvement in the transport business. Around five years earlier Sergi had bought a semi-trailer for 'five or six thousand dollars' but on its first trip the vehicle had an accident in Canberra that caused it to roll over and burn. There had been many reports about the accident in Canberra involving a clapped-out truck from Griffith that appeared to be carrying much more than wine; the fact that the truck mysteriously caught fire was considered highly suspicious, as was the pungent smell of cannabis smoke. According to Sergi, the truck was loaded with wine and liquor worth about $18,000 and all was destroyed. The insurers, however, valued it at between $15,000 and $16,000 and so far were refusing to pay.

Sergi was deliberately vague when asked what he knew about his brother-in-law Rocco Barbaro's arrest for growing marijuana on Farm 1774 and his father-in-law, Giuseppe Scarfo's, arrest for growing marijuana on Farm 20. He denied ever having set foot inside the shed on Farm 20 in which marijuana was dried and packed. He was no more helpful on why mail addressed to Pasquale Agresta, one of the men found guilty of growing the multimillion-dollar Coleambally crop, was being forwarded to his address. He denied having asked his nephew, 'Young Tony' Sergi, to visit Patrick Keenan on his behalf.

■ ■ ■

Names were a constant problem for reporters and photographers covering the royal commission. The Sergi family tree provided to the media by the commission included five Francescos, four Antonios, four Giuseppes, three Giovannis and three Domenicos. At the time the commission was sitting in Griffith there were nearly twenty Antonio Sergis living in the district 'aged from eight to 80 years'. Inevitably, reporters picked up on the nicknames used by the Italians themselves—such as 'Winery Tony' and his nephew, 'Young Tony'—to distinguish family members with the same names.

Press and television photographers were forever confusing the images of witnesses, leading to numerous apologies and the odd court case. No one could escape being 'snapped' as they arrived at the courthouse in Griffith. Some witnesses were less than friendly: Winery Tony was pictured in full flight running from the media pack after giving evidence.

The royal commission was especially keen to establish how members of the extended Sergi family, who made a living from growing vegetables, found the money to move from a dilapidated farm house to big new brick homes, so-called 'grass castles'.

Among the rags-to-riches stories uncovered by investigators was that of Giovanni 'Johnny' Sergi (born 8 February 1927 in Platì), the youngest of five brothers who had migrated from southern Italy to live in Griffith. Johnny Sergi was interviewed twice by detectives gathering statements for the Woodward Royal Commission during October. The interviews were conducted in Italian and translated into English in preparation for Johnny's cross-examination by counsel assisting the commission, Bill Fisher, QC.

Johnny Sergi owned Farm 1775, which adjoined Rocco Barbaro's Farm 1774 at Tharbogang, where several acres of peach and apricot trees were removed to make room for a commercial crop of marijuana. Sergi told investigators that as well as owning several blocks of land in Griffith, he had borrowed \$100,000 from a solicitor (whose name he couldn't remember) in the western Sydney suburb of Fairfield to buy a block of eleven flats in Fairfield. He also claimed to have received a large sum of money from his mother-in-law in Italy. Johnny Sergi was questioned about this in his second interview with Investigator Lorenzutta:

Lorenzutta: Have you returned to Italy since you came to Australia?

Sergi: Yes, I went back twice. The first time was about six years ago, I was away about three months, and I did a trip around Japan . . . The second time was two years ago . . . I took my mother-in-law back to Italy after her mother-in-law died here. I was away about two to three months.

Lorenzutta: Did you bring any money back from Italy during one of these trips?

Sergi: Yes, on the last trip I brought back $60,000 . . . My
mother-in-law gave it to me . . . She gave me the $60,000
and said: 'half is for Frank [Barbaro] and half is for you'.
Lorenzutta: Do you know where your mother-in-law got
this money?
Sergi: No.

Sergi told the commission investigators his mother-in-law
was Maria Barbaro and that she had died more than a year
earlier; he didn't remember her address but she lived in Platì.
She had given him the money in cash, 62–63 million Italian
lire in 10,000, 20,000, 50,000 and 100,000 lire notes. Asked
by Investigator Lorenzutta how the money had been stored,
Sergi answered, 'In a paper sack.'

Not surprisingly, Johnny Sergi was unable to produce any
documentation for his windfall. He claimed to have changed his
lire to Australian dollars during the two and a half months he
was in Italy, converting lire 'all over the place, Reggio Calabria,
Bovalino, Locri, Catangaro . . . Taonnina'. He remembered
changing ten million lire with 'a man who sells clothing in
Messina'. Returning to Australia with $60,000 in cash, he filled
in the required entry card but failed to declare the money.

Despite the obfuscations, the Woodward Royal Commission soon built up a detailed understanding of how La
Famiglia worked, and of how the police in Griffith had
turned a blind eye to its activities. Counsel assisting, Bill
Fisher, QC, confirmed that five large marijuana plantations
in the Griffith district in the past five years 'were all organised and financed by the same group of people' and that
'poor quality work by the previous local police force had
allowed the industry to go undetected'. He exposed the rort
that had allowed 'relatively minor people in the industry . . .

to volunteer for blame and keep silent about organisers' in return for payments of thousands of dollars. He also blamed local police for having 'supported and even enlarged upon these people's portrayal of themselves as poor, hard-working farmers who hardly knew what they were doing'.

The commission's detectives, Fisher said, had reinvestigated the cannabis seizures at Tharbogang, Hanwood, Coleambally and Euston and come to significantly different conclusions to the police.

Rather than the makeshift, even accidental business suggested by Detective Sergeant Ellis, Fisher described an 'integrated industry generating millions of dollars'. On the subject of the Tharbogang and Hanwood crops, Fisher was amazed that the Griffith police had not just accepted but 'even enlarged on' the idea that the crop was supposed to be 'a new brand of tomato'. Nor had they found anything suspicious in the fact that after buying a rundown farm with $43,000 of borrowed money, Rocco Barbaro's 'first act was to bulldoze down peach trees, which were seemingly his only source of income', in order to form a 3.5-metre high wall that 'effectively stopped anyone seeing into the property from the road'.

The people involved in both crops had come 'almost without exception' from two generations of Calabrian families and possessed large sums of money which they attributed to:

- lucky bets on horses, roulette and pontoon;
- gifts and inheritances from 'wealthy' relatives in what was well known to be the poorest part of Italy;
- loans from relatives that were never repaid, for which no interest was paid and which were almost all paid in cash from money kept in the homes of people with ordinary jobs; and

- payment from the trading account of Trimboli, Sergi & Sergi, a firm of market stall holders at Fairfield whose account was used to launder the proceeds of cannabis crops.

■ ■ ■

In just a few weeks, the royal commission had unearthed more about La Famiglia and its operations than Griffith's detectives had managed in several years. But behind the scenes, the commission's investigators were frustrated by their inability to enter and value 'grass castles' and by the Commonwealth government's refusal to share bankruptcy and immigration records and information about the flow of currency in and out of the country.

Not all the 'grass castles' had been built in Griffith. Rocco Barbaro owned a luxury 60-square home in Canberra, described by Fisher as 'a big two-storeyed establishment situated at 3 Jordan Place, Spence, in Canberra, with a three-car garage and a large basement cellar' worth 'at least in the $100,000 range'. An inspection by the manager of a Canberra finance company found Barbaro's house to be 'luxurious and tastefully furnished'. Barbaro also owned a 25-acre (ten-hectare) property at St Marys near Sydney.

Barbaro was typically vague about how he had got the money to buy the house. A 'man with a semi-trailer' used to buy his tomatoes, always paying in cash. Barbaro had also visited a gambling club in Sydney 'three or four times' and won more than $40,000—more than $27,000 of it on a single night—but he couldn't remember the name of the club or where it was, or which card game he had played.

Rocco Barbaro's neighbour and brother-in-law, Francesco Barbaro (both were married to sisters of Winery Tony), was another whose 'grass castle' was closely examined by Woodward's investigators. Woodward ordered counsel assisting to release photographs of the house 'so the people of Griffith can actually see what you are presenting in evidence'. Valued at $191,000, the house was replete with luxury fittings including a gold-plated chandelier. 'At one time it would have been called a palace,' Fisher said. 'No expense appeared to have been spared.'

For years Francesco and his wife, Elizabeth, had scraped a living from Farm 1773, a 22-acre (nine-hectare) property described by Fisher as 'barely economic'. At times the couple had been so poor that they couldn't pay their fruit pickers' wages, yet in July 1973 they were able to buy Farm 1760—a farm without crops—for $40,000. A year later Barbaro's accounts showed a profit of $16,000, followed by profits of $32,000 in 1974 and $48,500 in 1975. In 1976 he had made a profit of $27,000 while paying just $207 in wages. 'These figures,' Fisher concluded, 'are quite unbelievable.'

Francesco Barbaro's account of his newfound wealth was as improbable as Rocco's: he claimed to have received $18,000 after his mother died in Italy and to have brought the money back with him in a 'bag with a couple of shirts'. Like Rocco, Francesco had been lucky on the horses, winning $22,000 during an eight-day period in June, although he 'could not remember the name of the race, the horse, or the exact day involved in some of his winnings'. He was also the beneficiary of various interest-free and un-repaid loans, including one of $10,000 from Bob Trimbole.

With no evidence to the contrary, Fisher told Justice Woodward that his submission to the inquiry would be that Francesco Barbaro was 'most likely' a principal party to drug trafficking in the Griffith area.

Discussion of 'grass castles' and black money soon brought Nunzio 'Norm' Greco into the picture. A member of a bricklaying family, Greco was Griffith's leading builder of 'grass castles', paying and being paid cash-in-hand. This made him an important player in the process by which black money from the sale of marijuana was laundered.

In his first interview Greco was questioned in detail about 'black money' cash payments he had received for his work on 'grass castles', in particular a house he had built for Leonardo Gambacorta, the Coleambally cannabis grower, at Grimison Avenue, Griffith.

Several days later Greco returned to the commission, apparently at his own request, to continue his evidence. Observers watching the comings and goings at Griffith Court immediately noticed a change in the builder's appearance: Greco had shaved off his beard.

Terry Jones recognised Greco straight away and published 'before' and 'after' pictures of the now clean-shaven builder in the *Area News*. One night an obviously alcohol-affected Greco approached Jones in the La Scala restaurant and threatened violence.

'Come on, Norm,' said Jones. 'Aren't you already in enough trouble? Can't you all see what's happening in Griffith . . . all because someone thought it was a good idea to do away with Don Mackay.'

Greco was still spoiling for a fight and had to be dragged away by friends.

The next time Nunzio Greco gave evidence before the commission, it wasn't just the *Area News* that carried his picture; his clean-shaven face was in all the metropolitan papers.

Exactly what occurred between the builder's two appearances could only be guessed, but some guessed that Greco had blundered in naming a friend, Pat Zirilli, as a source of money given to him to pay tradesmen working on Gamba-corta's 'grass castle'. Justice Woodward noted that Greco had 'stated that there were certain things he desired to correct in the previous record'.

Greco kept large sums of cash which he claimed to have won by gambling, telling the commission's investigators he had backed a horse called 'Piemelon Bay' when it won three times in a row at Rosehill. 'I always got . . . eleven to two for it,' he said. 'I was over twenty grand in front after about six months.'

Much of the paperwork for Greco's building work was obtained from his solicitor, Simon Mackenzie, whose firm was closely involved in the building of 'grass castles' for men who were doing time in jail for the supply of drugs.

Greco was unable or unwilling to supply documents to support his claims; his behaviour towards the commission was 'arrogant', Justice Woodward said, and 'some of his evidence and the manner in which he gave it clearly indicate that he was deliberately lying'.

The only relevant document Greco claimed to possess was a workbook which he kept in a drawer until it was torn up by his sister's young children. The builder had been investigated by the tax office and Woodward concluded he had probably 'destroyed all his records in order to avoid the consequences of such an investigation'.

Greco's far-fetched tale of having made a killing backing Piemelon Bay three times at Rosehill unravelled under ques-tioning, as the commission gradually pieced together an explanation for the cash Leonardo Gambacorta was splash-ing on his new house at Grimison Avenue.

Justice Woodward concluded, 'The figure of $209,000 would appear to be reasonably accurate, taking into consideration the $107,000 as a minimum spent on the construction of the house, the cost no doubt of furniture and furnishings within the house, and the expenditure of $83,000-odd in the payment of income tax. The conclusion therefore to be drawn from the above figures is that, as the result of the involvement of Gambacorta in the marijuana trade in Griffith, a sum of approximately $209,000 came into his hands, which otherwise is incapable of a legitimate explanation.'

On 29 November 1977 it was Pasquale Sergi's turn to be interviewed by the commission's investigators. In the record of interview, Sergi was asked about the purchase of a property at Hughes Street, Fairfield. He claimed to have bought it in partnership with his brother Antonio Sergi of 2 Diprose Street, Fairfield (born 25 September 1944) and Robert Trimbole. When questioned about the source of the money, Sergi had been evasive, saying only that he had received it 'off Bob Trimbole'.

When Sergi appeared before the royal commission two months later Justice Woodward concluded, on the evidence he had seen, that Trimbole had provided the entire amount of $177,000 used to buy 75 Hughes Street.

Pasquale Sergi also admitted that in October 1975 he, his brother Antonio and Bob Trimbole had paid $55,000 for a property at Lot 3, Mamre Road, St Marys. Asked where the money came from, Sergi answered, 'The same way we bought the other property—through Bob's punting.'

As the royal commission ground on, the word on the streets in Griffith was that the heads of La Famiglia in Griffith were mortified by the ongoing disclosures of their personal and business affairs. Approaches had been made to Al Grassby by some of the Calabrian community to intercede, if he could, but there was little chance of the former parliamentarian taking on Justice Woodward or his counsel assisting, Bill Fisher.

In the newsroom of the *Area News*, Terry Jones had heard that Grassby was being urged to come forward with evidence—whatever that might be—that could take the pressure off the Calabrians. But Grassby had his own problems. The leader of the Country Party, Leon Punch, had attacked him in parliament, reminding members that Grassby, as Minister for Immigration, had signed entry permits for three people 'all named Barbaro' who had previously been refused entry to Australia on character grounds. One of the men, Domenico Barbaro, 'came out only to deposit money in Australia before returning to Italy, where he was arrested for the kidnapping of an Italian industrialist three months before being allowed back into Australia by Mr Grassby'.

The granting of the entry permits by Grassby was 'not unconnected with the marijuana growing scene in the Riverina', Punch told parliament. As a result of his mauling by Punch, it seemed unlikely that Grassby would dare come to the defence of La Famiglia.

■ ■ ■

Fisher's criticism of the Griffith police had led to calls in parliament for both Sergeant Ellis and Constable Borthwick to be suspended, but it was not until April 1978 that Ellis was brought before the commission's investigators. There was a lot they wanted to ask him: Ellis's interview extended over three days.

After coming to Griffith in 1962 as part of the Riverina District Police Force, Ellis seemed to live a pretty ordinary life. He and his wife raised a family. Outside work, Ellis enjoyed a day at the races, often in the company of Griffith's prince of punters, 'Aussie Bob' Trimbole. One thing that did catch the investigators' attention was the improvement over the previous five years in Sergeant Ellis's financial situation, something Justice Woodward said he could reasonably assume, in the absence of a satisfactory explanation, had come from 'unaccountable and therefore improper sources'.

Ellis's financial affairs were not complicated. Besides his salary as a serving police officer, he received a share of profits from Joanne Gift Store, a business established by Mrs Ellis in 1969, which was sold in January 1976 to Archie Molinaro, Bob Trimbole's business partner in Atlantic Amusements.

In July 1974, around the time the first drug crops were found near Griffith, Ellis began making a 40 per cent salary deduction each fortnight to the Police Department Employees' Credit Union Limited, with no withdrawals.

As a regular punter, Ellis had working accounts with the TAB as well as a telephone betting account. His modest 'flutter on the ponies' averaged around $350 per week between December 1977 and April 1978. While combing his financial records, investigators found a bookmaker's cheque for $8000, purportedly won on a race at Rosehill on 16 April 1977. They checked with the bookmaker, who could find no record from that day of a payment of $8000. In fact, the race meeting on 16 April 1977 had been at Randwick, not Rosehill. The bookmaker kept an 'unpaid bets book' but there was no entry in it for $8000.

Woodward's investigators spoke to the bookmaker at Randwick but neither he nor his clerk could remember a winning bet by Sergeant Ellis. However, Bob Trimbole made at least two bets that day. The only plausible explanation seemed to be that Ellis had given the bookmaker cash and in return had received a cheque for $8000. Ellis claimed to have won the money at Randwick three days earlier and to have asked the bookmaker to look after it for him.

There were other anomalies. Accountants working for the commission discovered that the Ellises' combined assets had increased by nearly $100,000 between June 1973 and March 1978. During the same period, there appeared to be a shortfall of around $55,000 between their known income and their expenditure. Suspicions were also raised by a cheque for $3000 written by Sergeant Ellis to his former colleague in the Riverina Police Force, Detective Arthur O'Sullivan of Wagga Wagga. Ellis described this cheque as a loan to O'Sullivan, who was being investigated by Police Internal Affairs for his associations with Bob Trimbole and Winery Tony and with the former Griffith detectives Brian Borthwick and John Robins.

With damaging publicity from the Woodward Royal Commission making life uncomfortable for La Famiglia, the cannabis growers were forced to change their business methods. Terry Jones had been tipped off about small, easily concealed 'cash crops' of marijuana being grown in order to keep supplies ticking over. It was too dangerous for the growers to use their own vehicles, so rental vans and cars were booked for drug runs to Sydney and to various country towns. The 'cash crops' were not confined to the area around Griffith, Hillston and Hay but extended west to the Murray River and even as far as the New South Wales–Victoria–South Australia border. Jones passed this information to the Australian Federal Police.

■ ■ ■

While the net tightened around La Famiglia and the corrupt detectives, one man seemed to have emerged unscathed: Robert Trimbole. Aussie Bob had been interviewed on 25 November 1977 and had answered questions about his betting activities, naming several bookmakers as holding his money when he gambled. Up until late 1976, Trimbole appeared to bet only in cash. After that, he regularly bet on credit. Trimbole's records stopped after 1976, so there was no reliable record of his bets during the period of the royal commission. According to Trimbole, he had been advised not to keep records, lest it be to his 'financial disadvantage' or impose upon him 'an obligation to contribute to the national economy'.

According to one bookmaker, Robert Blann, Trimbole's bets usually ranged between $200 and $10,000 and he had lost money overall. Around 90 per cent of Trimbole's bets were placed by a man named Tony Calabria. Blann's records showed that between November 1976 and July 1977 he paid cheques to Trimbole amounting to $227,075. It was not possible to reconstruct Trimbole's cash betting with Blann for that period.

A similar story was told by another bookmaker, Bruce McHugh. Again, Trimbole's bets were placed by Tony Calabria. McHugh said, 'Over the period of time that I have been accepting bets from Mr Trimbole I would have won money from him.' McHugh took a large amount of cash to the races and sometimes cashed cheques for Trimbole when he ran short. McHugh's records showed Trimbole had lost $83,855 during 1977, but Trimbole himself claimed to have won $30,000.

Another bookmaker, Terry Page, told the commission that Trimbole had started out making small bets in cash but had quickly switched to betting on a much larger scale, always in cash. Eventually Trimbole became 'one of the biggest cash and credit bettors' on Page's books. Trimbole appeared to bet on every race and often backed more than one horse in each race. According to Page: 'Bets of $50,000 were not uncommon.'

Just because a cash bet was noted in Trimbole's records and a corresponding notation of a bet was found in a book-maker's sheet, it did not follow that the punter had in fact had a winning bet, Justice Woodward said. A person could claim to have made a cash winning bet after seeing—or being told about—an entry on the bookmaker's sheets. (It was not even essential to inspect the sheets, as cash bets were usually 'called' and could be noted by an astute bystander.)

The investigation of Bob Trimbole's betting activities had unwelcome consequences for Winery Tony, who had been the recipient of several large cheques from Trimbole. Suppos-edly the proceeds of winning bets placed by Trimbole on Sergi's behalf, the cheques looked suspiciously like payments made in the course of their marijuana business. 'I did not believe Trimbole,' Justice Woodward would comment, 'nor did I believe Sergi. My conclusions were that both of these men have lied in relation to the transaction.'

The commission's investigators also scrutinised Trim-bole's off-course TAB betting between July 1975 and October 1976, a period that spanned the Coleambally drug seizure. It was also a time when Trimbole was widely rumoured to be fixing races. In Griffith, Trimbole had been heard to boast of having 'ten to a dozen' jockeys on his payroll and of having had 27 winning bets out of 28 bets placed.

Trimbole produced what he said was an accurate record of his betting on course and at the TAB between July 1975 and December 1976. Analysing the four books, which totalled 166 foolscap pages, occupied as many as four financial investigators at once. The books showed that during this period Trimbole placed 1254 losing bets at a cost of $2,018,350. At the same time, he placed 772 winning bets for a return of $3,522,249.50. His net winnings over the period were $1,503,899.50. Much of the alleged 'winnings' was deposited in Trimbole's personal account at the Liverpool branch of the Bank of New South Wales.

Justice Woodward, however, was not convinced. 'I am unable,' he said, 'to accept that the records produced by Trimbole in relation to his betting transactions are genuine or complete.' Not only Trimbole but 'Winery Tony' Sergi and other La Famiglia members in Griffith had 'wagered to win and launder money' on the same horses on identical dates. Bob Trimbole was an insatiable gambler but betting alone could not explain the vast sums of cash passing through his hands.

CHAPTER 10

A clairvoyant and a royal commission

Despite one of the biggest rewards ever offered in New South Wales, the police investigation into the presumed murder of Donald Mackay had hit a brick wall. 'There's been nothing fresh for some months,' Detective Sergeant Parrington told the *Area News*. 'We are receiving very little, very little information at all.'

Frustrated by the lack of progress, the media created their own leads. In February 1978 the investigative journalist Dick Wordley obtained an interview with the Dutch clairvoyant Gerard Croiset Junior, whose father, also a clairvoyant, had been involved a decade earlier in a failed attempt to solve the mystery of the missing Beaumont children.

Wordley's story, based on a three-hour interview with Croiset in the Netherlands, claimed that 'Griffith drug crusader Donald Mackay was executed by a bullet fired into his spine and was buried near water under a pile of stones. His killers were three men, one a VIP well respected in social and political circles. Mackay was murdered as he tried to keep a rendezvous with the VIP near Griffith on 15th July last year. The rendezvous was a death trap established by the VIP because Mackay had learned too much about the illegal drug market in Australia.'

Croiset also gave Wordley a pen drawing of the killer and drawings of possible grave sites. Details of Croiset's insights were passed on to the New South Wales Homicide Squad; Barbara Mackay—after an international phone call, during which the clairvoyant allegedly gave a detailed description of her bedroom—was said to have 'welcomed' Croiset's intervention.

Six months later the News Limited-owned 0–10 TV network combined with Sydney-based News Limited newspapers to bring Croiset to Australia, ostensibly to offer his 'expert' evidence to the Woodward Royal Commission. On 25 July, the *Daily Telegraph* published a lengthy story by journalist Shelley Neller under the headline 'Clairvoyant joins search for Mackay'.

Journalists at the *Area News* scoffed at Croiset's Australian visit as a 'stunt', but that didn't stop Jones assigning reporters and photographers to meet the Dutch clairvoyant at the airport.

Television crews from the 0–10 network followed Croiset to the Mackays' furniture store, the car park at the Griffith Hotel, and to Lake Wyangan, where Mackay's body was suspected of having been dumped. Within minutes of arriving at the picnic ground beside Wyangan Lake, the clairvoyant said he was convinced it was the place where Mackay was shot in the back. The assassin, he said, was the man who drove Mackay from the Griffith Hotel.

Drifting in and out of trances, Croiset often had to break away from the cameras to recover his focus. At the end of a long day he retired exhausted to rest. Seemingly drained both physically and mentally, Croiset managed to drag himself back out to describe the images that had flashed through his mind's eye. It made gripping television but would be a cause of predictable anguish to Barbara Mackay and her family as it departed more and more from the facts established by the police.

When asked by reporters whether she intended to co-operate with Croiset, Barbara replied, 'We have had enough of publicity pranks . . . I wish they would leave me and my children out of it.'

■ ■ ■

Despite the failure to find Mackay's body, the New South Wales Probate Registrar declared two days before the anniversary of the businessman's disappearance that he would grant probate in Mackay's estate because it would be 'unrealistic' to withhold it. Probate documents showed that Mackay left an estate valued at $205,967, all of which was left to his widow, Barbara.

The decision reflected the views of everyone concerned with the investigation and confirmed what Barbara had believed from the beginning. Some had criticised her for saying publicly, in the absence of proof, that her husband was dead. But it was only by accepting the worst that Barbara felt that she and the children could come to terms with what had happened. She had seen the evidence and knew that hope alone could not bring her husband back.

The anniversary of Don Mackay's disappearance offered an opportunity for more soul-searching in Griffith. The *Area News* published a four-page wrap-around, which included a heartfelt plea from Barbara: 'Someone in Griffith knows the answer.'

Parrington had been hoping that the Woodward Royal Commission would unearth new information, but it failed to produce any leads, or to coax out new informants.

At the *Area News*, Terry Jones and June Webster were becoming frustrated with Parrington's lack of progress and, in particular, his apparent reluctance to look at the person they considered to be the prime suspect: Bob Trimbole. Jones and Webster still had faith in the Griffith chief of detectives, Sergeant Jim Bindon, but they worried that Bindon had been sidelined by both the Mackay investigation and the royal commission.

On 14 July, the paper expressed the editorial opinion that any hopes of finding Donald Mackay alive had been 'completely erased' by the Supreme Court's decision to grant probate. Sergeant Parrington had long since reached the same conclusion. Appearing before the royal commission, he was asked by Justice Woodward whether he had any doubt as to whether Donald Mackay was alive:

Parrington: I do not know if anyone cares what I personally think.

Justice Woodward: I do. I am interested to know.

Parrington: I am sure he suffered a serious head injury there. I think it must be a strong presumption he is dead, not because of the available evidence, but because he has never been seen since. The blood and the expended bullets give a strong presumption. I think his Honour in the other court put a lot of weight on it.

Bill Fisher (counsel assisting): Did any evidence at all of significance turn up to support any other hypothesis?

Parrington: None at all.

The consensus that Don Mackay had not 'disappeared' but had been murdered served to highlight Parrington's failure to identify—let alone catch—his killer. This failure, the *Area News* told its readers, was 'of grave concern in this town' and contributed to a climate of 'fear in the community . . . that persons who have been responsible in some way for Mr Mackay's death, might still be among us'.

On the same day that the *Area News* declared its belief that Don Mackay was dead, Terry Jones published a letter from the Mackay family's solicitor, Ian Salmon:

Sir,

Just one year ago, here in Griffith, Don Mackay was murdered and his body stolen away. It is a practical certainty that there lives in Griffith today somebody who either did this wicked deed, or at least knows who did it.

While the body remains concealed the Mackay family lives in anguish. While the murder is unsolved a cloud hangs over the Griffith community. Many of us hope, and pray, that this horrible state of affairs can be brought to an end.

One person can do that. One person who is good enough, and brave enough, to come forward with the vital clue that will solve the crime.

Business was feeling the effects of the 'cloud' hanging over Griffith. The arrival of the royal commission seemed to have put the whole town on edge. The commission's team of investigators had served subpoenas and warrants on local banks and accountancy firms to obtain files. There was hardly a professional adviser or counsellor in Griffith—solicitors included—who had not been called to tender documents.

Those with money to spend were choosing not to buy a new car or tractor or to replace an old piece of farm machinery. Nobody wanted to attract attention for fear of having their finances investigated.

The once-booming economy of Griffith was looking fragile. Famiglia members who had been happy to flaunt their affluence suddenly became more guarded. Spending on 'grass castles' came to an abrupt halt, at the expense of many honest local businesses. Tradesmen who until recently had had more work than they could handle were struggling to find a job.

■ ■ ■

Justice Woodward's attention, meanwhile, was turning back to the Griffith detectives, and especially to Sergeant Jack Ellis. Ellis had already been questioned in November 1977 and April 1978. On 21 November 1978 he was brought back to the royal commission for another grilling.

In his previous appearances Ellis had been steadfast in his explanation of income and assets that did not tally with the pay he received as a serving police officer. He always put it down to 'basically betting wins', while failing to produce corroborative evidence or documents to support his story. The only documentary evidence he had so far managed to show the commission was a batch of betting tickets relating to one horse in 1977, which had lost. Woodward was willing to accept that Ellis was a consistent punter, but not that he had been a successful one. A more likely explanation for Ellis's extra income was his relationships with Robert Trimbole and Winery Tony.

Justice Woodward's counsel assisting, Bill Fisher, QC, and commission investigators subjected Ellis to intense questioning over corruption allegations made against him in relation to the Tharbogang and Hanwood marijuana crops.

It was known that Ellis had been named in a dossier prepared by the Concerned Citizens of Griffith and handed by Don Mackay to the then state attorney-general, John Maddison. Justice Woodward commented: 'At an early stage in my inquiry into Griffith, the conduct of the police investigation into the Barbaro and Scarfo crops was the subject of adverse criticism, centring particularly on the conduct of Sergeant Ellis, as well as the conduct of his subordinate officers, Detective Constables Brian Borthwick and John Robins.'

Asked on his third appearance before the commission whether he regarded Trimbole as a friend, Ellis replied, 'I have no reason to be unfriendly with the man.' He said something similar about Winery Tony. The only way to make sense of Ellis's conduct, Woodward concluded, was in the light of his friendships with Trimbole and Sergi.

When asked, 'Did you ever receive any money corruptly for anything that you did in relation to that [marijuana] growing operation?' Ellis insisted he had not. Justice Woodward did not believe him. Rejecting claims by Ellis's lawyer that the evidence against him was circumstantial and unproven, Woodward declared that in 'many instances' Ellis had lied and 'lied deliberately' during his evidence to the commission.

■ ■ ■

Initially intended to run for six months, Justice Philip Woodward's Royal Commission of Inquiry into Drug Trafficking had to be extended twice in order to hear evidence from 565 witnesses, including many overseas. Justice Woodward's final report was presented to the governor of New South

Wales, Sir Roden Cutler, on 31 October 1979. One week later the premier, Neville Wran, tabled the three-volume report in parliament, bringing it under the protection of parliamentary privilege. In the hours before the report was tabled, reporters from radio, television and the press went into lockdown in Sydney to study Woodward's findings.

In the newsroom of the *Area News*, Terry Jones was facing a dilemma that would have been the envy of every newspaper editor in Australia. He had obtained, from a source inside the royal commission, a 50-page extract from Justice Woodward's report. Hand-delivered by courier, the package put Jones in an awkward position: he could publish and risk being prosecuted for contempt of the commission or of parliament; or he could lock the pages in a drawer, obey the embargo and turn his back on the biggest scoop of his career.

It wasn't the first time that Jones's journalistic contacts had come through for him. When reporters were desperate for a photograph of 'Aussie Bob' Trimbole, it was Jones who managed to get hold of one through his contacts in the police. But this was different. The courier had travelled all the way from Sydney to deliver the package to Jones in person, but what was it worth to the *Area News* to be able to publish a day before its rivals? Jones had given the courier $300 cash to cover his expenses, but the bigger question remained unanswered.

The paper's newly appointed manager, John Kelly, who had just taken over from June Webster, was anxious to play it safe. Neither he nor Jones wanted to end up in jail.

Under Jones's editorship, the *Area News* had been scrupulously even-handed in its reporting of the Mackay case and the Woodward Royal Commission, refusing to give space to the barely disguised racial bigotry that had come to the surface since the Mackay killing. As far as Jones was concerned, the leaked pages from Woodward's report were the paper's reward for having done its job properly. But the risk of publishing a detailed account of the report before it was tabled seemed too great for a little country paper like the *Area News*. Jones decided to write a short 'pointer' story for the front page saying scarcely more than that Justice Woodward's report would be tabled that day.

While journalists from all the major dailies were in Sydney reading the three huge volumes of Justice Woodward's report, a media scrum descended on Griffith to cover the local reaction. Most found their way to the office of the *Area News* on the corner of Olympic and Kooyoo streets. Laurie Wilson arrived from Canberra to report for the Australian Broadcasting Commission. 'Well, Terry,' he said, 'I bet you can't wait to read what Woodward has to say.'

Wilson watched in stunned silence as Jones showed him the sheaf of photocopied pages from the report. 'Mate, where did you get this?' Wilson asked as he started reading.

Jones replied with a shrug.

■ ■ ■

The first newspapers to hit the streets of Sydney on Tuesday 6 November with details of Justice Woodward's report were the city's afternoon tabloids, the Fairfax-owned *Sun* and the Murdoch-owned *Daily Mirror*. Both seized on the most explosive of Woodward's findings: that Donald Mackay had been murdered on the orders of an Italian-based organisation known as the 'Honoured Society' (L'Onorata Societa). Woodward named six Italian men as 'influential' members of the society. All six lived in Griffith. The six 'influential' Italians were:

- Francesco Sergi, born 24.1.35;
- Domenic Sergi, born 3.3.39;
- Antonio Sergi [Young Tony], born 4.2.50;
- Antonio Sergi [Winery Tony], born 29.10.35;
- Francesco Barbaro, born 8.9.37; and
- Robert Trimbole, born 19.3.31.

According to Justice Woodward, the organisation 'planned and directed a "commercial" cannabis growing and distribution network' and 'might have concluded that the elimination of Mackay would permit it to conduct its marihuana enterprise without further law enforcement interference'. Woodward declared: 'I am . . . satisfied that . . . Donald Bruce Mackay was disposed of, by members of, or on behalf of, that organisation.'

In parliament, the premier, Neville Wran, promised that the royal commission's report would 'not gather dust'. He went on: 'Every line of investigation opened up by the commission will be pursued exhaustively . . . Every suggestion for legislation or other action by the government will be thoroughly considered.'

Terry Jones squeezed everything he could onto the front page of the *Area News*, highlighting the murder of Don Mackay and the attempt by Detective Sergeant Ellis and some of his colleagues to cover up for the men behind the marijuana crops.

In a section of the report headed 'Police', Justice Woodward noted that there had been 'poor quality police work' by some Griffith police involved in the arrest of the cannabis growers. His criticism, however, was 'not extended to all local police, nor to the drug squad or to the force generally'. On the evidence given to the commission, Woodward was satisfied that Detective Sergeant Ellis—whom he did not accept as 'a witness of truth'—was involved in 'covering-up' for Winery Tony , either as an 'active participant in a conspiracy to cultivate cannabis' or in order to 'aid and abet Sergi in his involvement in that crime'. He considered the former proposition more likely.

The report continued:

> An examination of the record of proceedings against [Giuseppe] Scarfo and of the affairs of a sergeant of police named Ellis, then stationed at Griffith, and of other evidence, revealed that the behaviour of the sergeant and two other police officers left much to be desired and justified a belief, which existed amongst a large group of the townspeople (both Australian and Italian), that there was an organisation in existence, involved with the growing of marihuana, which was receiving benevolent treatment from certain members of the local police force.

Woodward was satisfied that in the proceedings against Scarfo and Barbaro, the court was 'manipulated' and 'the accused were treated leniently' as a result of false information given by Ellis. He did not accept that this was the result of a 'negligent performance by Ellis of his official duties' but rather that he 'acted deliberately and . . . was activated by a dishonest motive'. Detectives Borthwick and Robins, he said, were either 'co-adventurers' or 'knew that he was involved in some criminal activity and were not prepared to inform upon him' or, thirdly, 'knew what was going on but were prepared to turn their backs upon it'. After dismissing the third option, Woodward concluded that 'in either event they are untruthful and the purpose was to assist [Winery Tony] Sergi in his illegal enterprise'.

On the subject of the marijuana crop at Scarfo's farm, Justice Woodward had no doubt that Patrick Keenan had seen Winery Tony 'assisting in the harvesting of marijuana' and that Keenan's evidence had been deliberately suppressed to protect Sergi. Woodward was 'comfortably satisfied' that:

(a) Ellis in some way or another was able to assure Sergi that there would be no difficulty in keeping the fact of his involvement out of the proceedings;

(b) Some arrangement was made between Ellis and Sergi that if Scarfo pleaded guilty it would not be necessary to call Keenan and so disclosure of Sergi's involvement could be avoided;

(c) Ellis assured Sergi that he would do what he could to speak in favour of a plea of guilty by both [Giuseppe] Scarfo and [Rocco] Barbaro; and

(d) In due course Ellis was no doubt rewarded.

In a section of the report dealing with the growing of marijuana in the Riverina, Justice Woodward confirmed what the Concerned Citizens of Griffith had known since 1974: that between 1974 and 1977 an organisation 'comprised almost exclusively of persons of Calabrian descent, and based principally in Griffith, but partly in Sydney . . . was engaged in the illicit cultivation, trafficking and marketing of marijuana'.

The organisation, Woodward said, was 'directly responsible' for the marijuana plantations found at Farm 1774, Griffith (Rocco Barbaro); Farm 20, Hanwood (Giuseppe

Scarfo); Coleambally (Leonardo Gambacorta); and Euston (Vincenzo Ciccarello).

The growing side of the marijuana operation, which was controlled from Griffith, was 'supervised principally by Antonio Sergi [Winery Tony], of Farm 1305, Tharbogang', while 'the distribution and marketing of the drug was controlled from Sydney, supervised principally by Robert Trimbole, also known as Bruno Trimbole'.

Justice Woodward's report also shed light on the intricate financial arrangements used by La Famiglia to launder the proceeds of its marijuana operation, noting the use of company structures; 'loans' from friends and relatives; gambling 'wins'; cash payments to tradesmen; and the intermingling of illicit funds with legitimate earnings to launder drug profits.

In his report Woodward described the account of Trimboli, Sergi & Sergi at the Bank of New South Wales in Fairfield as a 'major source' of finance to those involved in growing and distributing marijuana. Between 14 March 1974 and 14 March 1977, a total of $1,907,900.59 was paid out of the account, which functioned as a 'major "laundering" outlet'.

Despite the mass of evidence gained by Woodward's investigators, some refused to accept the royal commission's findings. The officer-in-charge of Griffith police, Inspector Ken Hewitt, told the *Area News* that he was 'unaware of the existence of a secret Italian society, L'Onorata Societa, which was named in the report'.

■ ■ ■

The backlash against Justice Woodward's report was not long in coming. On 22 November Terry Jones received a phone call from Sydney. The caller was Jim Madden, a reporter on the *Sun*. 'Terry,' he said, 'I'm outside Central Court. There's a young bloke handing out a typed statement signed by Jennifer A. Sergi. Do you know her?'

'Sure,' said Jones. 'She's the wife of "Young Tony" Sergi.'

Jennifer was not Italian. Before marrying Tony Sergi she was Jennifer Joliffe. She worked in a takeaway shop called Nibbles in Banna Avenue. Jennifer was very popular. Lots of young Italian men went there to buy food, just to talk to her.

'I've got a copy of her statement,' said Madden. 'Do you want me to read it over the phone? I reckon you'll find it pretty interesting.'

Madden read out what appeared to be an open letter. It began, 'Dear Sir, I am Australian and married to Antonio Sergi, who is one of the men named in the Royal Commission as being an influential member of an "Honored Society", which supposedly is responsible for the murder and disappearance of anti-drug campaigner Donald Mackay.'

The statement went on to say that Jennifer and her husband had been in Surfers Paradise at the time of Mackay's disappearance and were 'as shocked as any to think that something like that could happen in Griffith'. She took issue with the suggestion that some of the six named were 'conveniently' out of town at the time Mackay went missing. '[T]his is the normal time of the year for farmers to go for their holidays,' Sergi wrote, 'as there is very little work and so there is nothing so really suspicious at all. I think the Royal Commission should have been a little more sure of its facts before it made such damning accusations because there is no such secret society as it claims, and none of our families had anything to do with the disappearance of Mr Mackay.'

The people who had condemned the six were 'becoming a lynching party', Sergi wrote, 'ready to condemn and punish these men without question or proof'.

Accusing Barbara Mackay of lying in her comments to the press and of stirring up 'vigilante groups' against the six men, Sergi claimed to have received threatening phone calls and letters and asked, 'What has happened to the Aussie "fair go"?'

The statement continued:

I have been married for five years now and was going steady with my husband for four and a half years before that, and in the nine and a half years that I have been part of a Calabrese family, I have come to admire my husband's people very much.

I have never known a people to work so hard and so continuously. The family is the whole basis of their whole life.

This special family bond that they have has been interpreted many ways and is often mistakenly said to have sinister underlying meanings.

But this is because, I am sure, of the inability of the interpreter to begin to understand our closeness ... The secret society or Honorata as it has been called is a figment of people's imaginations, fantasy is often substituted for fact when the observer is unable to comprehend the truth.

Jones took about half an hour to type the dictated transcript before sending his copy to the typesetters for publication the next day in the *Area News*. Unable to reach Jennifer Sergi to confirm that the statement was hers, Jones decided to consult June Webster.

'It's the first time we've had anything from the Sergi family since Don disappeared,' Jones told Webster. 'And she's right. A lot of the reporting has been pretty one-sided. But it's the code of silence—everyone has been up against it.'

Jones published Jennifer Sergi's statement in full under the front-page headlines 'MACKAY DEATH: SIX INNOCENT, SAYS MRS SERGI' and 'Accused man's wife issues statement'.

After the paper came out, Jones tried again to contact the Sergis, but without success. The war of words—which had begun with Ellnor Grassby denouncing the royal commission on the current affairs show *This Day Tonight*—was hotting up. Terry Jones wasn't the only one worried about how it would end.

CHAPTER 11

Another body

Less than three months after the premier tabled the report of the Royal Commission of Inquiry into Drug Trafficking, Griffith suffered another blow. Early on the morning of Sunday 27 January 1980 the body of Frank Nugan was discovered slumped over the steering wheel of his luxury Mercedes car in the foothills of the Blue Mountains, west of Sydney. It appeared that Nugan had died from a single gunshot wound to the head.

Rumours swept Griffith that Griffith City Council and other local businesses may have had millions of dollars in money tied up in the Nugan Hand Bank, the merchant bank Frank Nugan had set up with Vietnam veteran Michael Hand.

As soon as he heard about the discovery of Nugan's body, Terry Jones called his close friend Len Ashworth, editor of the *Lithgow Mercury*. Ashworth had already assigned a reporter to the story. Nugan's car had been found parked off the old Forty Bends Road by police on a routine patrol.

Lithgow police were describing his death as suicide: they had found Nugan's hand resting on the gun and the blood pattern indicated the shot had been fired inside the car. But it was clear from evidence found in the car that Frank Nugan had been rubbing shoulders with some influential people in Sydney. Ashworth told Jones there had been a diary or notebook with some interesting phone numbers, although police were not saying whose they were. The inquest was going to be held in Lithgow.

Ashworth reckoned the story of Frank Nugan's suicide would not sell many papers in Lithgow, but in the newsroom of the *Area News* it was the only subject of conversation. As usual, June Webster knew more than most. She had heard on the Griffith grapevine that Frank's brother, Ken, and his wife, Michelle, had left Griffith very quickly the previous morning to attend to a 'personal family matter'. It was being said that Ken Nugan had rushed straight to his brother's home in Sydney's eastern suburbs, and also to the office of the Nugan Hand Bank in central Sydney.

'We know Ken and Frank were both under investigation by auditors and the Corporate Affairs Commission,' June said. 'My guess is Ken got word that Frank was dead and raced to Lithgow, then Sydney to do a once-over of Frank's office and files.'

Whatever had driven Frank to suicide, it was certain to make things difficult for Ken. Both brothers were facing charges of having conspired to defraud the Nugan Group Limited and certain shareholders of the Nugan Group Limited at Sydney between July and October 1977. Eight weeks had been set aside for hearing defence evidence.

A story headlined 'FRANK NUGAN FOUND DEAD IN CAR' was splashed across the front page of the *Area News* on Tuesday 29 January. As well as outlining the conspiracy charges against Frank and Ken Nugan, George Gay's story mentioned that Frank Nugan's home had been broken into on Sunday night. Burglar alarms at the house had allegedly been triggered about 10pm on Sunday night, but both the Vaucluse area police station and the police public relations branch denied having heard reports of a break-in.

Rumours had begun to circulate that the diary found inside Frank Nugan's Mercedes contained the names of high-ranking officers belonging to the US Central Intelligence Agency. It was known that former admirals and generals were high up in the Nugan Hand Bank. Some doubted whether the body found inside the Mercedes was Frank Nugan's. There was talk of a big life insurance policy, and of Nugan having faked his own death before fleeing overseas with his associate, Michael Hand, taking millions of dollars of bank funds. It was also being said that Nugan had been murdered, but that his death had been made to look like suicide.

Nearly two years earlier the *Australian Financial Review* had reported Nugan Hand's claimed turnover of $1 billion per annum, commenting, 'At that rate Nugan Hand will soon be bigger than BHP.'

Such a turnover would certainly have been amazing for a firm whose founders, an Australian lawyer and a former US soldier, had no experience of basic banking, let alone merchant banking on a global scale.

As interest in the case mounted ahead of a formal inquest at Lithgow, more facts emerged about the events that occurred immediately after Frank Nugan's death. June Webster's tip-off was correct: as soon as Ken Nugan heard about his brother's suicide, he had rushed to Sydney to find the keys to Frank's home and office.

Although the Nugan brothers were both due to appear in Sydney's Central Court on 5 May, police had made no attempt to secure either place. Frank's wife, Charlotte, was not home or even in Australia, but was living in Tennessee with their two children. By the time Sergeant Bill McDonnell was belatedly sent to the multimillion-dollar mansion in Coolong Road, Vaucluse, Ken and Michelle Nugan were already inside the house with a legal clerk, Brian Alexander, from the law firm of John Aston, a solicitor with a growing criminal practice.

Alexander, who would become notorious as the middle-man between corrupt police and Terry Clark's 'Mr Asia' heroin syndicate, was known to Sergeant McDonnell as a person of interest in a Commonwealth police inquiry into drug trafficking. Alexander had also come to the attention of Australian Customs investigators looking at the movement of drug money between Australia and Asia. (At a subsequent coronial inquest into the murder of two drug couriers police would use documents seized from John Aston's office to show that Aston and Alexander had conspired with the Nugan Hand Bank to import drugs into Australia and to launder the proceeds.) Aston's links to Nugan Hand and the Mr Asia drug syndicate were detailed in the report of Justice Stewart's royal commisison.

It was obvious to Sergeant McDonnell that he had arrived too late to seal off the home. He spoke to Ken Nugan, who told him that Frank had just returned from Europe having signed off on a 'big bank expansion deal'. Ken described his brother—whom he had seen just hours before he shot himself—as 'quite happy and untroubled' but 'terribly tired and suffering from jet lag'. Ken acknowledged, however, that the recent indictment by the Corporate Affairs Commission had 'weighed heavily' on Frank.

It did not occur to Sergeant McDonnell to secure the city office of the Nugan Hand Bank. This was the next destination for Ken Nugan, who went there the following morning and removed documents that, he claimed, concerned the brothers' 'joint criminal defence to the stock manipulation charges, and nothing else'.

At 8.30am Frank Nugan's private secretary and administrative aide, Patricia Swan, received a call from Nugan Hand's vice-president, Stephen Hill, asking her to come into the office, despite the fact that it was a public holiday. Swan would later testify, 'I arrived at 9am to find Hill, Ken Nugan and a goodwill ambassador for Nugan Hand, Dennis Pittard, inside the office gathering masses of official documents . . . When I went into the office I found my desk drawers open—to my surprise. Only I and Frank Nugan had keys to those drawers. I can only assume Ken Nugan had obtained Frank Nugan's keys from police. Ken Nugan was taking out of the office the masses of papers pertaining to the Nugan Group litigation. He also asked me if I could find the document that Frank and he had put together, showing dates and amounts of money that Frank had advanced to Ken, and what amounts Ken had paid back. I was unable to locate this document and to my knowledge Ken Nugan did not find it. Steve Hill then told me to go through all the filing cabinets and drawers in my room and Frank's room and "take out anything that might implicate you or go against you".'

Not really knowing what she was looking for, Swan went quickly through the filing cabinets in her room while Hill stuffed 'cash books or ledgers or journals' into cartons that Pittard carried downstairs. Hill expected either the police or corporate affairs investigators to arrive at any moment.

The next day Michael Hand allegedly ransacked the office for anything the others had left behind.

It would later emerge that the merchant bank had been a sham from the start. Cheques had been passed around the boardroom table, but there was no money in any of the company's accounts to cover them. Through skilful management of the money market, the merchant bank had been able to trade with as little as $105 in share capital, often while insolvent. With the help of compliant auditors, Frank Nugan had created the illusion of a bank worth at least $1 million if not $1 billion. Before long, the Nugan Hand Bank was opening branches outside Australia. Among these was an office in Chiang Mai in northern Thailand, convenient to the Golden Triangle, source of much of the heroin smuggled into Australia by the Mr Asia syndicate and others. Neil Evans, who worked for a time in the bank's Chiang Mai office, would later admit, 'I was never under any illusion at any time that I was to go over there for any other purpose but to seek out drug money.'

■ ■ ■

In the days before the inquest opened in Lithgow, the *Area News* picked up on reports in the Sydney tabloids that lawyers for the Nugan Hand Bank intended to argue that Frank Nugan had been murdered. According to a story in *The Sun-Herald*, no fingerprints had been found on a spent cartridge case found in Nugan's car. Huge sums of money were said to be owed to Frank Nugan and questions were being asked about a mysterious $1 million insurance policy on his life.

The media scrum that descended on the small coal-mining town of Lithgow rivalled those that in recent years had converged on the drug trials, inquests and royal commissions in Griffith. Alec Shand, who had successfully defended

Frank Sergi over the 1976 Coleambally drug crop, appeared at the Nugan inquest for Sun Alliance Life Assurance Ltd.

The most eagerly awaited witness was Frank Nugan's American business associate, Michael Hand. With Nugan not there to contradict his evidence, Hand accused his late partner of having 'fraudulently misappropriated a vast amount of money from the company and other companies in the group without my knowledge. The embezzled money was paid to certain of his personal companies and to himself.'

Hand went on to say his legal advisers had told him it would be a 'long and involved process' to recover moneys even if that were possible. Up to $3 million had been 'loaned out to persons or companies whose identity is either unknown, or without formal documentation . . . prospects of recovering these moneys is extremely remote'. Frank Nugan's surviving records, he said, were 'incomplete and misleading'.

Alec Shand asked, 'All this embezzlement, on top of a stock fraud indictment that was pending against Nugan, might seem to create a motive for him to commit suicide?'

Hand, however, insisted that his partner 'more likely had been murdered. I believe that Mr Nugan was a fighter and would have kept going.'

The coroner disagreed, finding that Frank Nugan had died 'of the effects of a gunshot wound, self-inflicted and with the intention of taking his own life'. Nugan's body had been positively identified after Ken Nugan told the police that his brother had two webbed toes. But this was not the last word on Francis John Nugan. A year later, a Sydney businessman claimed to have met the merchant banker in a bistro in Atlanta, Georgia in November 1980, ten months after Nugan's supposed burial in the Northern Suburbs Cemetery at North Ryde. Ignoring the objections of the police and the pleas of Nugan's widow to leave her husband's body in peace, the attorney-general, Frank Walker, ordered the body to be exhumed. Dental records confirmed that it was the body of Frank Nugan.

The stench from the Nugan Hand Bank threatened to engulf the Nugan Group, although it was six years since Frank Nugan had been a director of the Nugan Group. In a statement given to the *Area News*, Ken Nugan distanced his fruit distribution company from the now notorious merchant bank, saying that the board of the Nugan Group Ltd 'viewed with concern' the public linking of the company and the bank. At no stage, he said, had he or the Nugan Group or any of its subsidiaries held any interest in Nugan Hand Limited; nor had Nugan Hand ever been a shareholder in the Nugan Group.

Not everyone believed his denials.

CHAPTER 12

Mr Asia

Despite some uncomfortable moments during the Royal Commission of Inquiry into Drug Trafficking, the marijuana growers were still in business. A few days after Frank Nugan was found dead in his Mercedes, a Bilbul farmer was arrested near Liverpool in possession of a truckload of marijuana worth an estimated $750,000. The village of Bilbul was six kilometres from Griffith. In court police alleged that the truckload was part of a crop worth at least $6 million found on a property at Coonabarabran. The farmer, 25-year-old Nunzio Greco, was charged with possession and supply of Indian hemp. Described by the police prosecutor as being part of a 'large organisation' handling large sums of money, Greco was already notorious as the builder of some of Griffith's most conspicuous 'grass castles'. According to police, he was the owner of the Coona-barabran property where the crop had been grown.

A month later Greco was further charged with having conspired with others to grow Indian hemp at Griffith and other places between 1 November 1979 and 30 January 1980. It did not escape the notice of journalists covering the case that Greco's alleged cultivation of a multimillion-dollar cannabis crop in the central west of New South Wales coincided neatly with the delivery of Justice Woodward's report to parliament.

■ ■ ■

In March 1980 the *Area News* reported yet another significant marijuana bust under the headline 'RIVERINA POLICE IN AMBUSH ON S.A. DRUG CONVOY'. Tipped off by the officer-in-charge of Griffith detectives, Sergeant Peter Yeo, Terry Jones published a detailed account, with photographs, of a police swoop on a convoy of three vehicles alleged to be carrying marijuana across the border from South Australia.

The ambush had taken place between 5am and 6am on Saturday near Gunbar on the road between Hay and Goolgowi. Police from Griffith and Wagga, reinforced by heavily armed officers from the Sydney Crime Intelligence Unit, waited in darkness as three vehicles with South Australian number plates drove along the Mid-Western Highway towards Goolgowi. Five men were arrested and taken to Sydney for questioning. Although armed with pistols, they were taken by surprise and did not offer any resistance. Police found large bags containing marijuana in a white van and a blue station wagon.

The Gunbar ambush was a good result for Yeo, who was working hard to restore confidence in Griffith police after the corruption allegations made against Ellis and his mates. Less satisfying was the sight of the arrested men being removed from custody in the Riverina and whisked off to

Sydney, along with the cache of marijuana that would be the main evidence in the prosecution case.

Terry Jones had heard from his own sources that police in Sydney had been planning their own 'sting' and were unhappy about having to give way to a bunch of 'country coppers'. Still, it was highly unusual for both the arrested men and the key piece of evidence against them to be spirited out of the area so quickly.

By the time the *Area News* went to press again on 19 March, the Gunbar ambush story had been overtaken by something more sinister: the shotgun death of 33-year-old Vincent Peter Ferraro of Fairfield in Sydney's outer west. Ferraro, who had been called to give evidence before the Woodward Royal Commission in both Griffith and Sydney, was found dead on the floor of his flat by his nineteen-year-old girlfriend, who had gone to investigate the sound of a gun blast. A single-barrel shotgun was lying beside the body.

Questioned about the source of a bank deposit of around $75,000 in old banknotes, Ferraro had refused to answer and was charged by Woodward with contempt and with conspiring to give misleading evidence to the commission. Lately he had been interviewed again by police.

While the Fairfield police were publicly ruling out any suspicious circumstances to the death, in Griffith it was common knowledge that Ferraro knew more than was healthy about the sudden rise to riches of Giovanni 'Johnny' Sergi and his family. It was also remembered that Ferraro had not stood up well under cross-examination at the Woodward commission. Although officially his death looked like suicide, some were suggesting that police should be checking the whereabouts of certain people at the time the gun went off. Nevertheless, a coronial inquiry on Ferraro's death would find that he died of an intentionally self-inflicted gunshot wound to the head. Evidence given by his young de facto wife referred to his 'depression', which she attributed to 'business worries'.

By the end of March the five men (four from South Australia and one from Victoria) arrested in the Gunbar drugs ambush had been released on bail at Lidcombe local court in western Sydney. All five intended to plead not guilty to all charges.

The net was now closing around Francesco Sergi, who had so far gone unpunished for his role in the Coleambally cannabis crop, and around the corrupt Griffith detectives who had attempted to cover up for the men behind the Hanwood and Tharbogang crops. The attorney-general, Frank Walker, was now open to the idea of a third trial for Sergi, and the Independent Member for South Coast, John Hatton, was calling for former Detective Sergeant Ellis to be prosecuted for perjury over his evidence to the royal commission.

Outside parliament, inconsistent penalties made a mockery of the existing drug laws. A twenty-year-old labourer pleaded guilty at Griffith Court to smoking cannabis in a car pulled over by Detective Constable Peter Bowtell in April. Bowtell was also the arresting officer in a case involving three eighteen-year-old youths who had driven to the Riverina on a shooting expedition. After stopping the car for a traffic offence, Bowtell smelt burning cannabis and found several rifles in the boot, including a loaded .22. The fines imposed on the young men for possessing and using cannabis were scarcely different to those imposed on Barbaro and Scarfo for growing commercial crops of the same drug.

■ ■ ■

The third anniversary of Don Mackay's murder passed without any charges having been laid. There had been no response to the New South Wales government's latest offer of a $100,000 reward for information. It had been another year of 'appalling silence', according to a reader's letter published by the *Area News*. Another reader commented that 'as a community we are held in contempt . . . Today, the network still holds tight, money buys silence, and the community goes on as though nothing has happened . . . We are showing future generations that we do not care enough about truth and justice to fight for it.' Yet another observed, 'This week marks the third year since Don Mackay disappeared from Griffith in such shameful circumstances. In the intervening years, we have witnessed an amazing amount of emotion, bad feeling, heartache, political mileage, hope, disillusion-ment, conjecture, hypocrisy etc. Through all this confusion, one fact emerges plainly for everyone to see: our legal system is not working . . . The same greed and ruthlessness that caused Don's death will return with renewed confidence and power—and our own apathy will be to blame.'

Dismay over the failure to find either Donald Mackay's body or his killer brought calls for the premier, Neville Wran; his attorney-general, Frank Walker, and the police minister, Bill Crabtree, to visit Griffith for a public meeting aimed at restoring the town's 'good name'. Some citizens were not satisfied with the offer of a public meeting: according to a report in *The Australian*, 'residents of Griffith, the NSW country town tagged the drug factory of Australia, say they are ready to run the drug bosses out of town at gunpoint'. The plan was to 'close the town on either August 25 or 26, to hold an armed rally and run out of town at gunpoint about 50 people . . . known to be involved in the drug trade'.

Before the 50 so-called drug bosses could be 'run out of town', the attorney-general issued long-awaited warrants for the arrest of former Griffith detectives Jack Ellis, Brian Borthwick and John Robins, as well as two men identified as 'Griffith farmers'. Police arrived from Sydney armed with warrants alleging that the three detectives had conspired with Antonio Sergi (Winery Tony) of Farm 1305, Tharbogang, to pervert the course of justice between 1 February 1974 and 24 November 1979. Detectives went to properties at Tharbogang and Hanwood but neither of the farmers was at home.

In a statement outside the court after he had been charged, Ellis claimed that his arrest was the result of political pressure on the state government and told reporters, 'I am entirely innocent of any charge whether criminal or at departmental level.'

Less than a week after Ellis was charged, the New South Wales Police Association protested that the three police arrested in the Griffith drug case conspiracy charge had not been given 'the rights of a common criminal'. The association was 'disgusted' that news of the arrests had appeared in the media before the three were told.

In Sydney, Borthwick and Robins were charged with having conspired with each other and Winery Tony and John Kenneth Ellis to pervert the course of justice. Sergi was charged with having conspired with Borthwick, Robins and Ellis to commit the same offence. He was also charged with having conspired with Michael and Giuseppe Scarfo and other people between 1 August 1973 and 19 February 1979 at Tharbogang to supply Indian hemp. No pleas were entered and Borthwick and Robins vowed to prove their innocence.

■ ■ ■

With the net tightening, La Famiglia turned once again to Al Grassby for support. Despite the damning findings of the Woodward Royal Commission, Grassby continued to deny the existence of the Calabrian mafia in Australia while doing all he could to frustrate attempts to investigate its activities. Since 1979 Grassby had been peddling gossip that implicated Don Mackay's widow, Barbara, their son Paul and the family solicitor in Mackay's murder.

The following year he redoubled his efforts, trying without success to persuade politicians in three state parliaments to table an unsigned document accusing the widow, son and solicitor of being behind the murder. On 10 August Grassby's persistence paid off, when *The Sun-Herald* ran a story under the headline, 'Mackay killing: Not the mafia'.

The smears being spread by Grassby against the Mackay family were old news in Griffith, but the prospect of their being tabled in parliament horrified Terry Jones, who found it hard to believe that anyone would put their trust in the as-yet anonymous document.

While reporting the gist of the allegations, the *Area News* warned that a former state government crime adviser had 'serious reservations' about the motives behind the release of the document. The adviser was Bob Bottom, who identified the mafia apologist Grassby as the source of the document given to Mr Michael Maher, the New South Wales Labor MP for Drummoyne. In a radio interview Bottom said, 'It was Mr Grassby who was gloating about it and it was his responsibility to explain where he got it, what his motives were and what it was all about.'

■ ■ ■

Mackay's was not the only killing in which 'Aussie Bob' Trimbole was implicated. In August Trimbole was subpoenaed by Victorian homicide detectives to give evidence at a Melbourne inquest into the deaths of two drug couriers. Douglas and Isabel Wilson were alleged to have been lured to their deaths in April 1979 for giving statements to police about the Mr Asia drug syndicate.

At the inquest in Rye, Victoria, a woman known as 'Miss X' had identified a picture of Trimbole and given evidence of a conversation between Trimbole and the alleged leader of the Mr Asia network, Terry Clark.

Described at the inquest as a 'shopkeeper' of Cabramatta in western Sydney, the 50-year-old Trimbole had in fact spent the past three years cultivating a new career for himself as a kingpin in the Mr Asia syndicate. As well as boasting valuable connections to corrupt police, Trimbole had an established cannabis distribution network that was easily adapted to selling heroin for the Mr Asia syndicate. Trimbole also had associates such as Frank Tizzoni, who did not baulk at murdering any who posed a threat to the network. Within a year of meeting Terry Clark, Trimbole had become a trusted member of the syndicate, recruiting prospective couriers; passing on tip-offs from corrupt police and customs officers; arranging false passports (he seemed to have an unlimited supply of government birth certificate forms); and organising the murders of those Clark no longer trusted. As the number of killings escalated, internal tensions began to affect the syndicate's operations. Bodies that were never supposed to be found turned up, incriminating Clark and others. When Clark decided it was too dangerous for him to remain in Australia, Trimbole was an obvious choice to take over.

The subpoena to give evidence at the Wilson murder inquest represented a serious threat to the Cabramatta 'shopkeeper', who would eventually flee the country to avoid facing charges related to the execution of the two couriers.

At the inquest, Chief Inspector Paul Delianis described a series of alleged meetings between 'Miss X' and a man called Bob Jones, whom they both identified as Robert Trimbole. One of the meetings was said to have taken place in a London flat in July 1979. According to 'Miss X', Clark had been present at the meeting and had complained about the botched murder of the Wilsons, whose bodies were not meant to be found. 'Jones' had been unable to find the hitman who had done the job in order to discover what had gone wrong.

Trimbole resisted having to give evidence at the inquest and was eventually excused on the grounds that it might incriminate him in the murders. Brian Alexander, the law clerk who had corruptly obtained tapes of the Wilsons' statements and passed them to the syndicate, was also excused, on the same grounds. (After the coroner, Mr Kevin Mason, SM, concluded that Trimbole and Alexander could have given information helping to identify the Wilsons' killers, the Victorian government decided to review the law allowing a person to refuse to give evidence in court.)

In Trimbole's absence Victorian Assistant Commissioner of Police, Rod Hall, gave detailed evidence about the self-styled shopkeeper's role in the Mr Asia drug syndicate. The Mr Asia network, he said, was responsible for the importation of huge amounts of heroin into Australia: evidence from one of Clark's associates revealed that during one nine-month period in 1978–79, the network smuggled 48 kilograms of pure heroin into Australia.

Hall told the court that Clark's organisation had links to both the Griffith marijuana growers and to the Nugan Hand merchant bank. Clark's ability to corrupt police and others had enabled him to operate with 'relative impunity' in Australia and much of the truth about his activities was still not known. According to Hall, Bob Trimbole had effectively 'controlled' the syndicate from the moment Terry Clark left Australia after hearing of media reports linking him to the Wilson murders.

On 29 August the coroner, Mr Mason, ruled that the Wilsons had died from gunshot wounds 'feloniously, unlawfully and maliciously inflicted' by a person unknown together with Terrence John Clark. Mr Mason recommended a warrant be issued for the arrest of Clark, who was now awaiting trial in England for the murder of another former associate, the New Zealander heroin trafficker Marty Johnstone.

'Miss X'—the pseudonym given to Clark's former lover, Alison Dine, who had been a heroin courier and recruiter of couriers for the Mr Asia syndicate—told the inquiry that Clark had paid $25,000 to have the Wilsons killed after learning that the pair had given details of his organisation to police in Brisbane. She believed Bob Trimbole had arranged the murders. Dine also described the murder of drug courier and dealer 'Pommy' Harry Lewis, whose handless body had been found in bushland at Port Macquarie in March 1979.

After Mr Mason found there was 'no doubt' Trimbole was involved with Clark in the Mr Asia heroin syndicate, the New South Wales police had little choice but to announce that it was looking again at the recent career of the Cabramatta shopkeeper.

■ ■ ■

Closer to home, the Griffith district coroner handed down his long-awaited finding about a fire that had burnt the old Coro Club to the ground in April. Terry Jones and his colleagues at the *Area News* were among those who had fond memories of the once-popular Griffith watering hole, which had been a favourite haunt of 'Aussie Bob' Trimbole before it closed. Since December 1978 the building had been hired out for engagements and bucks' parties for twenty dollars a night.

A month before the Coro Club burnt down, another mysterious fire had destroyed the nearby St Mary's Hall. Both were insured for $50,000.

The Coro Club blaze had always been suspicious, with the notorious 'Calabrese Candle' suspected by locals as being the most likely culprit. The coroner found that the fire, which had broken out around 2am on 17 April, was not the result of an electrical fault but had been set by a person or persons unknown. A police officer attending the fire had smelt diesel and another witness, Mr Miller, reported hearing an explosion shortly before he saw flames. Immediately after the explosion, Mr Miller had seen a white Falcon utility with three people in the front driving slowly away from the club. He noticed a similar vehicle return to the scene after the fire brigade had arrived. Inside were two men of Italian appearance, one young and the other much older.

After hearing the coroner's findings, few doubted that the 'Calabrese Candle' was up to his tricks again.

As the date for Francesco Sergi's re-trial approached, a last-minute attempt was made to have the charges against him dropped. A petition was circulated around Griffith, although few were willing to sign and some were fiercely opposed. The *Area News* tried to find out the source of the petition but nobody—not even Sergi's wife, Santa—would admit to it. In any case, it failed, and on 24 November 1980 Francesco Sergi went on trial at Sydney District Court over his involvement in the 1975 Coleambally cannabis crop.

In Griffith it had long been argued that Frank Sergi would escape a jail sentence over the Coleambally marijuana crop, but Archie Molinaro was not so sure of Frank's chances 'third time around'. Molinaro had confidently predicted a 'No Bill' after Sergi's first trial; when the case finally went back to court he was again 'pretty sure' Frank would win. But Molinaro had taken note of Woodward's inquiry into Coleambally. The commissioner had visited Gambacorta's Coleambally farm and seen the big shed with its trusses marked with the name 'Sergi'. Bags of fertiliser found at the farm had also been traced to Sergi. As the third trial got under way in Sydney Molinaro told Terry Jones, 'Frank looks gone this time.'

Both Jones and Molinaro knew that the jury at the first trial in Griffith included someone who was obscurely related to Sergi—a fact that had been raised in the New South Wales Parliament and at Justice Woodward's Royal Commission.

Woodward had come up with compelling evidence of Frank Sergi's involvement in the Coleambally crop—evidence that meant previous admissions by Sergi, subsequently withdrawn, were less important.

A week and a half later the jury found Sergi guilty of conspiring to sell marijuana. Sentencing him to three years' jail with a non-parole period of thirteen months, Judge Godfrey-Smith said, 'Your role was a behind the scenes one, out of the limelight, but you were still standing to make enormous profits quickly.' The news for Sergi was not all bad. As a result of his conviction for conspiring to sell

Luigi Pochi, Giuseppe Agresta and Pasquale Agresta were convicted for their role in the 1975 Coleambally marijuana crop, the biggest ever found in Australia.

Part of the 13-hectare Coleambally drug crop. Donald Mackay was the source of the tip-off that led police to the property.

Living quarters and vehicles used by the Coleambally drug growers. Three men were arrested at the property but others escaped.

The Agresta brothers, Giuseppe and Pasquale, with the owner of the Coleambally property, Len Gambacorta.

Harvesting of the Coleambally drug crop. The New South Wales Government eventually footed the bill for its destruction.

Co-author Terry Jones, editor of *The Area News* at the time of Don Mackay's murder.

Donald Mackay was involved in sporting, charity and community organisations and was determined to stand up to the drug growers.

Local MP Albert Jamie 'Flash Al' Grassby owed his political power to the Italian vote and acted as a stooge for the mafia.

Fruit inspector Patrick Joseph Keenan gave evidence that he had seen Antonio 'Winery Tony' Sergi packing marijuana in Giuseppe 'Old Joe' Scarfo's packing shed in 1974. A man with the same name was later found drowned in a drainage channel.

Nunzio 'Norm' Greco, builder of 'grass castles' and marijuana grower, is believed to have been murdered by La Famiglia.

(From left) Don Mackay, former Griffith Co-op manager Herb Turton and Al Grassby at a dress-up swimming carnival charity event.

On the morning of 16 July 1977, Don Mackay's blood-spattered mini-van was found abandoned in the car park of the Griffith Hotel. Mackay was never seen again.

On 26 July 1977 around 6000 people attended a thanksgiving service for Don Mackay on the lawns of the Griffith Base Hospital.

Investigative journalist Wendy Bacon (left, standing) was one of many prominent speakers invited to Griffith by the Concerned Citizens to talk about crime and the drug trade.

TV personality David Frost interviewed Barbara Mackay on his show *Frost Over Australia*, which was recorded at Griffith's Yoogali Club. Frost had recently filmed a series of explosive interviews with former US President Richard Nixon.

Nearly 2000 people crammed into the Yoogali Club to watch the recording of *Frost Over Australia*. Among them was Al Grassby (front row, third from left).

Paul Mackay has campaigned without success for the prosecution of the six Griffith men named by Justice Philip Woodward as being responsible for his father's murder.

Justice Woodward (wearing hat) visited the site of the 1975 Coleambally cannabis crop in the course of investigations by the Royal Commission of Inquiry into Drug Trafficking.

Justice Woodward and the leader of the Mackay murder investigation, Senior Sergeant Joe Parrington (centre), in the car park of the Griffith Hotel.

Justice Woodward at the Sergi winery in Tharbogang. 'Winery Tony' Sergi (second from left) was identified by Woodward as an 'influential' member of L'Onorata Societa.

Barbara Mackay (right) at a meeting of the Concerned Citizens of Griffith.

The murder of Don Mackay inspired many Griffith citizens to protest against the marijuana growers and traffickers.

Mackay employee Bruce Pursehouse was lured to Jerilderie in a failed attempt to ambush Mackay. Pursehouse's detailed description of the alleged killer was covered up by New South Wales detectives.

Dr Richard Smith was a leading figure in Concerned Citizens.

Dutch clairvoyant Gerard Croiset was flown to Australia to help with the search for Don Mackay. Croiset concluded that Mackay had been shot at Lake Wyangan.

Police divers searching for Don Mackay's body in the Murray River at Tocumwal six years after the murder.

A coronial inquiry found that Vincent Peter Ferraro died from a self-inflicted gunshot to the head. Some who knew of his evidence to the Woodward Royal Commission were not so sure it was suicide.

BISTRO
HOTEL GRIFFITH
QUALITY FOOD
WINES SERVICE
Monday–Saturday
Lunch–Dinner
PHONE 62 1011

TREVI
Spumante
FRESH and
SPARKLING
AS A FOUNTAIN
Available at your wine outlet

THE AREA NEWS

Registered by Australia Post Publication No. NAC 1635

Published Tuesday, Wednesday, Thursday, Friday.
Incorporating the Griffith Times.

PRICE 30c   Griffith, Tuesday, May 8, 1984.   PHONE 62 1733; 62 1384 GRIFFITH.

Police recover two bodies

EARS CUT FROM MAN FOUND BY FISHERMEN

Divers find second body

Police recover the second body of a man from the Murrumbidgee River, yesterday afternoon.

8th May 1984

GRIFFITH TILE CENTRE
Tiles and bathroom fittings shower screens, vanity units.
Benerembah St.
PHONE 62 3620

INCORPORATING THE GRIFFITH TIMES

Published Tuesday, Wednesday, Thursday, Friday.

Price 15c

Griffith, Wednesday, November 7, 1979.

Phone 62 1733; 62 1384 Griffith

ALIPRANDI'S PHARMACY

THE GRIFFITH COSMETIC HOUSE

Wran tables drug probe report

SIX NAMED IN MACKAY DEATH PLOT

Six men have been named as influential members of an organisation responsible for the murder of Griffith businessman and anti-drug campaigner, Mr Donald Mackay.

They are Francesco Sergi, 44, Domenico Sergi, 40, Antonio Sergi, 29, Antonio Sergi, 44, Francesco Barbaro, 42 and Robert Trimbole, 48.

The six men were named in the NSW Royal Commission into Drug Trafficking report that was tabled in ●liament yesterday.

●sion, which was headed by Mr. ●p shortly after the

●6.30 pm on
●Griffith

POLICE IN DRUG CASE COVER-UP

Griffith police involved in the apprehension of some people involved in cannabis growing and recommended that the affairs of three former Griffith policemen be investigated.

Mr. Woodward has called for the continuation of investigations into the Griffith organisa-
●n that he says has made money out of drug ●king and has been prepared to resort to ●courage interference.
●would be a mistake to permit the
●he activities of the organisa-
●publication of his report
●h had had its appetite
●the few years prior
●n prepared to
●erference was
●tiva by an

- **Francesco Sergi, 44**
- **Domenic Sergi, 40**
- **Antonio Sergi, 29**
- **Antonio Sergi, 44**
- **FrancescoBarbaro,42**
- **Robert Trimbole, 48**

'Don Mackay was murdered'- Woodward

Griffith anti-drug campaigner Mr. Donald Mackay, who mysteriously disappeared on July 15, 1977.

7th November 1979

marijuana, the remaining charges against him relating to the Coleambally crop were dropped.

■ ■ ■

For the police in Griffith the new year began the same way the previous one had ended: with a prosecution for cannabis. Marijuana crops were a regular topic of discussion among staff of the Water Resources Commission, which managed the irrigation channels to farms where cannabis had been found in the past. After receiving a tip-off from three WRC workers, police paid a visit to Farm 598 at Tharbogang on 1 January 1981, fully expecting to find marijuana plants growing on the property. But the plants, if they had ever existed, were gone by the time they arrived.

Detective Bowtell told Robert Romeo he had received information that Indian hemp was growing on the farm. Romeo replied, 'I do not know anything about it'—words that suggested to Bowtell that he was on the right track.

Bowtell told Romeo he had a search warrant and intended to search the farm for the drug. Bowtell walked to a paddock, accompanied by Romeo, but could not find any cannabis. It was obvious to him that whatever marijuana had been growing was harvested before he arrived. Bowtell then told Romeo he would search the farmhouse. Romeo responded, 'I don't think you will find anything.'

Romeo was wrong. Bowtell found marijuana seeds in the pocket of an army-style greatcoat. Asked what they were, Rome answered, 'Seeds.'

Detective Bowtell asked, 'Who owns the coat?'

Romeo said, 'I do, but I don't own the seeds.'

Asked whether anyone else wore the coat, Romeo replied, 'No.'

When they walked outside, Romeo's brother asked what was going on. Romeo told him, 'They found some seeds.' His brother said, 'Tell them nothing', and then spoke to Romeo in a foreign language. He told Romeo, 'They can't prove anything.'

Bowtell told the court that while being interviewed at Griffith police station, Romeo said, 'I don't know anything about the plants. What happens if I tell you about the seeds?'

Bowtell said, 'You'll be charged.'

Romeo asked, 'What if I tell you nothing?'

'You'll still be charged,' said Bowtell.

Asked whether he wished to make a statement, Romeo said, 'I can't read or write. I'd better not. My brother told me to say nothing.'

Romeo's lawyer tried to suggest that the seeds could have been in the coat pocket without Romeo's knowledge, but the magistrate disagreed, accepting the prosecutor's argument that Romeo had 'dominion over the coat and contents of the pockets' and fining him $250 for possession of Indian hemp seeds.

Although a gratifying success for Bowtell, the Romeo case was dwarfed a few days later by the discovery of 1500 marijuana plants worth an estimated $500,000 at a property near Euston. Two men were charged, while three more fled when detectives raided the farm after a tip-off. They found a crop that was ready to harvest and distribute to outlets in New South Wales and Victoria. Some of the plants were two metres high. The paddocks were fenced and police found irrigation equipment nearby.

It was less than four years since the police had raided a six-hectare crop of marijuana at Euston. Despite the royal commission, nothing seemed to have changed in the Riverina: the marijuana growers were still in business. Two men charged in connection with the latest crop were released on bail to appear in the Euston court, but the case was a sideshow to the long-awaited committal of the three former Griffith detectives Ellis, Borthwick and Robins; 47-year-old Detective Sergeant Arthur Andrew O'Sullivan of the Wagga scientific squad; and 40-year-old Antonio Sergi of Tharbogang on conspiracy charges.

The committal took place at Sydney's Castlereagh Street court. Among the first witnesses to be called was Rocco Barbaro, who declined to answer a number of questions—including whether or not he knew Detective Sergeant Ellis—on the grounds that he might incriminate himself. Back in Griffith the report of Barbaro's evidence, given with the assistance of an interpreter, was greeted with mirth. It was well known that Rocco Barbaro understood English and could speak it fluently. Barbaro was not the last Calabrese confronted by law enforcement over the cultivation, possession and supply of marijuana who would pretend to be unable to understand English.

Patrick Keenan, the fruit inspector who told Griffith police that he had seen Winery Tony packing marijuana into bags in Giuseppe Scarfo's big shed, endured a torrid day in the witness box at the hands of Sergi's lawyer, Barry Larbalestier. Seizing on every slip, Larbalestier tried to paint Keenan as not just an unreliable witness but as a man who was prejudiced and even envious of Sergi's success. It was Keenan's misfortune to have reported his sightings to corrupt detectives who were willing to fabricate an alibi for Sergi. With only Keenan's word against Sergi's, the odds were always against Keenan, who had taken a big risk both by speaking to police and by giving evidence against Sergi in court.

If Paddy Keenan hoped the worst was over, he was mistaken. After a short adjournment the committal resumed only long enough to be sensationally aborted when the magistrate disqualified himself. Proceedings collapsed after a letter signed by Mr J.D. Cummins, QC, counsel for Bob Trimbole, was delivered to Mr Henry in his chambers. Trimbole had been due to give evidence in the conspiracy case. The letter, which was addressed to him and purported to come from Bond & Bond Solicitors, contained extracts from the Woodward Royal Commission that could only be seen as prejudicial to the corrupt police and Sergi.

As soon as they learned of the letter being sent to the magistrate, both the defence and prosecution lawyers assumed Mr Henry had read the letter and as a result asked him to remove himself from the hearing. After studying the letter silently in court Mr Henry agreed to disqualify himself on the grounds that the letter contained 'information which is not evidence in the proceedings before this inquiry'. The conspiracy committal was estimated to have run up costs of half a million dollars before it was aborted. Few in Griffith believed that the collapse of the hearing was accidental.

CHAPTER 13

Special tomatoes

The collapse of the committal proceedings against Winery Tony and four corrupt detectives was a setback, but the Concerned Citizens of Griffith were becoming used to setbacks. They had seen the Woodward Royal Commission come and go and few were holding their breaths for a break-through in the three-year-old Mackay murder investigation.

The prime minister's announcement of a joint Common-wealth–state royal commission, the Royal Commission of Inquiry into Drug Trafficking, chaired by Justice Donald Stewart, had been greeted with a mixture of hope and scep-ticism. Set up in response to revelations that emerged during the inquest into the murders of Douglas and Isabel Wilson, the Stewart Royal Commission was to begin its first public hearings the following year. Its principal target would be the Mr Asia syndicate.

In the meantime, petty cases of drug use and possession continued to come before the Griffith court while men and women with links to Griffith's Calabrian families were being implicated in major cannabis crops in New South Wales and other states.

The ongoing charade of the long-delayed conspiracy case seemed merely to confirm what the Concerned Citizens already knew: that organised crime was running rings around the institutions of law and order.

■ ■ ■

In February 1981 Bob Bottom—by now the author of the controversial bestseller *The Godfather in Australia: Organised Crime's Australian Connections*—visited Griffith to talk about the mafia. Pointing out that the mafia had been active in Australia since the 1920s, Bottom warned that historic links between US mafia organisations and Griffith were still strong but that these had been ignored by Australian authorities until the murder of Don Mackay. Griffith, he said, was conspicuous for 'ancillary' crimes that commonly went hand-in-hand with more orthodox forms of organised crime such as prostitution, drugs and gambling. 'The claims for arson against insurance companies from Griffith rate as the highest in Australia,' he told a packed audience at the Griffith Ex-Servicemen's Club, popularly known as the Exies. 'Government Insurance executives have also noted an extremely high incidence of claims for vehicle accidents in this area.'

Reminding his listeners of the town's unwanted reputation as the 'pot capital' of Australia, Bottom pointed out that the marijuana trade generated more profits than the heroin trade. Blame did not rest solely with the marijuana growers, he said. Businessmen and bankers 'wallowed in wealth', knowing exactly where the money was coming from.

Asked what the citizens of Griffith could do in the fight against organised crime, Bottom suggested they lobby for the formation of a crime commission, adding that California's crime commission had had some notable successes.

Bob Bottom's recommendation was the catalyst for a coordinated push for action against the mafia. Local Apex clubs, keen to honour Don Mackay (himself a former member), had already pledged to help raise $350,000 to establish a crime commission. The following week the president of the town's Chamber of Commerce and Industry, Mick Whalan, announced that Griffith businessmen would 'strongly support' moves for a crime commission.

Stung by accusations that they had 'wallowed in wealth' derived from illegal sources, and alarmed by reports of 'notorious criminals' who had visited Griffith from overseas, businessmen and community leaders now threw themselves behind the push for the commission.

According to Mick Whalan, Bottom's speech had prompted much soul-searching from businesspeople who were just beginning to realise that not only had they done nothing to help Don Mackay in his campaign against the marijuana growers but they had personally prospered from the drug trade. They had been prepared to sit back and take the money, Whalan said, but were now anxious to 'make whatever amends they could'.

What they had in mind was a crime commission consisting of local citizens—largely businesspeople and other professionals—who would hire professional staff to keep watch on the conduct of law enforcement agencies and public officials. One of its primary targets would be corruption. The commission would not be a vigilante group but would cooperate with law enforcement to improve all aspects of the criminal justice system: law enforcement, the courts, correction, parole and crime prevention.

While it sounded impressive, some members of the chamber doubted that such a commission could be effective without drastic changes to libel laws. Nevertheless, the chamber unanimously passed a resolution calling on Wade Shire Council to hold a public meeting to discuss the creation of a crime commission.

Bob Bottom's lurid depiction of Griffith as a town in thrall to organised crime shocked many citizens, but how true was it? After completing a six-month community project funded by the Department of Youth and Community Services and Wade Shire Council, researcher David Phillips concluded that the town's notoriety was based on 'an illusion of widespread criminal conspiracy, corruption and racial conflict'. It was 'vital to state, at the outset, that this illusion is false and bears little resemblance, if any, to the true situation'.

According to Phillips, the picture painted of Griffith was the result of 'misconceived and ill-researched observations by reporters . . . and of the pragmatic needs of editors and producers . . . Unfortunately, the superficial sensational stories were attractive to editors and producers, while the mundane but realistic picture of a rural community was not.'

Nobody in Griffith would have been surprised by Phillips's finding that 'there is a high degree of social interaction of intermarriage, of acceptance and of tolerance', but many were puzzled by his failure to consider the subject of marijuana, ostensibly because 'the alleged illegal activities are presently before the courts and are therefore subjudice'.

Eyebrows were also raised at Phillips's division of Griffith society into six 'strata':

First, the upper and middle class Anglo-Australians;

Second, the class of Italio-Australians that have been assimilated into the Anglo-Australian culture;

Third, the lower class Anglo-Australian;

Fourth, the Northern Italian;

Fifth, Southern Italian; and

Sixth, the Aboriginal.

Analysing Griffith's crime problem without reference to marijuana was seen by Phillips's critics as an exercise in futility and wishful thinking. Some felt that terms such as 'ill-researched' and 'superficial' used by Phillips to criticise reporting by visiting journalists might have been better applied to his own conclusions.

While David Phillips's community project was soon forgotten, plans were moving ahead for the creation of a citizens' crime commission. In March 1981, a bank account under the name of the citizens' crime commission—to be known as the Australian Crime Commission—was opened in Sydney with community and business leaders as signatories. Mick Whalan announced that an office of the new crime commission would be established in Griffith within weeks.

A decision by the Griffith business community to 'stop the town' for two hours to enable citizens to discuss the crime commission made headlines not just in the *Area News* but in newspapers in Sydney, Melbourne and Adelaide. Residents were said to be 'seething' at the failure either to apprehend Don Mackay's killers or to break up the organisation identified by Woodward as having ordered the murder. 'Certain people intend to take matters into their own hands to rid the town of undesirables', one 'leading figure' told the *Australian*. 'If necessary they'll resort to fast cars and shotguns. The town is absolutely sick of being fobbed off by the Government when the finger has been pointed so clearly at individuals.'

Only the Wade Shire Council seemed unmoved, with councillors refusing to support a public meeting because the subject to be discussed lay outside the responsibilities of local government.

The meeting—promoted with the slogan 'If you care, be there'—proved to be an anti-climax, attracting far fewer than the 10,000 hoped for by the organisers. But the publicity had an unintended result: it spurred a return visit by Detective Sergeant Joe Parrington, still in charge of the Mackay murder investigation and apparently no closer to finding the body or identifying the killer.

Parrington was anxious to follow up some startling disclosures made in an English courtroom. In the grand hall of Lancaster Castle, reputedly Britain's most secure court-room, Terry Clark was on trial for the murder of Marty Johnstone, the original 'Mr Asia', whose handless corpse had been found in a Lancashire quarry, and for conspiring to import and traffic heroin. After a six-month trial Clark would be found guilty of both and sentenced to 37 years' jail.

What had caught Parrington's attention, however, was the naming of 'Aussie Bob' Trimbole as a Mr Big in the drug trade who had helped organise murders in Australia for Terry Clark. Trimbole was revealed as the mastermind when it came to obtaining false passports and enabling drug and cash couriers to bypass airport customs searches, not only in Australia but also in New Zealand and the United Kingdom.

After Clark moved to England in 1979, Trimbole was said to have offered as much as $30 million to buy the Mr Asia heroin business. Trimbole had travelled the world without detection using an array of forged passports in made-up names; it was claimed that he had as many as 50 aliases.

Intending to stay for three days, Parrington invited members of the public to contact him with any information about the Donald Mackay case or other matters. The response forced him to extend his visit and to promise another in the near future.

It would have helped Parrington to have known that the New South Wales Bureau of Criminal Intelligence had surreptitiously intercepted calls made by Trimbole in the weeks before he escaped overseas. Among the calls intercepted during May 1981 were several Trimbole had made to Detective Jack Ellis, still awaiting his day in court over allegations of conspiracy to pervert the course of justice. Taps were understood to have occurred around 7 May, when Trimbole was allegedly tipped off by friendly police to flee the country before he could be called to give evidence to the Stewart Royal Commission.

Terry Jones heard about the phone intercepts from Bob Bottom. Although the taps had been illegally obtained, they confirmed much of what Jones and others already suspected about Ellis's corrupt relationship with La Famiglia.

Within a few months Ellis was back in court, with his three colleagues and Winery Tony, to face a fresh committal hearing. The hearings took place in Sydney at the Castlereagh Street magistrates' court before magistrate Kevin Waller. On 4 December 1981 Waller held there was a prima facie case against Ellis, Borthwick and Robins and committed them to stand trial on charges of having conspired with each other and persons unknown to pervert the course of justice between 1 February 1974 and 21 May 1974. Detective Sergeant Arthur O'Sullivan and 'Winery Tony' Sergi were discharged.

Three weeks after the three Griffith detectives were committed for trial, the police minister, Peter Anderson, announced that an inquest would be heard into the death of Donald Mackay. After studying a report of Parrington's murder investigation, Anderson had decided a coroner should be given the opportunity to hear all the available evidence in the case. The inquest, however, would not be able to start until the completion of several related cases that were still before the courts. Anderson said he expected those proceedings to be finalised within three months.

■ ■ ■

The start of 1982 brought a flurry of drug-related arrests. In the most serious case, a 49-year-old Griffith man appeared in Windsor Court, in north-western Sydney, charged with cultivating Indian hemp. He was Carlogelo Scuderi, one of three men arrested after police discovered marijuana plants worth about $3 million on a property at Putty near Windsor. The other two appeared in Liverpool Court on similar charges.

Drugs were also on the move at street level in Griffith. Two men were arrested after the discovery of marijuana plants growing in a shed in Groongal Avenue, West Griffith where it was alleged seventeen Indian hemp plants had been seized, some more than two metres tall. Police allegedly found a quantity of Indian hemp and implements for smoking the drug in the house. The men, aged 31 and 22, were charged with cultivating Indian hemp, possession, smoking and having utensils.

In another incident, a 31-year-old man was arrested after police stopped and searched his vehicle in Kookora Street, Griffith, finding a quantity of Indian hemp.

On 9 February, a twenty-year-old man from Yenda, fifteen kilometres east of Griffith, was arrested for culti-vating marijuana. Two days earlier he had been charged with smoking cannabis.

As a parade of smalltime drug users and addicts passed through the court, 'Winery Tony' Sergi was finally cleared of all charges in Sydney's Central Court. After an application from the prosecution magistrate, Bruce Brown dismissed the charge against Sergi of having conspired to supply marijuana at Griffith in 1974.

Both attempts to prosecute Winery Tony over his involve-ment in the Tharbogang and Hanwood marijuana crops had come to nothing. So ended Tony Sergi's part in the legal saga that had embroiled a trio of Griffith detectives for the past eight years. Many in Griffith were dismayed to see Sergi walk out of court a free man. It was widely felt that the one witness who had stood up to the marijuana growers, Paddy Keenan, had been hung out to dry by corrupt police.

■ ■ ■

With Winery Tony's exoneration, the last impediment to the long-delayed trial of Ellis, Borthwick and Robins had been removed.

Their trial began on 10 May 1982 in the Sydney District Court, with all three pleading not guilty. The prosecutor, Richard Burbidge, QC, accused the three detectives of using their position to ensure the growers of marijuana crops received preferential treatment when they came before the court. The men, he said, had 'turned their backs on their duties as police officers and attempted to shield various persons'.

The Royal Commission of Inquiry into Drug Trafficking had uncovered 'serious irregularities' in the way the three detectives had investigated the Tharbogang and Hanwood marijuana crops, Burbidge said. Instead of trying to find out who had financed the Tharbogang crop and organised the marketing, Ellis and his colleagues had 'made up a story for Rocco Barbaro to deceive the District Court judge who sentenced him'.

It was alleged that Ellis and Robins had gone to Barbaro's farm by private car on the evening the crop was discovered. 'What they did at the farm is not known,' said Burbidge, 'but it is clear that they, or one of them, was in contact with local Italian people and in particular, Antonio Sergi, the brother-in-law of Barbaro . . . arrangements apparently were made with Sergi, or others . . . that the following morning a large number of Italian men would turn up at the Barbaro farm and harvest the five acres.' Barbaro was taken into custody on the morning of the harvesting and charged with the 'comparatively minor' charge of selling Indian hemp. Barbaro had later signed a record of interview which was 'false' and 'presumably composed by Ellis'.

The second crop of three acres of marijuana had been discovered on a farm in Hanwood owned by Giuseppe Scarfo, the father-in-law of Winery Tony. It was found by Paddy Keenan, who had seen Scarfo, his son Michael and Winery Tony stripping dried marijuana plants. After being told about the crop by Keenan, Ellis and Robins had gone straight to the farm. Scarfo was not taken into custody until much later under circumstances Burbidge described as 'unbelievable'. There was no proper investigation of the crop and a story was 'made up' for Scarfo, who was the only person charged.

The Sydney jury heard evidence from a string of prosecution witnesses, including Keenan, who had not been asked to make statements or give evidence at the Scarfo and Barbaro trials. Keenan stuck to his story of having seen Winery Tony packing marijuana into bags, and of having received an intimidating visit from 'Young Tony' Sergi the morning after.

When it was Barbaro's turn to give evidence, he repeated his earlier claim to have been given seeds by 'a Greek man' named Michael Poulos at a club in Canberra and to have believed he was growing 'a species of special tomatoes' rather than marijuana. Barbaro insisted that at the time he was arrested he still believed he was growing special tomatoes, even though the plants by then had reached a height of nearly two metres.

Giuseppe Scarfo also claimed to believe he was growing tomatoes, telling the court through an interpreter that he had been given 'a handful of seeds' by 'two men passing by on the street'. According to Scarfo, the men told him they were 'American tomato seeds'. Asked by Burbidge how he had grown about two acres of marijuana from just 'a handful of seeds', Scarfo said he did not know how much marijuana he had grown. 'I planted them because I thought they were tomatoes,' said Scarfo, 'but when I saw them growing up, I didn't care about them. I left them alone.'

The Sydney trial lasted eight weeks, with 39 witnesses called by the Crown and sixteen by the defence, including the three accused. The case was followed avidly in Griffith, despite the fact that the alleged conspiracy was nearly eight years old and that most of the evidence had been given many times before. The *Area News* regularly sold out.

After the dismissal of charges against Winery Tony there was a strong feeling in the town that the trial of the three detectives was a watershed moment for justice in Griffith. The Concerned Citizens were in no doubt that in 1974

La Famiglia had had Detective Sergeant Ellis in its pocket. They had seen Rocco Barbaro and Giuseppe Scarfo escape serious punishment after the discovery of the Tharbogang and Hanwood crops. They knew that detectives had socialised with senior members of La Famiglia on the night Donald Mackay was murdered. And many of them had read the report of the Woodward Royal Commission, which confirmed what was already suspected about the origins of the money that built the 'grass castles'. Anything less than a conviction would have proved that in Griffith the mafia could get away with anything.

On Thursday 8 July, the jury retired to consider its verdict. Ten hours later the jurors returned to the courtroom to declare all three defendants guilty. It was an important day for justice and for Griffith, and Terry Jones commemorated it with a huge headline printed in red ink: 'DETECTIVES GUILTY'. The front page carried photographs of Jack Ellis, Brian Borthwick and John Robins.

While the corrupt detectives had been convicted, the trial left many questions unanswered. What, for example, had become of the marijuana plants harvested and supposedly burnt by 'ashamed Italians' at Tharbogang? The harvesting of Barbaro's crop had been carried out not by police and staff from the department of agriculture but by the growers themselves, including Bob Trimbole and Winery Tony, apparently at Ellis's invitation. Between them, the two crops could have been worth millions of dollars on the street, yet Judge Muir and the jury could not be certain how much of the marijuana at Barbaro's farm had been destroyed. (It was rumoured in Griffith that plastic bags containing marijuana had been held for a time in Detective Borthwick's home garage.) The truth was, nobody really knew—or would ever know—what had happened to the marijuana grown at Thar-bogang and Hanwood.

Concerns that Ellis, Borthwick and Robins would be let off with light sentences were hardly allayed by the news that the trio had been taken to Silverwater Detention Centre, a minimum security establishment, to await sentence.

The conviction of the three detectives, and the anniversary of Donald Mackay's disappearance, brought renewed calls for an inquest into his death. Finally, it was announced that an inquest would begin in Griffith on 6 December.

While Ellis, Borthwick and Robins waited to learn their sentences, another prominent Griffith man, Ken Nugan, had his own fate decided by a Sydney judge. On 18 June Nugan had pleaded guilty before Justice Roden in the Central Criminal Court to three charges of fraudulently appropriating company funds between 1975 and 1976. Two months later, on his 42nd birthday, Nugan was sentenced to six months' jail for fraudulent appropriation of $11,700.36 while he was a director of the company. The court was told that false fruit and vegetable delivery dockets had been processed through the accountant's office and cheques were drawn to fictitious payees. The cheques were cashed and the money was put in a metal box in the office strong room, where it was said to be available to Nugan.

Ignoring pleas by Nugan's barrister that his client should not go to jail because he and his family had suffered 'significant public humiliation', Justice Roden said that Nugan had shown no contrition for his crime.

The following week Judge Muir handed down his sentence for the three corrupt Griffith police. After acknowledging that all three were 'devoted family men' who had made 'considerable contribution to the community, by reason of your police service', Muir sentenced Ellis to six years' imprisonment with a non-parole period of two years; John Robins to four years' imprisonment with a non-parole period of one year; and Brian Borthwick (who he accepted had acted largely out of loyalty to Ellis) to three years' imprisonment with a non-parole period of nine months.

Explaining his recommendation that the three be taken to Silverwater pending assessment, Judge Muir emphasised that it was not to give them preferential treatment but to counter the 'special risk' each of them would face in prison.

In a provocative 'Opinion' column for the *Area News*, Terry Jones drew a clear link between the cover-up of the 1974 marijuana crops and the subsequent murder of Don Mackay:

From the evidence and findings in the trial, it can be seen that the jury accepted that Ellis, Robins and Borthwick conspired with two drug growers and the names which were mentioned during the trial—those of Antonio Sergi and Robert Trimbole—would suggest much more serious matters indeed.

As Sergi has been named in the Woodward report as the organiser of marijuana on a large scale in NSW and elsewhere; and Trimbole as the distributor of drugs, the failing of the three detectives must be looked upon in an entirely different light.

It could be argued that had Ellis acted when he had the chance in February 1974, when Antonio Sergi—according to a reliable witness—was seen on one of the two Griffith district drug farms, marijuana growing . . . might never have reached such a magnitude.

Griffith people will always remember that the disap-pearance in 1977 of a highly respected businessman,

Mr Donald Mackay, was accepted by Commissioner Woodward as being a result of his involvement in fighting the drug growers.

■ ■ ■

Within days of the corrupt detectives being sentenced, Terry Jones was being asked for information about a Griffith man visiting his family in Italy. 'Jonesy,' said the caller, 'there's been another mafia hit in Calabria. What do you know about a man called Angelo Licastro?'

The name was familiar. On 1 November 1977 Licastro had given evidence to the Woodward Royal Commission. He was 22 years old at the time, having come to Australia in January 1975 for an arranged marriage the following year to Anna Sergi, the daughter of Giovanni 'Johnny' Sergi. Licastro told Woodward about his wedding and about the $17,600 the couple received in wedding gifts from the hundreds of guests at the ceremony. Licastro said he worked on Farms 1774 and 1775 at Tharbogang, which were owned by Johnny, who was the father of Antonio 'Young Tony' Sergi.

While visiting the town of Platì, Licastro had been shot in the head. Gruesome newspaper pictures from Italy showed Licastro lying in a pool of blood. Various theories circulated about the likely motive for the murder. Licastro's cousins were thought to be related to Luigi Pochi, the partner of Winery Tony and 'Aussie Bob' Trimbole in a Canberra wine shop called Vignali Wines. The shop had been officially opened by Al Grassby just eight months after Pochi and others were arrested and charged over the Coleambally marijuana crop. Justice Woodward found that the money behind Vignali Wines came from the Griffith marijuana trade. Whether there had been a falling out between the Pochis and Licastro would not be known in Griffith outside the Calabrian community. Nothing was said by Licastro's widow, Anna, after she returned from Italy to live at Farm 1744.

If Licastro was the victim of a mafia vendetta, he would not be the last. But the mafia was not alone in having an impulse for revenge. In the wake of the convictions that sent Ellis and his colleagues to jail, Terry Jones was shocked to be taken aside by a friendly police constable and told, 'Watch your back, Jonesy.'

There were police in Griffith who still supported Ellis, Borthwick and Robins and who resented the way the three detectives had been portrayed in the *Area News*. Jones's name had been mentioned around the police station. The constable warned him to be careful.

Jones was worried. He was still living with his wife and kids on a remote farm in Hanwood. Most days he left for work around 7am. He was often in the office at weekends. The constable's warning had been too vague for him to be able to take any precautions, but it would have been foolish not to take it seriously.

The next day Jones told his editorial staff at the *Area News* that he'd been given a 'friendly warning'.

Griffith was a small town. Jones knew that the police would be aware of his routine. They would know he liked to drink after work with his reporters and advertising staff at the Jondaryan Club, playing snooker on Thursday afternoons. Sometimes they noticed him walking past the Griffith police station on his way to the Victoria Hotel, another favourite watering hole. They would see him drinking at the Area Hotel, a place also popular with police.

Journalists and photographers at the *Area News* enjoyed a good relationship with police that went back many years. The warning to Jones to 'watch your back' belied the mutual trust and professional respect that existed between them. The words came back to him as he drove home one night past Griffith High School and noticed the high beam of another vehicle in his rearview mirror. The lights had come out of nowhere, as if the car had been following with its headlights switched off. It was a police car.

Jones immediately pulled over, got out of his Morris Mini and walked back to the police car. Two officers emerged from the police car. Jones recognised one as Sergeant Evans; he didn't know the other. 'Hi fellas,' he called out. 'What's doing?'

Evans said, 'You were driving over the centre line.'

'What centre line?' asked Jones. 'There's none on this street, as you can see. It goes from two lanes down to one.'

Evans asked, 'Have you been drinking?'

'Oh,' said Jones. 'So that's what this is about. It's payback time, is it?'

'What are you talking about?' asked Evans.

'Don't play dumb. You've been planning for weeks to get back at me. I was warned.'

Evans said, 'This is a random breath test.'

'There's nothing random about this,' said Jones. 'You boys were out to get me because you didn't like what I published about your mates.'

The two police exchanged worried glances as Jones asked, 'What happens now?'

'We're going to take you back to the station for a breath test,' said Evans.

'You've been following me,' said Jones. 'I suppose you know I had a few drinks with Detective Bindon? I suppose you'll be stopping him, too?'

Neither of the policemen spoke as Jones collected his camera, locked his car and accompanied them to the police station.

Jones received a friendly greeting from the officer at the station desk. 'It's a bit late for you to be working, isn't it, Jonesy?'

'I'm not here on the job,' Jones replied. 'I'm here for a random breath test.'

'You're kidding. Who's pulled you in tonight?'

Before Jones could answer, Evans and his younger colleague walked in. They asked for the breathalyser unit to be set up and for an independent officer to conduct the test. Not many police were on duty that night but the few who were scattered. It seemed to Jones that nobody was keen to 'put him on the bag'.

As he stood there, Jones began to regret his decision not to report the payback threat to the officer-in-charge, Inspector Ken Hewitt. At one time it had even crossed his mind to report it to the police internal affairs branch. But it was too late now. He asked to make a phone call to Irene, who was expecting him home. Since Don Mackay's disappearance, Irene had been anxious about her husband's safety, but it was the Calabrese she was worried about, not the local police.

As well as undergoing a breathalyser test, Jones had his fingerprints taken, but when the arresting police suggested putting him in the holding cells, the duty officer refused.

After Evans had charged Jones with driving while over the limit, Irene arrived to take him home. He left the police station without being asked to make a statement. He had not been advised that anything he said would be recorded, nor had he seen Evans taking notes. Given the comments Jones had made at the time of his arrest, this did not surprise him.

It didn't take long for Griffith's bush telegraph to spring into action. Some police were clearly dismayed by what had happened. The next morning the phone hardly stopped ringing. Jim Bindon was among the first to call. 'Terry,' he said. 'What the hell happened last night?'

'Two of your uniformed police followed me after I left you. They drove without lights and pulled me over for a random breath test outside the high school.'

There was a long pause before Bindon said, 'Terry, this is crazy. I can only say we're all very sorry.'

Jones also got a call from the solicitor Simon Mackenzie. 'Mr Jones . . . I'm just ringing to let you know I can offer my services.'

'Thanks for the call, Simon. And the offer.'

'What the bloody hell's going on with our coppers?'

'It's about the jailing of Jack, Johnny and Brian. They still have a few Sergeant Plod mates who don't like the way we reported their case.'

'What did they expect?'

'Obviously they wanted it swept under the carpet. I was given a friendly warning there'd be payback.'

'You'll be pleading not guilty, won't you?'

'I don't think so. We both know you can't beat a breath-alyser reading.'

At the Griffith police station, many were aghast at Jones's drink-driving charge. The *News*'s police rounds reporter, Tori Horder, told Jones, 'They all know there was talk about payback for the way we covered the court case, but they can't believe anyone could have been stupid enough to go through with it. Jimmy Bindon and the Ds are just shaking their heads. They've been asking if something can be done.'

'It's a bit late for that now,' said Jones. 'They've already charged me.'

Glad as he was for the support, Jones knew that the police had their own reasons to be worried, since quite a few enjoyed a drink after work, sometimes with Jones, before driving home.

Asked by the *Area News*'s manager, John Kelly, how he planned to report his own arrest, Jones said, 'It will be reported as normal. Tori has got a few lines about a man being picked up by the RBT. When it goes to court we will cover it the same as we would any other case.'

Jones had not yet decided whether to mention the payback threat. Many Griffith police, including Inspector Hewitt, were worried that he would. There was a lot at stake, personal friendships as well as good working relations between the police and the press.

When the day came for Jones to appear in the Griffith Court of Petty Sessions, some felt that the Griffith police force was back on trial. Everybody seemed to know the real story behind Jones's so-called random breath test and there was plenty of apprehension about what he would say.

Jones was sitting outside the court waiting for his solicitor, John Eades, when Constable Fletcher—the man who had warned him to watch his back—walked over from the police station to talk to him. If the payback story came out in court, it could mean trouble for Fletcher.

'This isn't a good look, Jonesy,' said Fletcher.

'I know, Fletch,' he said. 'I appreciate you sticking your head out to warn me.'

'We go back a long time, Jonesy. I didn't like what I was hearing at the station. Someone had to tell you. What are you going to say in court?'

'You've nothing to worry about,' said Jones. 'I'm not going to put you on the spot.'

Fletcher said, 'I know the boss [Ken Hewitt] is pretty upset about this.'

'Ken's a good bloke,' said Jones. 'He's had enough on his plate with the conspiracy case. You can tell Ken I'm pleading guilty . . . I'll take it on the chin.'

Jones did as he'd promised. He was fined and had his licence suspended. The *Area News* reported the case, with Jones sub-editing the story and giving it a headline. Jones was philosophical about the result. He knew he'd been set up, but at the same time he could see that the case had forced other police, those who were not part of the Ellis–Robins–Borthwick clique, to question how they did their jobs. Maybe the era when the rotten elements of the Griffith police were untouchable was finally coming to an end.

CHAPTER 14

Aussie Bob on the run

Griffith was changing, or seemed to be. Two months after Jack Ellis was jailed for conspiring with others to pervert the course of justice, the man whose evidence he tried so hard to discredit was made a Freeman of the Shire of Griffith. A key witness in the Woodward Royal Commission of Inquiry into Drug Trafficking and in the trial of three corrupt detectives, Paddy Keenan had lived in Griffith all his life. He and his wife, Wendy, had three children. The honour, awarded in recognition of his services to the community, was a tribute to Keenan's courage in staring down both the marijuana growers and the police.

If Paddy Keenan represented a new future for Griffith, Al Grassby signified a return to its disreputable past. In the same month that Keenan was given the freedom of the shire, Flash Al announced he was contemplating a return to politics. Grassby's seven-year term as the federal government's commissioner for community relations had come to an end, although he had been asked by the Fraser government to stay on briefly as a special advisory officer. Bitterly disappointed by his failure to have his term in office extended, the former state Member for Murrumbidgee and federal Member for Riverina was now said to be weighing up his options. Many in Griffith were dismayed at the prospect of once again being represented in parliament by a mouthpiece for the mafia.

November 1982 brought more unsettling news: the indefinite postponement of the Mackay murder inquest. The announcement by the deputy chief magistrate, Bruce Brown, followed a request by Justice Stewart, whose Royal Commission of Inquiry into Drug Trafficking was exploring territory that was certain to be covered by the Mackay inquest. No new date was given, but Brown warned that hearings were unlikely to start before mid-1983.

With the inquest postponed, media interest swung back to Joe Parrington's now six-year-old homicide investigation, which was rumoured to be on the verge of a significant breakthrough. In June 1983 Parrington made another of his unpredictable visits to Griffith. This time he brought his colleague Fred Shaw with him. On his arrival in town Parrington's only comment to Terry Jones was, 'You'll see an increase in tempo during the next few weeks.'

Jones, as usual, had been keeping his ear to the ground with the help of friendly journalists in Sydney and Melbourne. Rumours of a breakthrough were coming from a variety of sources. Jones's mate Terry Gallaway, a radio reporter for 2GB in Sydney, confirmed his suspicions. 'I'm coming straight down to Griffith,' Gallaway said. 'From what I've heard, something's about to blow.'

It was impossible for Joe Parrington to be discreet in Griffith: with his rumpled suit and felt hat, the tall detective had become a familiar figure on his visits to the town, wandering between the Griffith police station and the courthouse across the road. Outside work, wearing a loose cardigan and no hat, Parrington often mingled with the lunchtime crowd on Banna Avenue buying food from Bertoldo's famous bakery. He wasted no time before calling on Barbara Mackay and her son Paul to bring them up to date with the investigation.

Jones was tipped off to have a photographer on stand-by for coordinated police raids in Melbourne, Griffith and else-where early on the morning of Tuesday 14 June. Among the properties raided were the Griffith home of Joan Trimbole, Aussie Bob's ex-wife, and the Tharbogang home of Winery Tony. Both were premises long identified as 'grass castles' by the Woodward commission.

The New South Wales police commissioner, Cec Abbott, told reporters he was 'personally overseeing inquiries' at Griffith and said that Parrington was 'keeping in close contact with Victoria and Federal Police'.

Two men had now been arrested and charged in relation to the murders of the Mr Asia drug couriers Douglas and Isabel Wilson. One of them, Gianfranco Tizzoni, had Griffith connections. Fearing for his family's safety, police identified him at first only as 'a Carlton businessman', but Jones quickly established that Tizzoni, a former associate of 'Aussie Bob' Trimbole, was the so-called 'Federal Agent' said to have told police about Peter Calipari's unlicensed pistol in 1974. Jones had also found out from a colleague at *The Age* that the other person charged was James Frederick Bazley.

Tizzoni had been picked up by police in March 1982 after a joint operation involving a marijuana plantation at Bungen-dore, near Canberra. New South Wales and Australian

Federal Police had been watching the crop for some time, and on 31 March were tailing vehicles they suspected of transporting marijuana. The vehicles were followed across the border into Victoria before being stopped by Victoria Police. Tizzoni was one of those arrested. Not long afterwards he 'rolled' and turned police informer. Jones and other reporters were aware that Tizzoni had made admissions about his role in Don Mackay's murder. There were strong suggestions that Tizzoni had been in Griffith with Bazley on the night Mackay disappeared.

With Tizzoni and Bazley in custody in Victoria, Parrington was under intense pressure to resume the search for Mackay's body. There was talk in Griffith of divers searching for Mackay's body in the Murray River; Parrington was understood to have told Barbara and Paul Mackay that he had 'some evidence to support the river theory'.

There was no denying the importance of the recent arrests in Victoria, but much of the evidence relating to the Mackay murder went back to the Mr Asia trial in London which had put Terry Clark in jail. The London trial had uncovered significant evidence about Trimbole's role in the Mr Asia murders. Parrington admitted, 'The Mackay case is being looked at in a completely new light in view of the Mr Asia trial.'

On the day after the Griffith and Melbourne raids, Parrington told the media that a search for Don Mackay's body would take place after the areas had been properly mapped and gridded to ensure nothing was missed. The search of the Murray River would begin at Tocumwal, he said, under the supervision of two detectives from the homicide squad and could take days or even weeks.

Parrington agreed to let the media have a 'free run' at the story, provided they did not interfere with the search. 'You can shoot and waste as much film as you like,' he said. 'Then get out of the way of police.'

After confirming that the aim of the search was to find Mackay's body, Parrington told reporters, 'We would love to find a murder weapon. But we have no information a murder weapon is there. Such a find would be a bonus.'

■ ■ ■

It was still dark on the morning of 17 June 1983 when Terry Jones and Terry Gallaway drove out of Griffith, crossing the Murrumbidgee River just after dawn at Darlington Point on their way to Tocumwal. The Murrumbidgee that day was as muddy as Jones had ever seen it. Jones and Gallaway discussed whether it might have been the 'Bidgee and not the Murray River where Mackay's body had been thrown six years ago. If the Murray was running the way the Murrumbidgee was, the police divers would have a hell of a job finding anything that remained of Mackay.

At the towns of Jerilderie and Finley, Terry Gallaway stopped to file radio reports. By the time the pair reached the Murray River at Tocumwal, journalists and photographers from both sides of the border were milling outside the police station. Some had been covering the Mackay story since the night he disappeared. The media pack followed police a short distance from the town to a spot downstream from Tocumwal bridge, then along a dirt road that followed the river between towering eucalypts, mostly red gums.

At a popular swimming hole called Pump's Beach, roughly three kilometres from the bridge, police divers wearing wetsuits and face masks and equipped with oxygen tanks were preparing to enter the sluggish brown river.

Working in pairs, watched by photographers and TV crews, the divers would spend between 60 and 90 minutes underwater before surfacing and handing over to the next pair. Underwater visibility in the slow-flowing river was terrible: the divers could hardly see their hands in front of their faces. Logs and other submerged objects were a constant hazard.

Reports from Melbourne of Mackay having been shot and wrapped in chicken wire, weighted with house bricks and dumped in the Murray had circulated widely in media circles. If it was true that Mackay had been murdered by a Melbourne hitman, Tocumwal was a logical dumping spot between Griffith and Melbourne. Victorian police were rumoured to be in possession of a page torn from a diary or notebook that pointed to Pump's Beach as the place where Don Mackay's body had been disposed of. But if Mackay's body had been tossed in the river, locals were sceptical that it would ever be found. The Murray flooded most years around Pump's Beach; those who knew the river reckoned a body would have been washed miles downstream in the first flood. Even if the body hadn't moved, they said, it would more than likely have been devoured by Murray crayfish.

After several days in the water, the divers had found no trace of a body. By 21 June Parrington was ready to scale back the search of the Murray River until more precise information could be obtained.

What Parrington had not told the press was that he now knew all the details of the plot to murder Donald Mackay, except for the whereabouts of the body. On 1 June Gianfranco Tizzoni had made a formal statement about his role, and that of Trimbole, Bazley and another well-known Melbourne criminal, George Joseph, in the Mackay and Wilson murders. Victorian detectives had given Parrington the information on a plate. A week after making his state-ment, Tizzoni repeated the allegations about Bazley to Parrington and Detective Sergeant Fred Shaw in a room at the Mid-City Motel in Ballarat.

By the time the coroner, Bruce Brown, began his inquest at Griffith the following March, the crucial information about Don Mackay's murder had been in Parrington's hands for nearly a year. Tizzoni and George Joseph, who owned a gun shop, had confessed to charges of conspiracy to murder Don Mackay and the Wilsons. While both men had implicated Bazley in the killing, the allegations against him remained uncorroborated.

The opening statement by the Crown repeated the account of the Mackay murder given to Parrington by Tizzoni. Within an hour of the inquest adjournment on the first day, the teleprinter in the newsroom at the *Area News* chattered into life with a 'memo to editors' from lawyers acting for Tizzoni. It began:

> As solicitors for Gianfranco Tizzoni we advise that publi-cation of proceedings of Mackay inquest at Griffith, NSW, may well constitute contempt of Victorian Supreme Court, due to fact that persons, including our client, have been charged in Victoria with criminal offences relating to Mackay murder.
>
> Advice has been obtained from senior counsel to this effect and you are requested to refrain from publishing any of the evidence or information provided to the said inquest.

The same memo had been sent to the *Melbourne Sun*, whose lawyers gave it short shrift, declaring that it was 'an unreasonable request and should be ignored', while stressing the need for 'careful handling' of material from the inquest. In order to avoid prejudicing the Victorian committal proceedings they advised that Tizzoni, Bazley and Joseph (who had all been charged with conspiring to murder Mackay) should not be named, and there should be no mention of a 'Melbourne connection' or of a $10,000 murder contract or of the Wilson murders or of Tizzoni's confession. The *Sun* decided to refer to Tizzoni's confession but followed the lawyers' advice on everything else.

The memo put Jones in a dilemma. The *Area News* had waited nearly seven years to tell its readers the full story behind the shocking murder of one of its most respected citizens, and now Jones was being warned that doing so might put him in contempt of court. Yet backing off would have felt like a betrayal not just of his own readers but of the town itself: he had to publish.

Jones headlined the paper's report with the facts that Mackay's body was never to be found and that the killer was paid $10,000. Tizzoni's account of the murder plot, told to Parrington in a Ballarat motel room, was quoted verbatim from the Crown's opening statement.

There was more to come from Tizzoni's lawyers. His barrister, Steven Rares, asked for the inquest to be terminated or at least adjourned until the completion of legal proceedings against his client in Victoria. Applying under Section 19 of the Coroners' Act, Rares claimed that evidence likely to come out in the course of the Mackay inquest would prejudice Tizzoni's chances of a fair trial.

The Melbourne committal was due to start in four weeks' time, and there was little doubt that the Mackay inquest— like the Northern Territory inquests into the death of Azaria Chamberlain—would generate intense interest throughout

Australia, and especially in Victoria. But as far as the coroner was concerned, the time to ask for an adjournment had been back in March, when he first called for appearances. Now it was too late; the inquest would go ahead.

While much of the evidence given at the inquest was familiar, some was new. Mackay's friend and fellow anti-drugs activist, Tom Erskine, told the coroner of having received anonymous warnings to give up his anti-drug campaign or else 'one day you will be found in a ditch'.

A Member of the Legislative Council from 1969 to 1978, Erskine had known Mackay all his life and had been involved with him in politics. He said the threats and warnings had started after the discovery of the Coleambally marijuana crop in November 1975. The tip-off had come from Mackay, who had received a letter containing information about the crop. Three people were charged and Mackay had been alarmed at the speed with which cash was produced for their bail. Soon afterwards Mackay started receiving threatening phone calls.

Worried that the situation was becoming dangerous, Erskine and Mackay discussed whether to suspend their campaign to change the drug laws and to ensure that traffickers were prosecuted. They decided to press on. Although Erskine did not receive any threats before Mackay's disappearance, afterwards he received several anonymous calls (one from a woman) warning him, 'you're talking too much'. The Griffith solicitor Simon Mackenzie had also given him a 'friendly warning' not to speak out.

■ ■ ■

Several witnesses, including Barbara Mackay, spoke about the attempt by the mysterious 'Mr Adams' to lure Mackay to

Jerilderie on 12 July 1977. An employee, Bruce Pursehouse, had driven to Jerilderie in her husband's place but Adams had not kept the appointment.

A local woman, Janice Barratt, gave evidence that on the day Mackay was supposed to meet Mr Adams at the Flag Motor Inn she 'noticed a man standing and walking near the cannon in the park opposite the motel'. Barratt described the man she had seen as '34–35 years of age, five feet eleven inches tall, medium build with short shiny black hair, dressed in dark trousers and a light-coloured jumper'. Janice Barratt's appearance at the coronial inquest lasted only a matter of minutes but her testimony would prove crucial.

In his own account of the would-be meeting with Mr Adams, Pursehouse did not add much to the evidence he had already given to the police, other than to recall that the day before he was to meet Adams, Mackay had noticed an article in the *Area News* headlined 'Attorney General files no bill in Sergi case'. After reading the article Mackay had told Pursehouse, 'Now I'm worried.' When asked why, Mackay had answered, 'Sergi's getting out.' At the inquest Pursehouse was asked to say which Sergi had been named in the article. Pursehouse replied, 'It was Francesco Sergi.'

Curiously, Pursehouse was not asked to give a detailed description of the man he had seen outside the Flag Inn in Jerilderie as he waited for Mr Adams. In his later statement to crown prosecutor Barry Newport, Pursehouse said he had been 'surprised that nobody asked me about the man at Jerilderie. After I gave evidence I walked out of the court. Parrington was sitting in the body of the court about halfway towards the back—as I walked past he tapped me on the leg, held up his hand and made an "O" with his thumb and forefinger and said, "Spot on, mate." Later, at the Griffith police station, Parrington said words to the effect, "you are a great witness, you have done a terrific job".'

Terry Jones was becoming convinced that the meeting at Jerilderie was going to be one of the keys to finding out who murdered Don Mackay. Tizzoni, Bazley and Joseph had all been charged with conspiring to murder Mackay. Photographs of all three had been published in the *Area News*, but so far there was no witness to connect any of them to the shooting. That was about to change.

Jones was sitting at the editor's desk in an upstairs office when Pursehouse walked in wanting to know how Jones had obtained a picture of Bazley that had appeared in the paper that day. Jones explained that it was a police mugshot and that the paper had had it for months. Jones had published the picture several times, often on page one.

Jones said, 'Why are you asking?' and was astonished to hear Pursehouse answer, 'He's the man from Jerilderie . . . The man in your photo is the man I saw at Jerilderie when I went to meet Ray Adams.'

Jones knew that Adams had never kept the appointment but it was the first time he had heard Pursehouse or anyone else identify the man outside the Flag Inn as James Bazley.

Pursehouse said, 'I gave Parrington a detailed description of the Jerilderie man but he left it out of my statement.'

Jones was speechless. As far as the coroner and most of the police were concerned, Mr Adams was still a mystery man. There were still some who believed that Don Mackay had been killed by the former Sydney detective Fred Krahe. Within days of Mackay's disappearance Krahe had been nominated as a potential suspect. Pursehouse's evidence proved that the man who had attempted to lure Mackay into an ambush at Jerilderie was James Bazley. Why would Parrington have withheld that evidence from the coroner?

Moments after Pursehouse left his office Jones called his journalistic staff together. They were as flabbergasted as he was to hear that Pursehouse had just identified Bazley as Adams. But what was he to do with the information? Jones felt that he couldn't publish without compromising the coroner's inquest. For now he decided to do nothing, to carry on reporting the inquest as he had from the beginning, at least until he'd had the chance to talk to Detective Parrington. When that might be was anyone's guess. In less than a week the inquest was scheduled to move to Sydney's Castlereagh Street court. Parrington would give his evidence in Sydney.

■ ■ ■

From the day the coroner began calling witnesses to appear at the inquest, no absence loomed larger than that of 'Aussie Bob' Trimbole. The alleged mastermind behind Mackay's murder had fled the country in 1981. The man of a thousand passports had slipped through the net by the simple expedient of manually altering the date of birth on the passport he was carrying. Three years later, police still had no idea where he was hiding. Few expected Mrs Vicki Greedy, described by the *Area News* as a 'housewife, of Doolan Crescent', to be able to throw any light on the subject.

Vicki's mother, Carmel Greedy, had long been known as a close friend of Joan Trimbole, Bob's ex-wife. Vicki herself was a surprise witness at the inquest. A family friend of the Trimboles, she had been called to verify a statement she had made to police on 4 May 1981, in which she said she had known Robert and Joan Trimbole since about 1974 or 1975. Vicki was still friendly with Joan and her daughters, Glenda and Gayelle, and had often visited their home.

There was laughter at the bar table when the coroner asked, 'I don't suppose you could tell us where Bob Trimbole is?'

The laughter stopped when Vicki answered, 'No . . . but I'd say if you asked his daughter, she would know where.'

Asked which daughter she was referring to, Vicki answered, 'Gayelle.'

The reason for her answer soon became clear. The day before Vicki Greedy gave evidence to the inquest, she had taken her car for a wheel alignment. The person who gave Vicki a lift home told her that while recently visiting the home of Trimbole's daughter Gayelle, he had noticed a photograph of Bob Trimbole with his grandson. Vicki told the inquest that the grandson had not been born until after Trimbole fled the country. A fortnight earlier, Glenda and Gayelle had visited Vicki at home and told her about a videotape of the grandson's birthday party which they were planning to send to Trimbole. Gayelle had also shown her a jumpsuit that Trimbole had bought for his grandson: the jumpsuit came from France.

Asked by David Shillington, QC, counsel assisting the coroner, whether she had any other information about Trimbole's whereabouts, Vicki Greedy replied, 'No.'

The mood in the courtroom darkened when Sergeant Raymond Brown took the stand. At the time of Mackay's murder Brown had been attached to the scientific section of the Technical Support Branch at Wagga. On the morning after Mackay disappeared, Brown had gone to the car park at the Griffith Hotel to photograph Mackay's blood-spattered mini-van as well as the bloodstains and drag marks on the bitumen. Sitting behind the family's barrister, Barbara Mackay wept as the photographs were tendered as evidence.

Barbara and her daughter Mary hurriedly left the court, followed soon afterwards by two of her other children, Paul and Ruth.

■ ■ ■

With a New South Wales state election approaching and the Mackay murder back in the headlines, it was no surprise when the Independent MP John Hatton arrived in Griffith to support the local Independent candidate Tom Marriott. Thanks largely to the so-called '*Age* tapes', organised crime was shaping up as one of the key issues in the coming election. Transcripts of illegal New South Wales police phone taps published by *The Age* in February 1984 pointed to widespread corruption in the state's criminal justice system. One of the phones tapped was Bob Trimbole's. The illegal phone taps, which were first exposed by Bob Bottom, confirmed that in May 1981 Trimbole had been tipped off by corrupt police before absconding.

Revelations about Trimbole's role in the Mr Asia executions and the conspiracy to murder Don Mackay reinforced Griffith's unwanted reputation as a hub of organised crime. It was a reputation Hatton was quick to confirm. Linking Griffith to both the *Age* tapes and the Mr Asia syndicate, Hatton told an audience at the Griffith Memorial Hall, 'All crime in NSW is organized and Sydney is where the organisation occurs. Sydney is the "money tree". Griffith is also a "money tree" . . . Organised crime involves illegal gambling, drugs, real estate, larceny, car theft and shoplifting, all parts of a multi-headed monster. It is integrated, it's free enterprise, it's competitive. The organisation can only be combatted through restructuring of the police force.'

Attacking the premier, Neville Wran, for his failure to act decisively on the findings of the Woodward Royal Commission, Hatton told his audience that the Commonwealth State Task Force had 'not bothered' to investigate Griffith. The only outside body to show any interest in Griffith, he said, was the Crime Intelligence Unit, which was collaborating with Joe Parrington in the Mackay murder inquiry.

In an opinion column alongside its report of the meeting, the *Area News* commented, 'To say that the Independent Member for South Coast, Mr John Hatton, left his audience sitting in stunned silence in Griffith on Monday night would be an understatement . . . So shocked were the 100 or more people in the audience that they could hardly mouth questions for him to answer.'

Amid renewed allegations of crime and corruption in Griffith, the Labor Party suffered a disastrous swing of around 20 per cent in Murrumbidgee, losing the seat to the Liberals' Adrian Cruickshank after 43 years of Labor domination. Cruickshank had learnt to speak Italian and understood the Calabrian dialect, making no secret of the fact that he enjoyed the company of Griffith's Italian voters and going so far as to Italianise his name. The little car Cruickshank drove around the electorate during the campaign had been emblazoned with signs for 'Adriano' Cruickshank.

■ ■ ■

Finding out where Trimbole was holed up was becoming a priority for the inquest. As a result of Vicki Greedy's throwaway suggestion, the coroner summoned the fugitive's daughters, Glenda and Gayelle, to appear. The coroner's decision to shift the hearings to Sydney made the lengthy reports of the inquest in the *Area News* even more avidly read than normal.

Glenda was the first to testify, telling the inquest how members of Trimbole's family had stayed in contact with a father they all loved and cherished. Unabashed by evidence that her father was a crime boss who had made his living trafficking marijuana and heroin as well as masterminding several murders, Glenda confirmed that members of the family regularly telephoned and even visited Aussie Bob while he was on the run.

She gave details of meetings with her father on the French Riviera and described a telephone conversation with him in January, when Trimbole rang her sister, Gayelle. The telephone call was 'unexpected', she said, adding that they did not know whether he was ringing from Australia or overseas.

'What did you say?' asked Shillington.

Glenda replied, 'How I loved him, everything is all right, don't worry about anything, everyone is good. Just the usual things you say to somebody you love.'

Glenda also confirmed that Gayelle had a photograph at home of Trimbole with his two-year-old grandson. The picture had been taken in June 1982 when Gayelle, her husband, John (Bignold), and their son visited Trimbole in Nice. Glenda, too, had visited her father a year earlier in Nice 'in flats . . . in units. I do not know whereabouts . . . on the waterfront'.

It turned out that 24-year-old Craig, the youngest of the Trimboles' four children, was also in regular contact with their father in France. The last time he had spoken to Trimbole was in January 1984, less than two months before the Mackay inquest began, when Trimbole telephoned him at the outer Sydney home of Craig's mother-in-law. Trimbole denied the call was 'by a prior arrangement', insisting that his father 'telephoned on a Saturday night and my wife and I have tea there regularly'. The phone calls were 'just to tell him that we loved him and he loved us,' Craig said. He rejected a suggestion from Shillington that Trimbole used to call him at his mother-in-law's home out of fear that Craig's home telephone might be 'tapped'.

Craig, who described himself as a florist living in Cabramatta, had been given power of attorney by his father before he left Australia in May 1981. In March 1983, while on his honeymoon, Craig had visited his father at a waterfront unit in Nice, staying with him for 'about five days'. He claimed not to know the address and to have 'no idea' why his father was there. Before visiting him in Nice, Craig had called his father to say he was coming, but he had since lost the number. He could remember only the first four digits: '3393'. Nor could he remember the address in Nice. 'I had it on a piece of paper,' he said, 'but I no longer have it.' Trimbole said his father had told him, 'it would be better if I did not know the number . . . He advised throwing away details of the address. He said it was in the event I was called before an inquiry and I could honestly say I didn't know where he was.' Trimbole told Shillington he had never spoken to his father about the Mackay inquest.

■ ■ ■

On Thursday 29 March 1984 Detective Inspector Parrington finally took the stand. Many Griffith citizens had waited years to hear details of the seven-year homicide investigation and resented the fact that Parrington would be giving evidence not in the Griffith courthouse but at Castlereagh Street court in Sydney.

Reading from signed transcripts of interviews with Gianfranco Tizzoni and George Joseph, Parrington told the inquest that Bazley had been paid $10,000 for murdering Mackay, and had paid 10 per cent to Joseph in 'commission'. Several months before Mackay disappeared, Joseph had sold Bazley a Unique-brand .22-calibre, short-barrel eight-shot pistol for $400. 'It was part of my stock at the Melbourne Firearms Centre,' Joseph told police during an interview on the third floor of Victorian CIB headquarters in Melbourne. 'It was written off in my books to another shop when in fact it was kept by me.' Joseph claimed to have 'bashed off' the serial number and threaded the barrel to take a silencer.

Tizzoni and Joseph had outlined the conspiracy during interviews at CIB headquarters, but the full picture had only emerged during interviews conducted by Parrington and Detective Sergeant Fred Shaw in Ballarat and Bendigo. Tizzoni allegedly admitted to being in charge of distributing marijuana in Victoria for a Griffith-based operation run from Sydney by Bob Trimbole. According to Tizzoni, Trimbole told him there was 'an endless supply in the Griffith area and that Tony Sergi [of the winery] had organised the growing part of it and the supply part of it' while Tony Barbaro had 'organised farmers' in the area and Trimbole managed the distribution.

Tizzoni said that each week he would receive between 400 and 500 pounds (180 to 225 kilograms) of marijuana that was delivered in panel vans rented from Avis and that before each shipment Trimbole would ring him and give the place and approximate time of the pick-up.

As a result of Don Mackay's efforts to disrupt the marijuana-growing operation in Griffith, Tizzoni claimed the organisation had been forced to bring in marijuana from

South Australia. Trimbole, he told Parrington, 'came down here about the middle of June 1977, he told me that Mackay was causing trouble and disruptions and that there was too much at stake and too many people in danger and that Mackay would have to go'.

When asked by Trimbole to arrange the murder, Tizzoni had replied, 'Yes, I probably know a person who can do it' but had suggested exploring other options—such as compromising Mackay with a woman—before resorting to murder. Trimbole's reply was that this would not work with Mackay.

Asked by Parrington what he thought of the decision to kill Mackay, Tizzoni allegedly answered, 'I regard it as part of the normal function of the organisation.'

Tizzoni told Parrington 'the money was right' and that the murder contract came with conditions that Mackay's body had to be disposed of; that Bazley had to return with some form of identification taken from Mackay to prove that the job had been done; and that a shotgun was not to be used in order to avoid casting 'any reflection on the Italian community'. Tizzoni said he had offered Bazley a deposit but Bazley said he would 'collect it after the job was done'.

Within a fortnight of Tizzoni's meeting with Bazley, Don Mackay was dead. The morning after Mackay's disappearance, the two men met in Park Hill Road, where Bazley handed over a driver's licence and a doctor's bill in the name of Mackay. He then 'apologised for taking longer than he expected', explaining that he had planned to murder Mackay at Jerilderie but that another person had come to the meeting in Mackay's place.

Tizzoni claimed not to know how or where Bazley had disposed of the body and told Parrington that on Trimbole's orders he had burnt Mackay's documents. But a notebook belonging to Tizzoni had been found to contain a sketch of the town of Tocumwal with a back road leading to the river. While in police custody in Melbourne, Tizzoni had urged Detective Chief Inspector Carl Mengler to search the Murray River near Tocumwal. When questioned about this by Parrington, Tizzoni claimed it was 'just a thought, which occurred to me to be helpful'. He claimed not to know whether the map found in his notebook was a map of where Mackay's body had been dumped. When asked by Parrington whether it was not 'a most extraordinary thing for a person to draw a map and not know anything about it', Tizzoni replied, 'No, except that I suggest to you, Inspector, that you dredge the river.'

For all the excitement that preceded Joe Parrington's appearance at the inquest, he added little to what had already been reported by the media in New South Wales and Victoria. Everybody except the coroner seemed to know that Parrington had doctored Pursehouse's statement to remove his identification of the man at Jerilderie. Many thought that Parrington had prevented Pursehouse from saying it because he wanted to drop the bombshell himself. Jones and his reporters were bewildered by Parrington's failure to mention Pursehouse's eyewitness testimony confirming James Bazley as the man who had waited for Mackay at Jerilderie. They felt that Parrington had given his evidence through gritted teeth, since most of what he told the coroner had been gifted to him by Victoria Police.

Pursehouse's statement to Barry Newport left little doubt that interstate rivalry was a significant factor in the Mackay investigation:

'In about September 1984 I received a subpoena to attend at Bazley's committal. I phoned Parrington and said words to the effect, "Are you going down to Melbourne for the trial?"

'He said, "No, I won't be going down there. [Detective Constable Rick] Campbell will be there as an observer. New South Wales has got nothing to do with it."

'I said, "Why is that?"

'He said, "We don't want to be involved in a case that will be thrown out of court."

'I then asked why did the NSW Police not want to be involved and he said words to the effect, "If we are involved and they loose [*sic*] him, we won't be able to try him ourselves."'

■ ■ ■

The day after Joe Parrington gave his evidence, the coroner found that 'Donald Mackay died on the 15th day of July, 1977, in the car park of the Griffith Hotel, at Griffith' and that 'a prima facie case of murder, in that each was an accessory before and/or after the fact, has been established against two known persons'. He found that Mackay had been killed as a result of his attempts 'to expose publicly persons responsible for the cultivation . . . and supply of large quantities of marijuana'.

As well as his findings about the murder of Don Mackay, the coroner made several other recommendations, including urging the prosecution of Winery Tony Sergi for his activities at the Scarfo farm, as alleged by Patrick Keenan. He also challenged the coroner's finding of 'accidental death' in the case of the other Patrick Joseph Keenan (not the fruit inspector), whose body was found in a Griffith drainage canal on 3 March 1974, exactly two weeks after his namesake reported seeing marijuana being bagged at the Scarfo farm. Brown said that in the light of subsequent events in the Griffith district 'substantial doubt' existed over the finding of accidental death and that new evidence pointed instead to an open finding.

Announcing his findings after hearing evidence from more than 60 witnesses in Griffith and Sydney, the coroner expressed his deepest sympathy for Mackay's family. Barbara and her daughter Mary were both in court to hear the result. Neither spoke to reporters as they left the court.

Few expected the coroner's to be the last word on the subject. Too many questions remained unanswered. Too many egos had a stake in the case. Before the coroner handed down his findings, Parrington claimed that the breakthrough had come the previous year when he interviewed two of the charged men in Victoria. Parrington's assertion caused eyes to roll, not least among members of the Griffith media who knew that Bruce Pursehouse had been prevented from telling the inquest that Fred Bazley had been at Jerilderie.

Terry Jones and his reporters argued over Parrington's motives for suppressing such important evidence. It was an open secret that the Mackay murder case had been a monumental embarrassment to the New South Wales police. It still rankled that Victoria Police had cracked the case. Many senior New South Wales detectives felt that Parrington's investigation had been mishandled from the moment he arrived in Griffith.

The paper's former general manager, June Webster, suspected Parrington didn't want news of Bazley's presence at Jerilderie leaking out before the trial of Bazley, Joseph and Tizzoni in Melbourne. Her theory was that if Pursehouse's evidence did not come out at the inquest and was not put before the committal hearing in Victoria, the three accused men might be acquitted at trial, leaving it open to Parrington to lay a murder charge against Bazley in New South Wales, with Bruce Pursehouse as his key witness.

As usual, Webster was not far wrong.

CHAPTER 15

Bodies in the river

Sunday phone calls to the *Area News* normally went unanswered. It was a stroke of luck for Terry Jones that he was in the office when the phone rang around lunchtime on 6 May 1984. Jones had dropped by the office on his way to buy the Sunday papers. He picked up the receiver. A breathless voice at the other end said, 'Jonesy, you'd better get a reporter and photographer down to the 'Bidgee. Benerembah Reserve . . . near Darlington Point . . . and fucken hurry!'

'Who's speaking?' asked Jones. 'Your voice sounds familiar.'

'It bloody should do, mate,' replied the caller. 'But I'm not saying at the moment. Just do what I say. Get a photographer down to the Point. If you move quickly, you'll be there before the coppers.'

'All right,' said Jones. 'Just tell me what I'm looking for.'

'We've been fishing at the river overnight, found a massive pool of blood, saw drag marks on the bank, threw a line into the water hole and hooked a bloke. His whole body just bobbed up out of the water. We fucken near shit our pants. He was in the fishing hole, a bit out from the bank. Poor bastard had been shot between the eyes, hands tied behind his back, fucken ears cut off. We've told the cops. They're on their way.'

By now Jones had recognised the caller: it was Don Plant, a legendary river fisherman who usually drank at the same hotel as the staff of the *Area News*. A keen fisherman himself, Jones often went overnight camping with Plant and others from the hotel's fishing club, working lines to capture native golden and silver perch, as well as the much sought-after Murray cod and crayfish.

'I know who you are,' said Jones. 'Thanks for the tip.'

'Never mind who I am,' said Plant. 'Just get on down here. Go to the Benerembah Reserve. It's off River Road, about sixteen kilometres downstream from the Point.'

'Will you be there?' asked Jones.

'Shit no, mate. I'll be at the Area Hotel. I need a stiff drink.'

'Were you alone when you found the body?' asked Jones.

'No, mate. There were two of us, but I'm not giving you the other bloke's name. If this is one of those mafia killings, we could be next.'

'Fair enough, mate,' said Jones. 'And thanks for the call. I owe you a drink.'

'Too bloody right you do,' Plant said, and hung up.

Jones took a deep breath. It was going to be the Mackay murder all over again: media from around Australia descending on Griffith like vultures, the words 'murder' and 'mafia' screaming from headlines, everyone pointing accusing fingers at 'the Italians'. It sometimes felt like the town was cursed.

The next deadline for the *Area News* was two days away, on Tuesday 8 May. That gave his reporters 48 hours to get the story. The top priority was sending a photographer down to the Benerembah Reserve before local police had the whole area taped off.

As a fisherman himself, Jones knew that the Murrumbidgee River was accessible from any number of public reserve roads. It would be almost impossible for police to keep the media out.

As usual, local radio and television would have the advantage; it could be another 24 hours before the Melbourne and Sydney papers had all the information they needed from the police.

Scientific investigators, led by Senior Constable Zane Douglas from Albury, began combing the riverbank from early on Monday. Detectives from Sydney's homicide squad arrived in Griffith around 11am to take over from Griffith detectives. When members of the police diving squad turned up an hour later to retrieve the body found by Don Plant and his mate, they were startled to discover a second corpse.

The front-page headlines on Tuesday's edition of the *Area News* said 'Police recover two bodies' and 'EARS CUT FROM MAN FOUND BY FISHERMEN'. A photograph showed government-contracted funeral directors loading body bags onto the back of a utility, surrounded by police wearing overalls and wetsuits.

Fingerprints sent to Sydney enabled police to quickly identify the middle-aged man whose ears had been cut off, although he had not yet been named. His body had been weighted with a car battery and a concrete block, both of which were tied to his waist with rope, and he had been stabbed in the stomach and the back of the neck. Police speculated that he had been tortured before being shot twice in the back of the head. His body was thought to have been in the water for about twelve hours.

The second body had been recovered from the same hole in the river, only a metre or two from where the first was found. The victim was around 45 to 50 years old. His hands were tied and he appeared to have been shot once in the forehead with a .22 bullet. His body had been weighted with a steel girder.

Both bodies were fully clothed. The first was wearing a white shirt, dark cardigan and trousers and tie; it was possible he was a waiter. The second was dressed in brown trousers, a white shirt and black boots. Both victims were described as being of European extraction, perhaps Italian. Police believed that both men were murdered near a camp-fire site and their bodies dragged for about 50 metres before being thrown into the river.

It wasn't long before the first victim had been named as Rocco Medici, the 47-year-old cousin of Marco Rosario Medici, who had been shot dead almost exactly a year earlier while driving his Mini Moke around his fruit orchard at Red Cliffs, near Mildura. Marco Medici was a senior member of the Calabrian mafia and was involved in the cultivation and distribution of marijuana. His 23-year-old son, Matteo, had been charged with the murder and was awaiting trial. (After two trials Matteo would be acquitted of his father's murder. The hit is thought to have been ordered by South Australian mafia bosses. Police suspect the rifle used to kill Marco Medici and the gun used to murder Don Mackay were supplied by the same man.)

Rocco Medici, of East Keilor, Melbourne, had convic-tions for assault and possessing firearms. His occupation was described as 'unknown' but he had recently been on workers' compensation after a back injury. Police believed he may have had his ears cut off for informing on his criminal associates. Some were speculating that Medici's ears were being kept for use as a warning to other potential informers.

The second victim was identified as 41-year-old Giuseppe Furina, also of East Keilor. Furina was Medici's brother-in-law.

The pair was last seen at 8.30pm on Saturday when they left Melbourne for Griffith in a 1975 brown and red Ford LTD. There was no sign of the car at Benerembah Reserve. The double execution was a 'messy job', police told the media, that did not look like the work of professional hitmen. Professional killers would never have been so sloppy as to leave blood and drag marks on the river bank and to have thrown the bodies in the river without enough weight to hold them down. But there was another theory: that the killers had intended their victims to be found, as a warning to those tempted to break Omerta—the mafia code of silence.

More information came out in the following days. The two murder victims were described by one detective as 'aspiring marijuana millionaires' who were involved in drug trafficking and might have decided to compete against the established syndicates. Police suspected they had been lured to Griffith on the pretext of a drug deal then ambushed, tortured and murdered. Although initially reluctant to describe the deaths as mafia killings, detectives were soon referring to both victims as members of L'Onorata Societa (the Honoured Society) who had fallen out with their mob bosses.

Medici was known to have been an associate of the Melbourne godfather Liborio Benvenuto, whose 4WD was blown up at the city's Queen Victoria Market in May 1983.

There were suspicions that Benvenuto blamed Medici for the blast and had given orders for him to be tortured and killed as punishment. Furina was thought to have been 'in the wrong place at the wrong time', perhaps brought to Griffith by his brother-in-law for company.

To outsiders, the murders of Medici and Furina reaffirmed all the old preconceptions about Griffith's Calabrian underbelly. The officer-in-charge of Griffith police district, Inspector Ron Robertson, defended the town's reputation in front of a battery of television cameras outside the Griffith police station: 'Griffith is no worse than any other town in New South Wales,' Robertson told the media. 'We just get the bad publicity because people remember the death of Mr Mackay.'

Robertson did his best to paint a positive picture of the town and to talk up the success of his detectives in making drug arrests. But Robertson, like many Griffith police, was a blow-in. 'If you mention you come from Griffith, someone makes a smart remark,' he said. 'I'd hate to be a local. It's bad enough being a policeman in a temporary position down here.' Locals could only roll their eyes as Robertson told reporters he did not believe major traffickers were still operating in Griffith and agreed with the claim that the town had 'cleaned them out'.

'Poor bugger', was how one of Jones's reporters described Robertson's performance at the media briefing. 'Robertson's a relieving officer in Griffith. Why couldn't they put someone up who knows that it's bullshit to say Griffith has cleaned out the big drug traffickers?'

Post-mortem examinations of the bodies revealed that Medici could have been in the water for as little as two hours before being snagged by Don Plant and his mate. It was another fourteen hours before police divers retrieved

Furina's body from the river; his body was deeply wrinkled from the immersion.

Efforts by police divers with metal detectors to find the murder weapon, or even used bullets, were hampered by the number of old tin cans lying on the river bed. Searchers found numerous brass .22 cartridge cases near the bank but all of them were old, probably fired by local hunters.

The early discovery of the bodies appeared to have given investigators a head start, but inquiries soon stalled. With nobody talking, the chances of a breakthrough in the case began to recede. The double murder was no closer to being solved when the committal of Tizzoni, Joseph and Bazley on charges of conspiring to murder Don Mackay opened in September.

■ ■ ■

On 6 September 1984 Terry Jones published a story looking ahead to the start of the committal in a week's time. Among the photographs was a picture of Gianfranco Tizzoni that caught the eye of local businessman Jim McCudden. One of Don Mackay's regular drinking school at the Griffith Hotel, McCudden was a commercial printer who had been a partner in the *Griffith Times* before its sale to Riverina Newspapers.

Non-regulars always stood out at the Griff and McCudden had a good memory for a face. Seeing Tizzoni's picture in the *Area News* convinced him that Tizzoni was the smartly dressed man (more smartly dressed, at least, than most of the Griff's regular drinkers) he had seen attempting to look inconspicuous in the Griffith Hotel on the evening of 15 July 1977.

McCudden wasted no time calling Jones. 'Jonesy, that photo you've been running of Tizzoni. I'm sure he was at the

Griff the day Don disappeared. I didn't know who he was, but I'm positive that's him.'

Jones was sceptical. 'It's not the first time we've run that picture, Jim,' he said. 'How come you haven't mentioned this before?'

'I suppose I never really looked at it closely before. But I'm certain Tizzoni was the man I saw. He was trying to be invisible but he stood out like a sore thumb.'

Jones said, 'A lot of people reckon it would have taken two men to kill Don and get rid of the body. Bazley would have been too small to do it on his own.'

'Yeah,' he said. 'I've read that.'

Jones asked, 'Are you going to tell the Ds?'

'I don't know. What do you think? Do you think it will make any difference?'

'Hard to say, Jim. It can't hurt.'

'OK. I'll think about it.'

Jones assured McCudden that it had been a confidential conversation and he wouldn't be writing anything about it.

A week later Tizzoni, who gave his occupation as 'farmer', pleaded guilty in Melbourne's Supreme Court to having conspired between 1 June and 15 July 1977 with Robert Trimbole and others to murder Donald Mackay. He also pleaded guilty to having conspired with Terrence John Clark, Trimbole and others to murder Douglas and Isabel Wilson.

Security around the court building was intense, with armed police stationed outside and five uniformed officers protecting Tizzoni during his fifteen-minute appearance before Judge Gobbo.

Tizzoni's barrister, John Walker, QC, told the court the guilty pleas were the culmination of a long and intensive police investigation during the last two years and five months. A year earlier Tizzoni had told detectives, 'I found I was in a situation where I became more deeply involved and found myself doing things which were against my upbringing and against my family beliefs . . . I realised this some twelve months ago when I began looking back over my life . . . When I was introduced to two police officers I realised I had an opportunity to make peace with myself and atone as far as I am able to for the acts I have committed against my family and society.'

Judge Gobbo agreed to extend Tizzoni's bail, which effectively meant returning him to the protective custody of police.

Two weeks into his committal hearing at Fitzroy Court, George Joseph emulated Tizzoni by pleading guilty. Both men escaped a maximum ten-year penalty, Joseph getting seven years and Tizzoni eight. The pair owed their reduced sentences, in part, to their willingness to give evidence against Bazley and the absent Trimbole.

Neither the Australian Federal Police nor Interpol appeared to have the slightest idea where—or even in which country— Aussie Bob was hiding. It was common knowledge on the streets of Griffith, however, that Joan and her children had kept in regular contact with Trimbole ever since he fled the country in May 1981 after a tip-off from corrupt police.

Jones often met Joan Trimbole in the busy main street; they always stopped for a chat, usually about her children, Gayelle, Glenda, Robert and Craig. The subject of Bob Trimbole usually came up but they were private conversations and Joan knew she could trust Jones to keep them private. Sometimes Joan would take issue with a story the family had read in the *Area News*: 'Terry, we know you have a job to do and we respect you for reporting fairly, but some of the stories you have been printing about Bob—they're unbelievable. According to your paper Bob is the Godfather of the Mafia, he's fixing races, trafficking drugs, rigging false passports, having people murdered. Bob would have to be 150 years old to have done everything you've been accusing him of.' As if she had a premonition of the next sensational allegation about her fugitive husband, one day Joan Trimbole told Jones, 'Next they'll be accusing him of the Fine Cotton ring-in.'

Within days Sydney's *Sunday Telegraph* published an exclusive story under the headline 'TRIMBOLE FINANCED FINE COTTON RING-IN'.

The previous month a horse masquerading as Fine Cotton had won a race at Brisbane's Eagle Farm track. The horse had started at 33–1 but as word of the switch spread, its odds plummeted to 7–2. After the race, stewards quickly saw through the amateurish disguise of white paint, peroxide and brown hair dye that had been used to mask the true markings of a much quicker horse named Bold Personality. After the fake Fine Cotton was disqualified, its trainer, Hayden Haitana, had gone on the run, triggering a manhunt across several states.

Keith Robbins's story in the *Sunday Telegraph* claimed that a 'standover man' being sought by two inquiries into the Fine Cotton ring-in had named Bob Trimbole as the ringleader responsible for 'putting up all the money'. Holed up on the Gold Coast, Haitana told Robbins that the standover man had told him about Trimbole's role in the ring-in.

Robbins's story fuelled the media frenzy surrounding what he described as 'the most amazing chapter in Australian racing history'. After Haitana agreed to appear on *60 Minutes* to tell his story of being forced at gunpoint to switch Fine Cotton for Bold Personality, Joan Trimbole unexpectedly gave an interview to the Sydney *Sun's* affable crime reporter, Steve Barrett.

Barrett had been among the first journalists to arrive in Griffith from Sydney after Don Mackay's disappearance. As well as reporting the Mackay murder, he had returned to Griffith to cover the various commissions of inquiry and inquests. Barrett was one of the few outside Jones and his staff to have persuaded Joan Trimbole to speak on the record about Bob.

In her interview with Barrett, Joan told of the effect on herself and her children of the allegations against her husband and proclaimed her deep sympathy for Barbara Mackay. Refusing to believe that Bob was a mafia boss and a principal in the Mr Asia drug syndicate, or that he was behind several murders, Joan Trimbole insisted that he had accepted the blame 'for other people in high places' and would 'come back to give his version . . . very soon'.

In Griffith copies of the paper quickly sold out. Few were convinced by Joan's insistence that she had no idea where Bob was and was not in contact with him; she freely admitted that three of her children had visited him overseas.

Those wondering why Joan Trimbole, who was usually so reticent about talking to the press, had spoken to the *Sun* might have recalled that it was the paper's tabloid stable-mate, the *Sun-Herald*, that published parts of a scurrilous document alleging that Don Mackay had been killed by his wife, son and family solicitor. A four-page copy of the document, written on government-issue paper, had been discovered in June 1983 by police searching the Trimbole family home in McNabb Crescent.

Reading Joan Trimbole's interview in the *Sun*, readers might have felt that her family was at it again. Asked by Barrett whether she believed that Mackay had been murdered, Joan replied, 'I feel it's a disappearance. I really can't accept the fact that the man's murdered. I really don't know. His family doesn't know either. I feel very deeply for his family. Who wouldn't? But we've done nothing to hurt them. I think his disappearance may have been a conspiracy within a conspiracy. I just feel that something's wrong some-where—there's too many loose ends.'

As to whether Bob could have been involved in Mackay's 'disappearance', Joan was adamant: 'No way . . . I refuse to believe that Bob would ever murder anybody, or organise to have anyone killed. Never, never, ever. He loved people too much.'

Whatever Steve Barrett may have promised her, many readers suspected that there was a reason behind Joan Trim-bole's decision to speak out, and that it had something to do with Bob. There were rumours in Griffith that Bob had been diagnosed with an incurable illness, believed to be prostate cancer. As she was making herself available for interviews, her daughter Glenda was away on yet another overseas trip. What Glenda did not know was that she was being followed.

From the moment she left Australia, Glenda's movements had been monitored by several police agencies. She arrived in Ireland on 8 October as her father was admitted to the Meath Hospital in Dublin for an operation for cancer of the prostate gland. Glenda and Trimbole's de facto, Ann-Marie Presland, booked into the Gresham Hotel in central Dublin. Both women visited Trimbole daily as he recovered from his operation.

On the day Trimbole was discharged, Gianfranco Tizzoni—nicknamed 'the Songbird' for the way he was singing to the authorities—returned to court in Melbourne to give evidence of Bob Trimbole's contracts to murder Donald Mackay and the drug couriers Douglas and Isabel Wilson.

After spending a night at the Gresham Hotel, Trimbole set off on Thursday 25 October with his daughter and de facto for Westport, but the trio were arrested before they left Dublin. Trimbole—using the alias Michael Pius Hanbury—was charged with firearms offences. Within hours the two women had been released, leaving Trimbole in custody.

Tizzoni's claim to have hired a killer to murder three people on Bob Trimbole's orders made it clear why Trimbole had been so anxious to disappear from Australia. Despite Tizzoni's assertion that the boss of La Famiglia in Griffith was 'Mr Sergi senior' not 'Aussie Bob' Trimbole, the feeling was growing that time was running out for Trimbole.

Most Australian media organisations had correspondents in the United Kingdom, but news of Trimbole's arrest sent big-name journalists from the Sydney and Melbourne dailies scurrying for flights to Ireland. In the grim Bridewell Remand Centre, a place usually reserved for IRA terrorists, Trimbole prepared for the hurriedly arranged court hearings that were to determine his fate.

Television pictures of the 53-year-old Trimbole showed a rumpled figure with a paunch and black bushy moustache, a brown cloth cap pulled low over his eyes. The years away from Griffith had changed him, but Terry Jones had no trouble recognising Michael Pius Hanbury as 'Aussie Bob' Trimbole—Australia's most wanted man.

■ ■ ■

The story behind Trimbole's arrest, recounted in the High Court in Dublin before Mr Justice Seamus Egan, hinted at the cock-ups ahead. Inspector Gordon and Inspector McGroarty of the drug squad had to argue there was a reasonable suspicion Trimbole was illegally in possession of firearms. Gordon told the judge, 'I formed a suspicion because of what Inspector McGroarty told me.'

About noon on Wednesday 24 October Inspector Gordon had met an Australian detective who told him that Trimbole was suspected of drug trafficking. That afternoon between 3.30pm and 4pm Inspector Gordon went to the Gresham Hotel but found no Trimbole registered. In the evening, he made inquiries at the Mater Hospital before finishing work about midnight. At 3.20am Inspector McGroarty was woken by a telephone call from a 'confidential source' who said that a man at the Gresham Hotel with an Australian or New Zealand accent had been given a gun between 4 and 6 o'clock the previous evening.

McGroarty did not immediately connect this tip-off with Trimbole. Although firearms offences were a matter for the Special Branch, McGroarty immediately called Inspector Gordon, who also failed to realise that the Australian in possession of a gun at the Gresham Hotel might be Trimbole.

About 2pm on Wednesday 25 October Inspector Gordon watched Trimbole and the two women leave the Gresham Hotel. Around the same time, Inspector McGroarty received another call from his confidential source, who said the man with the gun was in the company of two women. McGroarty passed this information to Gordon, who then arrested Trimbole six kilometres from the hotel.

Trimbole's appearance before the High Court in Dublin was like a flashback to his appearance at Justice Wood-ward's Royal Commission of Inquiry into Drug Trafficking, for which Aussie Bob had entered through a tradesman's entrance disguised as a cleaning woman in order to dodge the media scrum outside.

Trimbole told the judge he was Michael Hanbury, aged '21 years and upwards' and a resident of the village of Westport in County Mayo, an Irish citizen with an Irish passport to prove it. In response, Inspector Gordon was forced to admit, 'I can't say this man is Trimbole.'

Just before 10pm Judge Egan concluded the three-hour hearing by setting Trimbole free, explaining that he found the evidence against the accused 'unconvincing and invalid'.

It was an embarrassing rebuff for the Irish police, but Inspector Gordon was not finished. As soon as Trimbole left the court, Gordon served a provisional warrant for alleged offences in Australia and, amid a blaze of camera flashes, re-arrested him. Lashing out at photographers, the furious Aussie Bob was bundled into a police car and driven away. Trimbole's lawyers scuffled with journalists and photographers as they chased the police car across two city blocks to the District Court, where Inspector Gordon gave his opinion that the man in custody was Robert Trimbole.

In the new courtroom he faced thirteen charges including heroin smuggling, passport forgeries and the murder of Donald Mackay and Douglas and Isabel Wilson. This time he was named as Robert Trimbole. The District Court judge, A.H. Ballagh, heard the charges at 10.15pm and adjourned the court shortly before 11pm, having remanded Trimbole to appear before him again on 1 November when extradition proceedings would begin.

Speaking after his client's few minutes of freedom, Trimbole's high-profile barrister, Paddy MacEntee, said police use of the draconian Section 30 (Offences Against the State Act) were completely unwarranted. Usually used against members of the IRA, the law enabled police to hold a suspect for an initial period of 24 hours, which could be extended to 48 hours. Trimbole had been grilled for nine hours after being taken into custody by the police, while his daughter Glenda and Ann-Marie Presland each faced eight hours of questioning before they were allowed to leave.

To those watching events from New South Wales, the failure of the Irish police to make the case for Trimbole's detention in the High Court was an ominous portent of the legal battle ahead. Aussie Bob always seemed to be able to count on the best representation money could buy. Being on the run for three and a half years did not seem to have emptied his pockets.

■ ■ ■

Griffith, once again, was under siege, with the newsroom at the *Area News* acting as headquarters for radio, television and press journalists from all over Australia. There were hopes that Trimbole might come clean at last and reveal the truth behind the darkest episode in the town's history. Don Mackay's widow, Barbara, and his son Paul expressed relief at the news of Trimbole's arrest, which had 'ended long years of waiting, wondering and hoping'. But the Mackay family had been let down too often in the seven years since Don's murder for them to feel confident that Trimbole would ever face justice in New South Wales.

Many were apprehensive about what might happen to Trimbole if he dared speak out. It was less than six months since Rocco Medici's battered, earless body had been pulled out of the Murrumbidgee. Many predicted that a bullet, not cancer, would end Bob Trimbole's life if he ever decided to reveal what he knew about La Famiglia and its marijuana interests.

The marijuana growers would not have been alone in hoping Trimbole would keep his mouth shut. Paddy Keenan told Sydney reporter Joe Payne, 'I think a lot of our friends around here would be shaking in their boots; [Trimbole] has been linked with people in high places, particularly police and politicians. If he really talks it will implicate a lot of the people Justice Woodward mentioned in his commission.'

Keenan was speaking to the press in his capacity as deputy chairman of the Concerned Citizens of Griffith. By now a properly constituted organisation with a postal address and regular meetings, the Citizens had kept up the pressure on the government and courts to strip Trimbole and his fellow traffickers of their illegally acquired wealth. Failure to do this, the Citizens argued, had tarred Griffith with an 'unjust and false' reputation as the drug capital of Australia and caused 'the majority of its citizens [to] suffer a grave injustice'.

Meeting at the Griffith Ex-Servicemen's Club on 29 November 1984, the Concerned Citizens resolved 'as a matter of urgency' to request the newly formed National Crime Authority 'be given a directive to investigate all those responsible for the murder of Donald Bruce Mackay, the continued large-scale growing of marijuana and the esca-lating traffic in heroin'. Meanwhile the organisation, led by Dr Richard Smith, continued to work behind the scenes to assist the investigation. A CSIRO scientist who had attended the Uniting Church with Don and Barbara Mackay, Smith wanted to do everything he could for Barbara and the Mackay children. He was instrumental in organising big public meetings with high-profile journalists such as

Bob Bottom and Wendy Bacon and senior police like Fred Silvester as guest speakers. It was at these meetings that the community pitched in with donations to a fighting fund that reached as much as $20,000, with promises of more from other donors. Some of the money was used to pay for legal advice. It was largely through the group's efforts that Barbara Mackay was granted legal representation at the Bazley trial in Melbourne and the inquest in Griffith.

With Smith as chairman, the Concerned Citizens issued press releases and got petitions running. Reporters from the *Area News* would often go down to the CSIRO's Division of Water Resources to pick up Smith's press releases but, mindful of the risks they were taking, Terry Jones was careful never to identify who at the organisation was doing what. Not everyone was content to remain in the shadows. Perhaps recklessly, deputy chairman Paddy Keenan told Joe Payne that it was a tip-off from the Concerned Citizens of Griffith that had led police to Trimbole's Irish hideout. 'We passed the message to police that his daughter Glenda had gone overseas,' Keenan said. 'They didn't seem to be aware of it.'

With Trimbole safely in Irish custody, attention turned to getting him back to Australia. The lack of an extradition treaty with Ireland appeared not to concern the government, with a spokesman for the federal attorney-general, Senator Gareth Evans, saying there was no reason why Trimbole's extradition should not go smoothly despite there being no treaty.

As to who should be responsible for the extradition, Barbara Mackay and the Concerned Citizens were adamant that it should be handled by Victoria Police. Joe Parrington's failure to crack the Mackay case, despite seven years' trying, made them cynical about the ability of the New South Wales police to get Trimbole back to Australia. Few cheered the news that Parrington, now a detective superintendent, and Detective Sergeant Rick Campbell had packed their bags and flown to Ireland.

As part of the extradition process, staff from the attorney-general's department came to Griffith on Tuesday 30 October to take statements to be used to initiate proceedings. Terry Jones was among the citizens called to give evidence about Don Mackay's disappearance.

The media, however, were more interested in Joan Trimbole. Over the years the Trimbole children had rarely been approached for interviews. In the eyes of the Griffith community they were innocents not responsible for anything their father might have done. If anyone were to make themselves available, it had to be Joan; she was their mother and would speak for the family. But in the wake of Trimbole's arrest the rulebook was being torn up. Craig Trimbole was reported to have made a deal with 60 *Minutes* and to have flown to London with a camera crew. Rival current affairs programs were chasing other family members—especially Glenda—for rights to their stories.

Joan Trimbole, meanwhile, appeared to have left Griffith to spend time in Sydney, where it was rumoured that she was refusing to speak to anyone except the *Sun*'s Steve Barrett, the reporter to whom she had given the exclusive interview just days before her husband's arrest.

Although securely locked up in Dublin's Mountjoy Prison, Bob Trimbole was proving as elusive as his wife. While provisional warrants from Australia named the man in custody as the alleged crime boss Robert Trimbole, his barrister, Paddy MacEntee, continued to insist that his client was the Irish citizen Michael Pius Hanbury and that he would be representing him until otherwise instructed. Should he find that his client was not Hanbury, MacEntee said, he would 'seek further instructions'.

MacEntee had a good hand and knew how to play it. Even if it could be proved conclusively that the man in custody was not Michael Pius Hanbury, MacEntee was confident that Australian authorities would not be able to assemble the evidence needed in time to secure Trimbole's extradition. MacEntee appeared to have no intention of applying for bail for Trimbole, even though four Australian states, the Australian Federal Police and the Commonwealth government were all preparing warrants.

According to MacEntee, he expected the state solicitor to ask on 1 November for Trimbole to be remanded for another seven days. When that remand period ran out, Australian authorities would have just four more days before Trimbole, under Irish law, would be allowed to walk free. 'The ball,' MacEntee told reporters, 'I think is well and truly in the Australians' court.'

The mystery surrounding Joan Trimbole's intentions was solved when she turned up on *60 Minutes*. Terry Jones decided it was newsworthy enough to publish extracts of the interview in the *Area News*. Speaking to Jana Wendt, Joan trotted out the same answers she had given earlier to Steve Barrett in the *Sun*. 'It will all work out when Bob comes back,' she told Wendt. 'I don't understand how it's going to work out, but I know that everything will be uncovered. Everything will be uncovered.'

Asked whether her belief was 'blind faith', Joan said, 'True faith.' Insisting that everyone had been wrong, including the royal commissioners who had named Trimbole as a crime boss and drug trafficker, Joan described her husband as a 'very gentle, sincere man. He'd only help people. He wouldn't hurt them.'

On the other side of the world, Bob Trimbole was facing the prospect of spending Christmas in Mountjoy Prison. The case for extraditing him back to Australia was looking increasingly fragile. Not only was there no extradition treaty in place, but there was a question mark over the charges against him. Instead of the conspiracy to murder charges that emerged from the Victorian inquest into the deaths of Douglas and Isabel Wilson, it seemed that warrants for Trimbole's arrest contained nothing more serious than the passport and drug charges recommended by Justice Donald Stewart in 1982 (Justice Philip Woodward had not recommended charging Trimbole with anything).

Trimbole's legal team, led by the astute Paddy MacEntee, knew that if their client was extradited on the passport and drug matters, they would be the only charges Aussie Bob could ever face in an Australian court.

In the meantime, Trimbole was not exactly doing it tough in his Mountjoy prison cell. Newspaper reports coming back from Ireland said it was more akin to the life of Riley. The headlines said it all: 'TRIMBOLE'S "SWEET" JAIL LIFE'; '"HE CAN AFFORD IT"—PRISON OFFICIAL'. Trimbole was reported to have a fridge in his cell which he kept stocked with fine wines. Warders were said to have been sent on shopping trips to fetch him fillet and T-bone steaks. He also had an electric blanket to help him cope with chilly winter nights, as well as access to a television and daily newspapers.

And then, on 6 February 1985, it was over. Wagga's *Daily Advertiser* broke the story ahead of the *Area News* with a page one story headlined 'Irish court orders Trimbole freed'. The Australian extradition warrant listed eighteen counts alleging murder, conspiracy to murder, drugs importation offences and forgery, but Justice Egan of the High Court ruled that Trimbole was not available for extradition because of the 'conscious and deliberate violation of his constitutional rights' by Irish police.

Egan upheld Trimbole's appeal against extradition to Australia on the basis of an unlawful arrest used to hold him while special arrangements were made for extradition to Australia without a formal treaty.

The next day the full bench of the Supreme Court ruled unanimously that it had no power to hold Trimbole pending an appeal by the state against the High Court order to release him.

Patrick MacEntee asserted that the use of anti-terrorist legislation to hold Trimbole until special arrangements were made for his extradition because of the lack of a formal treaty was 'a gross abuse of the law and Trimbole's constitutional right to liberty'. He said his client had no intention of leaving the country.

Aussie Bob was not in court to hear the decision. MacEntee said he was 'a very sick man with cancer'.

For the citizens of Griffith, Trimbole's release from prison was yet another bitter pill. The former garage mechanic had cheated them again. As long as drug traffickers like Aussie Bob were free, the town would never be able to escape the notoriety of its name; it would always struggle to attract the best people to teach at its schools and technical college.

The only solution, in the view of one longtime resident, was to get rid of the town's name and choose another. Margaret Russell's suggestion, canvassed in an open letter to the *Area News*, was for the town to be renamed Wiradjuri after the Indigenous people who once lived and roamed over a large part of the Riverina.

The idea that a change of name could improve the town's fortunes would have brought a grin to the face of Michael Pius Hanbury.

CHAPTER 16

Aussie Bob: dead or alive?

As Australian authorities waited for the result of their appeal against the Irish High Court's decision to free Trimbole, rumours spread that he had already skipped the country. When it was put to Paddy MacEntee that Trimbole had fled, the barrister dismissed it as 'ridiculous, pure speculation . . . absolutely absurd'.

Yet MacEntee admitted that he had not seen Trimbole for five days. 'I don't know his exact whereabouts at the moment,' he told reporters, 'but I believe he is still in Ireland.'

The media were trying to keep up. It was known that Aussie Bob had had a brief meeting with his solicitor, Con O'Leary. O'Leary's secretary commented, 'He looked very sick and didn't want to spend much time in the office.'

According to the Irish press, Trimbole was in hospital. But Australian reporters, familiar with his record of escaping from tight corners, were sceptical. Although Aussie Bob was no longer thought to be of interest to the Irish police, a posse of Australian detectives, newly arrived in Dublin, was attempting to keep the fugitive crime boss under surveillance.

On 7 February Australia's ambassador to Ireland, Sir Peter Lawler, flew back to Canberra for 'consultations' with the federal government. Sir Peter professed to be in Australia for 'normal' mid-term ambassadorial talks, but there was little doubt that the main topic of conversation was the failed extradition case against Trimbole. The attorney-general, Lionel Bowen, promised that the government would do everything possible to bring Trimbole to justice in Australia.

Its efforts to date had made the country a laughing stock. Plenty had been written about the lack of a formal extradition treaty with Ireland (a draft extradition treaty initialled by both sides was found to have been sitting in the 'inactive' files in the Attorney-General's Department since 1982) and about the way Paddy MacEntee had run rings around the Australians in court. Now attention was turning to more sinister-looking omissions.

■ ■ ■

Journalists at the *Area News* had known since March 1984 that police had altered a vital witness statement to leave out the identification of hitman James Bazley during the Donald Mackay inquest in Griffith. It was not until February 1985 that Victorian authorities discovered the anomaly between the statement given by Bruce Pursehouse to the Mackay inquest and the statement he had given to Justice Woodward's Royal Commission of Inquiry into Drug Trafficking. The statement tendered to the coroner, Bruce Brown, was backdated to 17 July 1977, the date of Pursehouse's original statement, but there was no mention of his identification of Bazley at Jerilderie five days earlier.

Not for the first time, it was the investigative journalist Bob Bottom who broke the story. After Bottom stumbled on the information he rang Terry Jones, who told him about the day Pursehouse had walked into his office at the *Area News* and revealed that police had doctored his statement. The knowledge had been gnawing away at him ever since. It was a huge relief to Jones that the story had finally come out without his having to break the promise he had given to Pursehouse to keep their conversation private. Bottom said his report would be running on the front page of the *Sydney Morning Herald*.

Under the headline 'Mackay: vital evidence went missing', Bottom wrote: 'Authorities dealing with the bungled extradition moves against drug boss Bob Trimbole, have discovered that vital evidence was omitted from the NSW inquest into the murder of the Griffith anti-drugs crusader Donald Mackay.' He revealed that some statements of evidence given to the inquest had been 'backdated and re-signed by witnesses, and used to replace statements previously accepted by the Woodward Royal Commission'. As a result, a third set of statements including evidence omitted from the inquest had to be prepared for the Irish extradition battle for Trimbole.

Bottom's story did not identify Pursehouse as the witness whose original statement had been tendered by then Detective Inspector Parrington to the Woodward Royal Commission in July 1978. Woodward had been impressed by Pursehouse's evidence and by that of another eyewitness, Janice Barrett, both of whom had given statements 'very shortly' after the events they described at Jerilderie. The evidence from Jerilderie formed a cornerstone of Woodward's finding that Trimbole was involved in a conspiracy with La Famiglia to murder Mackay.

After Bottom's story was published, Joe Parrington hit back at allegations that he had doctored Pursehouse's evidence to the coroner. Noting that more than a thousand people had been interviewed during the seven-year homicide investigation, Parrington told reporters, 'It is true there was a hell of a lot of stuff put before the [Woodward] Royal Commission that was not put [to the inquest] because it would have taken years to hear.'

In the New South Wales Parliament, opposition leader Nick Greiner wanted to know whether 'key evidence which could have identified a murder suspect' had been withheld from the coroner and whether the government would reopen the inquest and set up an independent inquiry into the running of the first investigation.

The new attorney-general, Terry Sheahan, denied that 'anything untoward' had happened. While it was true, he said, that Pursehouse had not been asked by the coroner about his identification of Bazley at Jerilderie, 'failure to lead evidence from a witness at an inquest is a very different thing from an imputation . . . as to the suppression or deliberate omission of evidence'.

Asked whether the police had helped prepare Pursehouse's statement for the 1984 inquest, the police minister, Peter Anderson, insisted that the existence of the original statement had 'never been concealed' and that Pursehouse had 'read and signed the revised statement in March 1984, prior to the commencement of the inquest'. The fact that the revised statement still bore the date 17 July 1977 was an 'administrative error'.

As far as Trimbole's extradition was concerned, it hardly mattered. Since winning his case in the Irish Supreme Court, Aussie Bob had vanished. A police spokesman in Dublin told wire services, 'We've already started looking for him, but frankly we've no idea where he is. If I were him I'd be under a palm tree.'

When the full bench of the Supreme Court handed down a decision opening the way for Trimbole's recapture, Joan Trimbole told reporters that any new attempt to arrest her husband would also fail. 'They're not fighting Bob,' she said. 'They're fighting against God.'

■ ■ ■

The media's interest in Bob Trimbole since his arrest in Ireland had also revived interest in La Famiglia. Years spent working at the *Area News* and, before that, the *Griffith Times* had made Terry Jones a stickler for accuracy when it came to publishing names and photographs. He knew how many Sergis and Barbaros there were in Griffith and was aware that the majority had nothing to do with La Famiglia. But other editors—especially in the big cities—were less attuned to the risks attached to reporting on Griffith's Calabrian community.

In the wake of Justice Woodward's report, Sydney's *Daily Telegraph* published head and shoulders photographs of the six men Woodward named as being involved in the marijuana trade. The front-page story was headlined 'Murder Inc'. Unfortunately for the *Telegraph*, the Francesco Sergi whose picture appeared in the story was not the Tharbogang man who helped bankroll the 1975 Coleambally marijuana crop but Francesco 'Old Smoky' Sergi, a hard-working farmer from Hanwood.

The *Telegraph*'s story was later used as a 'prop' in an ABC current affairs program that featured an interview with Winery Tony. Once again, 'Smoky' Sergi found himself wrongly identified as a criminal. He sued both the *Telegraph* and the ABC.

Terry Jones was a good friend of Smoky's son, Tony 'Tank' Sergi, a talented local footballer, and knew how upset Smoky had been to see his picture on the front page of the *Telegraph*. Jones felt he had a good case against the paper but that his case against the ABC was weak. In the end, Smoky won $16,500 from the *Telegraph* but his failed action against the ABC cost him several times as much. It was a legal lesson that would not be lost on the Calabrese.

■ ■ ■

Meanwhile, Bob Trimbole's whereabouts remained a mystery. Glenda Trimbole's return to Australia after nearly a year away prompted a wave of speculation about her father's health. On 5 July the *Telegraph* told its readers that the crime boss, who weighed 'well over 90 kilograms before he disappeared', had become 'a sick, frail fugitive who has lost 20 kilograms . . . bedridden at times, frequently writhing with agony'. A 'source' in the Australian Federal Police confirmed that stories circulating in Griffith about Trimbole's health were 'substantially correct'.

On the same day, the Sydney *Sun* claimed that AFP officers had spent two days in Rome checking reports that Trimbole had died and been buried in a family graveyard in his 'home town' of Platì. Reading the *Sun*'s report, Jones had two good reasons to be sceptical: he knew that Trimbole had been born in Griffith, not Platì; and Joan Trimbole had said nothing about her husband being near death when she and Jones had chatted three days earlier on Banna Avenue. Bombarded with requests from the metro dailies to find out whether the 'Trimbole is dead' rumours were true, Jones sought a comment from Joan, who told him, 'the fate of Bob and the children is in God's hands . . . We are being looked after . . . I've said it before—God is taking care of us.'

As evidence of almighty protection, Joan Trimbole pointed out how easily Glenda and Craig and his wife, Josephine, had slipped through Customs on their return to Australia. 'Wasn't it beautiful they weren't harassed at all,' she said. 'That's why I know God is looking after us.'

Since coming back to Griffith, Glenda Trimbole had given no hint her father might be dead. When she left at the end of June 1984, Glenda had indicated she was travelling to the United States. After staying in Dublin throughout the failed extradition process, she had joined Craig in England. While the Sydney press remained fixated with rumours that Bob Trimbole was dead and buried, Glenda's 'healthy tan' led more than one Griffith reporter to conclude that her father had been boating on the Mediterranean.

It was the *Telegraph*'s Les Kennedy who declared on 14 July that the stories of Trimbole's death had been concocted by Trimbole's criminal mates to test whether federal police were tapping their phones. They were. Hoax conversations about Aussie Bob's 'death' sent officers from the Attorney-General's Department and police rushing to Platì in search of a grave reputed to contain Trimbole's remains. 'Police now concede that the reported death was false and deliberately spread around by Trimbole's friends,' wrote Kennedy.

■ ■ ■

The anniversary of Don Mackay's murder gave the Concerned Citizens an opportunity to refocus the nation's attention on what they described as 'eight years of government inaction against crime financed from Griffith'. Committee members Mike Hedditch, Paddy Keenan, Barbara Mackay and Richard Smith met the New South Wales opposition leader, Nick Greiner, for an hour over breakfast, winning his support for a resolution to be put to a public meeting in Griffith 'that all governments of Australia give a reference to the National Crime Authority to use its full coercive powers to investigate crime related to the murder of Don Mackay'. Such a reference, they said, was 'a last chance for the citizens of Griffith to have justice restored and the stigma attached to the name of Griffith removed'. A handwritten press release by Richard Smith noted that 'the committee members found Mr Greiner a deeply sincere and concerned person'.

The Trimbole 'extradition fiasco' was high on the list of topics raised at the public meeting held on 15 July 1985, along with the early release of corrupt former detectives Ellis, Borthwick and Robins 'after serving only a fraction of their sentences'; the lack of action against alleged marijuana growers and distributors named at the Woodward Royal Commission, the Mackay inquest and the Tizzoni committal hearing; and the 'inadequate co-operation of NSW with Victoria Police in the Mackay investigation'.

In the months following the public meeting 16,000 citizens signed a petition asking the Commonwealth government to use its direct powers to grant a reference to the National Crime Authority to investigate 'organised crime originating from Griffith'. In December Richard Smith and Don Mackay's daughter Ruth led a deputation to Canberra to deliver the petition to the prime minister.

There was an element of public vendetta in reports, in late July 1985, that Trimbole's wife and daughter were intending to apply for social security benefits. Reporters at the *Area News* had heard about Joan and Glenda Trimbole being interviewed by the department about their entitlement to welfare payments but had deemed it to be a private matter. The metro dailies had no qualms about reporting town gossip under headlines such as 'Town fury at Trimboles' and 'Dole bid by wife, daughter'.

'Griffith residents are furious,' Arthur Stanley wrote in the *Daily Telegraph*. 'The former wife and jet-setting daughter of Australia's most wanted man, Robert Trimbole, have applied for the dole. Mrs Joan Trimbole still lives in a split-level home and youngest daughter, Glenda, who drives a sports car, has just returned from a 12-month overseas jaunt. The pair registered for unemployment benefits last week.'

Capital city journalists rarely lived side-by-side with the people they were writing about. Staff of the *Area News*, however, could expect to bump into a member of the Trimbole, Sergi, Barbaro or Romeo families at least once a day. Jones's reporters knew that the dole story had legs but were reluctant to cross the line by attacking Trimbole's family. Jones was not too unhappy to be able to report, some days later, that the Department of Social Security had decided to reject the pair's bid for unemployment benefits on the grounds that neither Joan nor Glenda was actively seeking full-time work.

Joan Trimbole was not the only wife to be feeling the pressure of the media's insatiable fascination with Griffith. In the middle of August Jennifer A. Sergi, who was married to 'Young Tony' Sergi, hand-delivered a letter to the office of the *Area News*. On being told about the letter by the receptionist, Terry Jones hurried after her, hoping to be able to persuade Jennifer to agree to a photograph—and even an interview—to accompany the letter. Young Tony had never defended himself in public against allegations that he was a member of La Famiglia; maybe his wife would speak for him. Jones caught a glimpse of Jennifer Sergi as she walked away down Olympic Street, but it was clear that she had no intention of adding to what she had written.

It was the longest letter Jones had ever seen submitted for publication. If it were to be published in full, he guessed it would occupy a whole tabloid page. Given its obvious public interest, he sub-edited the letter and sent it to the typesetters to estimate how much space it would need.

On 15 August Jennifer Sergi's letter, published under the headline 'Matters of real concern', filled the letters page. It began, 'I am addressing my letter to all the concerned citizens of Griffith— the real concerned citizens.'

What followed was a heartfelt attack on the Concerned Citizens of Griffith and on the press for circulating 'rumours' and 'hearsay' about people who, she said, were 'trying very hard to mind their own business'.

'In the last eight years we have had royal commissions, court hearings, our houses turned upside down and gone through with a fine tooth comb, personal effects taken and not returned for months, bomb threats to our homes and businesses, threats to our families and our children, phone calls obscene and threatening, sometimes taken by our young children who are now very wary of answering the phone at all, having our homes measured inch by inch and valued item by item, our bank accounts gone through.

'Our businesses have suffered because many people are reluctant to have their names associated with ours, not even on a business level, let alone a personal one. Many people who were quite friendly before, now try, very obviously, to avoid being seen publicly with our families because they don't want their other friends to know they have any association with us.'

Scoffing at the idea that marijuana was still being grown in Griffith, Sergi blamed 'local vigilantes' for 'insinuations' that for the past eight years had made her family's life a 'nightmare'.

'Here we have a group of people, the "Concerned Citizens", who are calling for justice to be done, but do they see all the injustices they are creating along the way?

'Don't they see that by nominating a specific group of people as being guilty and indirectly causing them much heartache and harassment, they are taking justice into their own hands and bending it to suit their ideas?'

Turning to the 'grass castles', Sergi insisted that 'in order to build these homes their owners have lived sometimes up to 20 years or more in very old fibro or weatherboard houses, spending very little if anything on improvements, so they could afford to build a nice home'.

After thanking those who had phoned to express their sympathy for the way she and her family had been 'discriminated against during the past years', Sergi finished her letter by pleading for the people of Griffith to 'read more between the lines and question things they hear, not just follow the leader. Don't let this town and its people be led by a group of vigilantes—it could snowball into something very ugly (heaven forbid) . . . There is only one final judge—which one day we will all have to face.'

For all its special pleading, Jennifer Sergi's letter brought into the open a subject that Jones and his staff often talked about: the risk of public anger towards the drug traffickers spreading to the wider Italian community, and of Griffith becoming a divided town. Jones wondered how the *Area*

News's readers would react. Sergi was pretending that La Famiglia was nothing more than rumours and innuendo, but the paper's readers knew that it was real. Jones did not agree with Sergi's description of the Concerned Citizens as vigilantes, but he understood her reasons for saying it. If the Concerned Citizens were becoming more outspoken and activist, it was because they had lost faith in the government and the courts to protect society from criminals like Bob Trimbole and Terry Clark. The extradition fiasco that enabled Trimbole to escape Australian justice was just another example of the drug traffickers making fools of the government.

It was not just in Griffith that Jennifer Sergi's letter was being studied with interest. The letter came to the attention of the National Crime Authority, which discreetly asked Terry Jones to forward a copy of the 1979 letter by the same author that had been handed out on the steps of a Sydney courthouse. There was talk that the NCA had its eye on Al Grassby and that the 'scurrilous document' Grassby had circulated to newspaper editors and members of parliament might form the basis of a prosecution for criminal defamation and perverting the course of justice. The NCA was known to have obtained copies of the Grassby document, which it wanted to compare with the text of letters written by Jennifer Sergi. It suspected that Grassby was still doing the bidding of La Famiglia in Griffith. Jones speculated that the NCA's aim in comparing the two documents was to establish a criminal conspiracy between Grassby and La Famiglia.

■ ■ ■

While the NCA was busy investigating Grassby, Jones was looking at another person with interesting links to

La Famiglia: Gordon J. Aldridge. Aldridge's father, Jack, had been an old-school policeman who knocked around with the likes of Sydney detectives Fred Krahe and Ray 'Machine Gun' Kelly. Joe Parrington had once described Aldridge's son, Gordon, as being a 'Mr Fix-it' who had 'gone to the best schools' and had 'plenty of connections in business, politics and the police'.

Gordon Aldridge's business card described him as a 'Consultant' and gave an address in the Prudential Building in Sydney's Martin Place. Since turning up in Griffith, he had made a name for himself as a close associate of Winery Tony. Some people described him as Winery Tony's 'shadow', a trusted confidant who would tell anyone who cared to ask, 'I have power of attorney over Riverina Wines.'

Sergi's winery was a hot topic of discussion among the businessmen who met for a drink at the Jondaryan Club. Soon after his arrival in Griffith, Aldridge had boasted of having persuaded the Commonwealth Bank to lend him $400,000, which he then loaned to Winery Tony and his wife, Angelina. Aldridge had immediately begun a thorough reorganisation of the winery, telling people that Tony had asked him to take over the running of the business. It was Aldridge who had recommended changing the name Sergi Wines to Riverina Wines, given that Winery Tony had been under investigation by the tax office since the revelations of the Woodward Royal Commission. After being named by Woodward as one of the people behind the murder of Donald Mackay, Sergi had also run up huge legal bills defending himself against a charge of perverting the course of justice through his association with the three corrupt Griffith detectives.

Aldridge was clearly comfortable being seen with Sergi; Jones suspected that both men felt they had something to gain by their association, not least in their dealings with the Commonwealth Bank. It was unlikely that the bank manager, Kel Taylor, was as enamoured with the pair as they seemed to be with each other. As long as loans could be secured and the interest paid, the bank would do business with anyone; nonetheless, Taylor had a hard time explaining to the Concerned Citizens his dealings with La Famiglia.

The relationship between Gordon Aldridge and Winery Tony was one that Terry Jones was keen to explore in the pages of the *Area News* as a matter of significant public interest. Aldridge's links to La Famiglia had already caught the attention of another journalist, Marian Wilkinson, who had visited Griffith as a reporter for the ABC's *Four Corners* program to investigate the epidemic of third party motor vehicle injury claims in the Riverina region. The claims, which related to personal injuries sustained in car accidents, often between relatives, had been the subject of an Australian Federal Police operation code-named 'Trojan', investigating whether some of the accidents had been staged to defraud the insurance companies.

After moving to the *National Times*, Wilkinson had written a story about Gordon Aldridge. Headlined 'Operator with all the right connections', the report examined Aldridge's business record and noted his links with Winery Tony and others. As often happened when the national media wrote about Griffith, Terry Jones soon found himself chatting to the person under scrutiny. On this occasion Aldridge heaped scorn on the media, telling Jones, 'Gutter reporters should watch what they write. What the newspapers have been saying about people in Griffith is scandalous. I'm already involved in litigation. I'm recommending to several other people that they take action, too.'

This sounded to Jones like a threat. He knew that Aldridge had initiated defamation proceedings against John Fairfax and Sons for the article in the *National Times*, and for words allegedly said to him by a *Sydney Morning Herald* journalist, Stephen Rice. Jones challenged Aldridge, 'Are you telling me you're taking action against the *Area News*? I'd be sorry to hear that, as we're only reporting what we get from the police and courts and inquiries. It's all privileged.'

The pair discussed the 'Murder Inc' headline that had appeared in the *Daily Telegraph* and the mis-identified photograph of Smoky Sergi.

'I'm not saying people are going to sue the *Area News*,' said Aldridge. 'I suppose you have been pretty fair. But other papers haven't.'

Jones did not realise it at the time, but Aldridge had just alerted him to the start of a new Griffith 'cottage industry'—defamation action—to take the place of fraudulent third party accident claims and arson jobs.

Aldridge's defamation case went to court on 16 September. He was represented by Clive Evatt, the same barrister who had appeared for Smoky Sergi. According to Evatt, Wilkinson's article in the *National Times* had defamed Aldridge by suggesting that he 'wrongfully associated with persons of unsavoury, poor and questionable reputation and corrupt police officers, was guilty of criminal and wrongful activities and resorted to dishonest and underhand methods for and by his clients'. Evatt went on, 'Marian Wilkinson . . . telephoned Aldridge about the article . . . But he declined to be interviewed, although he spoke with her for a time. The next thing is that the article comes out and we say just kicks his reputation to pieces—destroys it for all time.'

Gordon Aldridge presented himself to the jury as 'a

businessman, a family man, a Justice of the Peace, a fellow of the Real Estate Institute, a fellow of the Institute of Directors and a fellow of the Institute of Management'. But when it came to explaining his dealings with Winery Tony, Aldridge was forced to agree with Fairfax's barrister, Henric Nicholas, QC, that Justice Woodward found Antonio Sergi had been involved in drug trafficking and in the murder of the anti-drug campaigner Donald Mackay, and that Sergi was a close business associate of drug boss Robert Trimbole. Aldridge also had to admit that in the general community, Sergi had a reputation as a criminal. Asked whether he considered three years' association with Sergi, a man reputed to be a criminal, would harm his personal reputation, Aldridge replied, 'No, I don't.'

After a three-day hearing, Aldridge lost his case against Fairfax, with costs awarded against him.

The failure of Aldridge's defamation action did not deter Griffith's next high-profile litigant, Arrigo 'Rick' Pillon, from taking Nationwide News to court over an article in the *Sunday Telegraph*.

A former schoolteacher and seasonal fruit picker, Pillon had once been Glenda Trimbole's boyfriend. The couple had worked together in a number of Trimbole family businesses set up with money from Bob Trimbole, including Pant Ranch, Forever Feminine and Denim Daks. (The report of the Royal Commission into Drug Trafficking noted that cash 'loans' and 'gifts' were used by Trimbole as a tool for laundering drug money.) Pillon was also the owner of Fonzies Leisure Centre in Banna Avenue, a business allegedly linked to the family of Sydney underworld figure Abe Saffron.

According to Pillon's lawyers, the article in the *Sunday Telegraph* defamed him by suggesting he was involved with a group of criminals linked to the murder of Donald

Mackay; that he had closed down his business Forever Feminine in 'dubious and suspicious circumstances'; and that he was 'criminally involved' in the disappearance of Donald Mackay. Pillon's barrister, Neil McPhee, QC, would describe the story in court as 'a pack of falsehoods'.

Unusually for a visiting journalist, the reporter had not checked his facts with Jones or one of his colleagues on the *Area News*. It seemed to Jones that the published article probably defamed not just Rick Pillon but a number of others.

Lawyers for Nationwide News told Jones they were going to defend the story on the basis that Pillon was an associate of La Famiglia and the notorious 'Aussie Bob' Trimbole in Griffith and of Abe Saffron's family in Sydney. News was represented in court by Alec Shand, QC, the same barrister who had defended accused drug growers after the discovery of the multimillion-dollar marijuana crop at Coleambally. Witness after witness was called by Mr Shand to attest to Pillon's alleged 'bad reputation' in Griffith, but the jury of one man and two women was not convinced. It believed Pillon's claim to have only found out about Bob Trimbole's criminal activities through the royal commission. On Wednesday 11 December, at the end of a six-week trial, the jury took just three hours to decide that Pillon had been defamed and to award him $350,000 damages. Mr McPhee described the offending article as 'sloppy and careless and as reckless a piece of journalism as one could imagine'.

News of the huge damages sent a chill through the offices of the *Area News*. While Terry Jones had seen the verdict coming, he also knew that even the most careful journalists sometimes made mistakes. After a payout like that, he wondered who would be next.

■ ■ ■

The Concerned Citizens, meanwhile, had something more important to celebrate. On 3 October the premier had promised a 'full-scale war on illegal drugs unmatched anywhere in Australia'. As well as establishing a State Drug Crime Commission to investigate and assemble evidence for prosecuting drug trafficking and other major associated crimes, the Wran government planned to introduce harsher penalties, including life imprisonment, for major drug traffickers and to enact laws enabling the seizure of drug profits.

The new provisions would provide for four categories of drug offences: possession or use; supply a prescribed quantity; supply a trafficable quantity; and supply a commercial quantity.

By distinguishing between trafficable and commercial quantities, the premier said the new laws would be able to punish the Mr Bigs of the heroin trade in a way that was not possible under the Poisons Act.

Five weeks later Wran announced that Cabinet had approved the introduction of a Crimes (Confiscation of Profits) Bill designed to strip the profits gained by offenders from serious crime. This was exactly what the families of those involved in the Griffith marijuana trade had feared. In 1979 the report of the Royal Commission of Inquiry into Drug Trafficking had exposed the 'money trail' that led from the commercial marijuana crops to the 'grass castles' and the buying of property, assets and businesses both inside and outside Griffith. Under the new seizure laws they could all be forfeited as 'proceeds of crime'.

The Commonwealth government had also beefed up its powers to confiscate assets from drug traffickers and other criminals, and 'Aussie Bob' Trimbole was top of the target list. Trimbole was thought to owe the tax office nearly

$2.5 million and by February 1986 federal authorities had moved to seize a rice farm near Griffith, valued at about $330,000.

Although no longer married to Trimbole, Joan remained the primary source of information about the family. Joan confirmed that it had always been Aussie Bob's ambition to provide for his children by buying each of them a rice farm. Ownership of a rice farm had long been seen as the ultimate aspiration of farmers in the Murrumbidgee Irrigation Area. It was a common saying that 'if you're a rice cocky, you're doing well'.

Bob Trimbole would not live to discover whether any of his children became rice cockies. A little over a year later, still a hunted man, Trimbole died, apparently of a heart attack, at a villa he shared with Presland and her daughter near Alicante, Spain. The family brought his body back to Australia for a funeral Mass at St Benedict's Catholic Church in Smithfield, Sydney that was notable for a bout of fisti-cuffs between mourners and reporters. The crime boss, who had cheated Australian justice simply by altering the date of birth on his passport, was buried at Pinegrove cemetery outside Minchinbury. As the coffin slid into the crypt, Father Massore said to the family, 'My message to you is to walk humbly in the Lord, and lead just lives.'

CHAPTER 17

Parrington pays

On Monday 3 March 1986 James Frederick Bazley pleaded not guilty to the murders of Douglas and Isabel Wilson at Rye or elsewhere on Good Friday 1979. He also pleaded not guilty to conspiring with Gianfranco Tizzoni, George Joseph, Robert Trimbole and others to murder Donald Mackay between 1 June 1977 and 15 July 1977. The jury at the Melbourne Supreme Court was told that the trial could last three months.

For readers of the *Area News* there was little new in Bazley's trial. Most of the evidence about the killings had already come out at the coroner's inquest and the committal hearings of Gianfranco Tizzoni and George Joseph. The trial was grinding towards a predictable conclusion when the normally reticent Bazley stood up to make an unsworn statement from the dock. Up to that point Bazley had refused to make any statements to police other than to deny that he had murdered the Mr Asia syndicate couriers Douglas and

Isabel Wilson or that he was part of the conspiracy to kill Donald Mackay. On Friday 4 April Bazley told the Supreme Court that he was an innocent man who had been set up. 'I have never fired a gun,' he said. 'I never killed anyone . . . I have nothing to fear in the eyes of God.'

Bazley's statement was the final evidence to be heard at the trial, which had heard 115 Crown witnesses and lasted fifteen days. Wearing a light grey suit and using gold-framed spectacles to read from his notes, Bazley told the court he did not know who had committed the crimes. 'I have been called a hitman by the Crown Prosecutor, by witnesses and by the press,' he said. 'These statements are not true. It is so easy to set someone up and the public are prepared to believe the worst. I have never killed anyone. I treasure the value and sanctity of human life.'

Bazley accused George Joseph of setting him up. He told the court, 'When I read the bodies were found in Rye, I thought I was being set up and I went to see Joseph and said, "You low bastard—you are setting me up for this."' Joseph laughed, he said, and told him not to worry, it wasn't true.

In his summing up, Bazley's counsel, Tony Graham, QC, scoffed at the 'bargain basement' fee. The Honoured Society, he said, 'was protecting a multi-million dollar marijuana industry. They could afford the top hitman money could buy. People could have come from Platì, the [Italian] home town of the Honoured Society. They could have come from the USA, the source of the Honoured Society's power. But the Crown had asked the jury to believe the Griffith-based branch of the society delegated the job of killing Donald Mackay to Bazley for $10,000—pin money by the standards of that organisation.' The final address of the crown prose- cutor was 'haphazard and repetitious', Graham said. 'What this case is all about is did Tizzoni and Joseph set up Bazley? Twenty years ago they used to call the person a patsy, a frame. Did Tizzoni and Joseph set up Bazley or has Bazley told you from the dock a pack of lies?'

The jury of five men and seven women took little time to decide that 60-year-old Bazley had told them a pack of lies. He was sentenced to life in jail for the Wilson killings and nine years for conspiring to murder Donald Mackay.

■ ■ ■

In Griffith, the guilty verdict brought mixed feelings. The six men named by Justice Woodward as 'influential members' of the Honoured Society that ordered Mackay's murder had never been brought to justice. Many hoped that Bazley's conviction would be the spur for further prosecutions.

Mackay's son, Paul, called for the men behind his father's murder to be charged and urged the police to prosecute drug dealers still operating in Griffith. 'Bazley's conviction is just the first step in bringing these people to justice,' Paul Mackay told the *Daily Telegraph*.

A statement from the Concerned Citizens of Griffith said that 'members of the Honoured Society had been identified and named by Justice Woodward in 1979 and have been renamed by Gianfranco Tizzoni at his trial in 1984 and again this year at Bazley's trial. The unanswered question is will the NSW government now exercise its responsibility for the administration of justice and bring this organisation to account?'

The group's chairman, Dr Richard Smith, together with Paul Mackay and his sister Ruth, were due to meet the premier and the police minister in Sydney, where Smith said he would urge the New South Wales government to give the

National Crimes Authority a brief to investigate the Griffith drug trade.

The Concerned Citizens had become expert at dealing with the media and Smith seized every opportunity to put pressure on Griffith City Council to face up to the town's marijuana problem. Smith was strongly rebuked by the council after an interview on *The Ray Martin Show* in which he linked Griffith to a marijuana crop at Armidale.

■ ■ ■

Bazley's trial, nine years after Don Mackay's murder, exposed all the failings in Joe Parrington's long and fruitless homicide investigation. The trial laid bare the interstate rivalries and conflicted professional loyalties that had dogged the Mackay investigation from the beginning. Not only had Parrington watched the Victoria Police claim all the credit for solving a crime that took place in New South Wales; he was also shown to have manipulated evidence that might have led to the case being solved years earlier and, as a result, was directly implicated in the judicial farce that allowed Bob Trimbole to walk out of Dublin's Mountjoy Prison.

A series of articles by Bob Bottom in the *Sydney Morning Herald* and the Melbourne *Age* began ominously for Parrington with a first instalment headlined, 'The vital evidence that went missing'. It recounted in detail the story of Bruce Pursehouse's eye-witness account of seeing Bazley at Jerilderie, three days before Mackay was murdered; of Parrington's failure to release a description or prepare an identikit based on Pursehouse's sighting; and of Parrington's deletion of the description from the statement given to the coroner's inquest.

Worse was to come. Bottom revealed that the Crown had refused to call Parrington as a witness because Crown lawyers attached to the Victorian Directorate of Public Prosecutions did not regard him as a 'reliable and truthful' witness. The decision was based on the 'conflicting accounts' given by Parrington and Pursehouse of how Pursehouse's description of Bazley came to be withheld from the inquest. Bottom quoted a damning exchange between Parrington and counsel assisting the inquest:

> Counsel: Now, you see you checked out all the things that were put before the Woodward inquiry, is that right?
> Parrington: No.
> Counsel: Well, you see, you're armed with a copy of the document, aren't you . . . the Woodward report?
> Parrington: I have one but I have never read it.
> Counsel: You've never read it?
> Parrington: I haven't had time.
> Counsel: In six years you haven't had time?
> Parrington: You're dead right.
> Counsel: Busy as could be, aren't you, underpaid and over-worked: did you ever have a look at the transcript?
> Parrington: No sir, I have portions of it.
> Counsel: It's like going for a ride without a horse, isn't it?
> Parrington: He covers many areas that are of not much interest to us.
> Counsel: Yes, but not all . . .

Readers also learnt of a conversation between Parrington and Pursehouse on the Monday when Pursehouse claimed to have looked closely at one photograph and told Parrington, 'This is the man I saw at Jerilderie.' Asked by Parrington,

'Can you be sure?', Pursehouse claimed to have replied, 'If I was under oath it would be hard.' Parrington then said, 'If you're questioned about this man while you are in the witness box, don't let them convince you that he was a specific height . . . If you are asked how tall he is, say he is over five foot two and under six foot . . . And make sure you say, "in my opinion he was this" or "in my opinion he was that". . . Don't be too definite with your description . . . Don't be too precise . . . We don't want to lose him now we've got him.'

Six months later, before giving evidence at the Melbourne committal hearing, Pursehouse had again been shown a booklet of police photographs, and had again picked out Bazley. When he told Victorian detectives that he had also identified a photograph at Griffith, they were astounded and said it was the first they had heard about it. A New South Wales detective senior constable, Rick Campbell, who had been one of Parrington's offsiders on the Mackay investigation and who had gone to Melbourne for the committal, immediately rang Parrington and his assistant, Fred Shaw, who denied that Pursehouse had ever positively identified Bazley. The conversation went on:

Campbell: What are you trying to do to us, mate?'
Pursehouse: What do you mean?
Campbell: You didn't identify any photograph. You may believe you did. Christ, mate, if you had identified Bazley, we, and especially Joe, would have been doing cartwheels around the room.

After Pursehouse complained to the New South Wales Attorney-General's Department, Parrington conceded that he had shown him photographs. Parrington's explanation hardly clarified the matter. 'It is the nearest thing I have ever seen in 30 years to a person identifying somebody and not doing it. He stopped at that page, came back to it, commented: "same face, different hair. No I can't identify anyone".'

Terry Jones couldn't help feeling sympathy for Detective Parrington. He had always found Parrington a decent bloke; a bit of a plodder maybe, but likeable and pretty straight with the press. From the word go, Parrington had been under enormous pressure from the top to solve the case, but he could never crack the Griffith code of silence. In the early days, he had made plenty of mistakes, barging in and changing the locks on all the doors, but it was easy to understand his paranoia.

Once Tizzoni had been arrested, Parrington was desperate to solve the Mackay mystery. He could see that Mengler in Victoria was ahead of him and he wasn't getting any help from the federal police. He had probably looked at the conspiracy to murder charge and thought, 'Why aren't we going after Bazley for murder?' Withholding Pursehouse's evidence from the coroner was a mistake and Parrington was going to pay for it. He would be lucky to have a career left when the media had finished with him.

One thing was certain: Joe Parrington would not be getting any support from the politicians in Sydney. The premier and the police minister already had their backs against the wall after agreeing to meet a deputation from the Concerned Citizens. Among the group were Paul Mackay, his sisters Ruth and Mary, and Paddy Keenan. They planned to demand a joint Victorian and New South Wales inquiry into the investigation of Mackay's death.

The chairman of the citizens' group, Richard Smith, told a Fairfax reporter, 'Bazley should have been charged with the murder of Mackay, but that could only occur in NSW, and only if NSW agreed to combine with Victoria. The Victorians have done a marvellous job. Without their persistence and integrity we would be down the tube in this State.'

It was no surprise to Terry Jones to hear Paul Mackay describe the meeting with Wran as 'the most unpleasant experience of my life'. According to Mackay the premier had been an hour late for the appointment. 'For the first hour Mr Wran abused us in the most foul way,' he told the *Daily Telegraph*. 'He accused us of having political motives and some of us of having political ambitions.'

Claiming to be 'personally disappointed' with Parrington's investigation, Wran committed his government to a judicial inquiry that would determine whether Parrington had failed to pursue the investigation 'according to accepted professional standards of technique, integrity and justice'.

It was clear to Jones that Joe Parrington was being lined up as the scapegoat.

The problem for the government was finding someone willing to lead the inquiry. Wran's preference was for a judge 'if one was available' or a person with legal qualifications who was 'independent of the Government'. Supreme Court judges, however, were understandably wary of becoming involved. The power of the government to set restrictive terms of reference for royal commissions and special inquiries left judges open to public criticism for not pursuing other avenues of inquiry. There was a growing feeling among New South Wales judges that they should adopt the Victorian stance of not participating in royal commissions.

Told by the chief justice, Sir Laurence Street, that current judges were unavailable due to their 'heavy workload', the premier named the former Supreme Court judge and royal commissioner John Nagle to head the Mackay inquiry, with Barry Toomey, QC, as counsel assisting.

Nagle's terms of reference directed him to examine whether any evidence to the 1984 coroner's inquest had been withheld or misrepresented, and to find out what had happened to the statement allegedly given to Parrington by Bruce Pursehouse on 17 July 1977. The shadow attorney-general, John Dowd, quickly branded the terms a 'whitewash'.

Still smarting from his ill-tempered meeting with Mr Wran, Smith said the Concerned Citizens were pleased with Nagle's appointment but predicted the group could 'expect further harassment'. Their doubts about the premier's good faith were hardly allayed when Wran hired La Famiglia's paid mouthpiece, Flash Al Grassby, as an ethnic affairs adviser.

The Nagle commission of inquiry began sitting on Friday 23 May 1986 at Sydney's Elizabeth Street local court. Strenuous lobbying by the Concerned Citizens ensured that Barbara Mackay, who had been denied legal aid for the 1984 coronial inquest, received legal assistance to appear at the inquiry. For the Concerned Citizens, the inquiry represented a final chance to 'put up or shut up' about Italian organised crime in Griffith, but the opportunity would be wasted unless Nagle could persuade the premier to expand the terms of reference beyond the alleged failings of Joe Parrington.

It seemed clear to Terry Jones that Wran, railroaded by public opinion into setting up the inquiry, had done all he could to hobble its power to investigate La Famiglia. He was doing to Nagle what he had done to Justice Woodward, who complained that he had less power of entry to Griffith's 'grass castles' than a fruit fly inspector. The question was, would 73-year-old Nagle be any more successful than Woodward in getting at the truth?

There was never any suggestion that Joe Parrington was corrupt but counsel assisting considered he had a duty to 'exclude the possibility'. Questioned about his finances, Parrington told the inquiry that his only car was a 1964 EH Holden worth maybe $500 and the only works of art in the home had been painted by Mrs Parrington and were unlikely to be worth anything. When his barrister asked Mr Nagle to protect Parrington's privacy by suppressing details of his financial affairs, the commissioner replied that the Mackay affair had caused 'enormous concern' in the Griffith area and he would be very hesitant to suppress anything.

Awkwardly for the government, the Nagle inquiry coincided with an investigation along similar lines by the ABC's *Four Corners* program. Describing his commission of inquiry as a 'Clayton's royal commission', Woodward told *Four Corners* that it was 'like many commissions that are established by governments, it's never intended that they should find out too much because anything that's found out which casts a slur upon any part of the administration of the country or state is accepted without question by the government as a slur on them'. Echoing John Dowd's criticism of the Nagle inquiry's terms of reference, Woodward said that the government expected his royal commission to be a 'whitewash'.

Reading the newspaper reports from Sydney, Terry Jones sometimes felt that he and his readers were doomed to keep re-living the events of 15 July 1977. For nine years the town had been tormented by the memory of what had happened that Friday evening in the car park of the Griffith Hotel. While the Calabrian drug bosses identified by Justice Woodward walked free, Joe Parrington was fighting to defend his reputation at the Nagle inquiry. But it was another crime, unconnected to La Famiglia, that would highlight the failings of the Mackay murder investigation.

■ ■ ■

On Saturday 20 June 1986, an eight-year-old Albury boy, John Purtell, disappeared from Griffith's Jubilee Park after playing in a junior football carnival. After a fruitless two-day ground search by 200 police and volunteers, crop duster planes made flights over Barren Box Swamp and Lake Wyangan. Helicopters and police divers would later be brought from Sydney.

In the newsroom of the *Area News*, Purtell's disappearance brought back memories of the abduction and murder of two Griffith schoolchildren in 1984. Mark Mott, twelve, and Ralph Burns, eleven, had vanished at the Griffith Show in September 1984, prompting a state-wide police search.

In October 1985 Mark Mott's body was found in Lake Wyangan. Two months later the body of Ralph Burns was discovered in scrub near the lake. Both bodies were unclothed except for football socks and running shoes. The boys' killer had never been caught. The similarities between the crimes, nearly two years apart, were close enough for police to suspect that whoever had murdered Mark Mott and Ralph Burns was involved in the abduction of John Purtell.

A $50,000 reward for information was offered by the government, matching the reward offered for information about the earlier abductions. Griffith police prepared a manikin dressed in clothes similar to those worn by the missing boy when he was last seen at Jubilee Park after playing football. Photographs of the manikin, with a photograph of John Purtell attached, were sent to all regional newspapers in an effort to uncover more information. The manikin itself was displayed at Griffith police station.

More importantly, the police were making every effort to publicly identify potential suspects. Interviews with boys who were in the showers at Jubilee Park just before John Purtell disappeared revealed that a man had come in and asked the boys to pass their underwear to him so he could wring it out. Detectives used the boys' descriptions of the stranger to create an identikit picture that was circulated throughout the state beneath the headlines 'THIS MAN IS WANTED' and 'SPECIAL POLICE PHOTO'. Three fourteen-year-old Albury girls were said to have noticed the man near the buses at about 2.25pm, fifteen minutes before John was last seen.

The stark contrast between the Purtell and Mackay investigations did not escape Jones. Not only did Parrington fail to circulate—in Jerilderie, Griffith or anywhere else—the description by two eyewitnesses of a man, possibly James Bazley, seen at Jerilderie three days before the murder, but no effort was ever made to construct an identikit image of a person who might have been Mackay's killer.

It was true that a wanted poster had been prepared with photographs of three Indian nationals working in Australia who were briefly (and wrongly) suspected of having links with Mackay. The three men had been observed driving at speed along Banna Avenue at about the time police believe Mackay was shot. The Indian seasonal workers (described as 'pickers') were quickly traced and found to have overstayed their visas, but police did not attempt to repeat their success with descriptions of more plausible suspects. It surely must have rankled with Parrington to read about information 'flooding in' from the public after newspapers published the identikit picture of the man seen lurking about Jubilee Park on the day of John Purtell's disappearance.

The investigation moved quickly after the New South Wales government doubled the rewards for information leading to the discovery of John Purtell and for information leading to the arrest and conviction of the murderer of Mark Mott and Ralph Burns. Perched in his office across the street from the police station and the courthouse, Terry Jones heard a whisper that a Griffith witness had come forward with vital information about a 36-year-old man who lived in a small house on a farm near Hanwood. The media were told to be patient.

After being interviewed by police the man had been allowed to return home, where he apparently overdosed on sleeping pills. After being treated at Griffith Base Hospital he was reinterviewed. As visiting reporters from radio, television and the press gathered in the newsroom of the *Area News*, a picture of the suspect began to emerge. A name—Michael George Laurance—was mentioned. Jones vaguely remembered Laurance as someone he had met at the Area Hotel.

Reporters were calling in updates on the half hour. The 2am, then 3am deadlines for the metropolitan late editions came and went without any suggestion that Laurance was ready for the 'walk', when he would be charged and led from the interview room. At 4am on Monday there was a call to the editorial office of the *Area News*. Laurance had confessed to the murders of all three boys. Just before dawn, community relations constable Paul Herring, scientific detective constable Dave Frost and Sergeant Mal Matthews emerged from the interview room with Michael Laurance. Clutching a grey blanket to his face, Laurance cowered from the TV lights and camera flashes.

An angry crowd of around 400 people hurled abuse as a police paddywagon drove Laurance less than 100 metres from the police station to the courthouse in Kooyoo Street. Security was the tightest ever seen outside the courthouse, which in recent years had hosted committal hearings into multimillion-dollar marijuana crops, an inquest into a mafia killing and two commissions of inquiry. Jones counted more than a dozen heavily armed members of the Tactical Response Group, as well as uniformed police with pistols and batons. Laurance's solicitor did not ask for bail.

A year later, Michael George Laurance would be found guilty by a Supreme Court jury of murdering Ralph Burns, Mark Anthony Mott and John Peter Purtell. The jury rejected his defence that he was guilty only of manslaughter due to a mental condition which diminished his capacity to understand and control his actions. Sentencing him to life imprisonment, Justice Slattery recommended that Laurance never be released. He would later commit suicide, hanging himself in Lithgow jail with a noose made from lengths of cloth taken from the jail's textiles workshop.

On 21 July 1986, Chief Inspector Cassidy wrote a letter to the manager of the *Area News*:

Dear Sir,
I write on behalf of all Police involved in the recent investigation into the disappearance of John Purtell, Mark Mott and Ralph Burns, to express sincere appreciation for the assistance you and your staff provided during the course of the investigation.

The assistance given by all sections of the community, particularly in Griffith and Albury, in this matter was overwhelming. The successful conclusion of this

> investigation is indicative of the results that can be
> achieved when complete co-operation exists between
> Police and the community we serve.
>
> Once again, thank you for your tremendous support.

It was a gratifying letter to receive, a reminder of the vital role the local newspaper could play in the life of a country town. Inevitably, it brought back thoughts of the Mackay case. While the cash reward might have played a role in encouraging informants to come forward, Jones was convinced that the turning point in the Purtell investigation was the decision to circulate the identikit picture. An identikit image of the man at Jerilderie, based on Pursehouse's eyewitness description, might have led to the early capture of James Bazley and a successful New South Wales prosecution for murder, rather than conspiracy to murder. The conspiracy that came undone as a result of Gianfranco Tizzoni's confession might have unravelled years earlier, enabling the police to arrest Bob Trimbole before he could flee the country. It gave Jones no pleasure to see Joe Parrington twisting in the wind but it was hard not to conclude that the Mackay investigation had been botched from the start.

■ ■ ■

On 16 July Jones himself was subpoenaed to appear before the inquiry. Fourteen years editing the town's newspapers had given him an intimate knowledge of Griffith and its inhabitants, but Jones felt there was little he could add to the thousands of pages of information already gathered by Justice Woodward and the coroner and by Joe Parrington himself. An awkward moment came when Jones was quizzed about a comment he had made a few days earlier to a reporter from the *Sydney Morning Herald*. Counsel assisting the commission, Mr Toomey, asked Jones what he had meant when he described the Nagle inquiry as 'bloody stupid'?

'What I meant,' Jones answered, 'was that it was stupid to the ordinary citizens in the town, particularly when a section would be sitting back laughing that the investigator [Mr Parrington] was now being investigated, and they were free.'

One man who was not laughing when Justice Nagle finally delivered his findings was Al Grassby, who was forced to quit his job as special adviser to the premier after being severely criticised by Nagle for circulating a document accusing Barbara Mackay and her son of killing Don Mackay. Nagle found that 'no decent man could have regarded the general attack on the Calabrians as justifying him in propagating the scurrilous lies contained in the document'. Chastised for his 'extraordinarily unsatisfactory and even evasive' evidence to the inquiry, Grassby was described by Nagle as being at best 'less than frank' and at worst of having 'concealed what he knew about the origins of the document'. In the New South Wales Parliament the opposition leader, Nick Greiner, accused Flash Al of having been a 'propagandist and apologist for the mafia' for twenty years.

The three people implicated in Grassby's 'scurrilous document', Barbara and Paul Mackay and their lawyer, Ian Salmon, sued Grassby for defamation and won. Grassby was later charged with conspiring with Jennifer Sergi and Giuseppe Sergi to pervert the course of justice between 1979 and 1981 by circulating the false document. The charges were thrown out by a magistrate before being reinstated on appeal. Grassby was convicted in August 1991 of attempted criminal defamation but acquitted on appeal twelve months later and awarded costs. In 1987 a National Crime Authority investigator, Bruce Provost, told a Sydney court that Bob Trimbole had given Grassby $20,000 before and $20,000 after the document was published in the *Sun-Herald*.

The Nagle inquiry's second scalp was that of Chief Superintendent Joe Parrington, who was found to have deliberately withheld evidence from the Mackay inquest, suppressed evidence and misrepresented people. After a 'cursory' reading of the report, the police commissioner, John Avery, said there was enough evidence to level departmental, if not criminal, charges against Parrington. Nagle concluded that Parrington had acted not to shield any wrongdoer but to 'gain credit' for himself. To Terry Jones, the motive was beside the point. Joe Parrington had been entrusted with finding and prosecuting Mackay's murderer and he had betrayed that trust by interfering with evidence. La Famiglia had a lot to thank him for.

■ ■ ■

The ABC reporter Marian Wilkinson was still speaking regularly to Jones about what was going on in Griffith. She was particularly interested in the town's long history of insurance fraud.

When Wilkinson visited Griffith, Jones pointed her towards sites in and around the town that had featured in insurance scams. One famous incident involved a large galvanised iron machinery shed that had mysteriously exploded before burning and collapsing. Marks on the ground indicated that derelict vehicles had been dragged from beneath nearby trees and parked in the shed before it was torched. As a result of the inferno all the machinery inside the shed was incinerated beyond recognition.

The fire was attributed to a certain Antonio 'Tricky' Treccase, a smalltime used-car yard owner and salesman whose passion for gambling rivalled that of 'Aussie Bob' Trimbole, and whom local police dubbed the 'Calabrese candle'.

In June or July 1979 an old utility belonging to Tony Treccase had gone up in flames, giving Treccase a $4000 insurance payout. The following year Judge Newton, in the Griffith District Court, fined three men $1000 each and placed them on $300 bonds for three years for setting fire to a vehicle with intent to defraud. All three had been used by a man the judge named as Tony Treccase, who was not before the court. Newton said he had considered jailing the trio because insurance fraud was a serious crime, but had decided it would be unfair as 'the real villain had escaped free'.

About the time of Treccase's shed fire, Griffith police were linking him with a number of suspicious house fires in which homes would suddenly explode in a fireball. At one failed fire, police discovered small bags of petrol strung like pearls on a necklace around the interior walls of a building targeted for arson. Flames ignited the bags in a chain reaction, allowing the blaze to catch hold before the fire brigade could reach the scene.

Another blaze occurred in March 1981 at a house in Nursery Road, Yoogali, east of Griffith, owned by Alberto and Saverio Treccase that burnt to the ground in less than 30 minutes. Firemen could not find any reason for the fire in what was described as a recently renovated four-bedroom home. It was later discovered that new appliances as well as family treasures and heirlooms had by a stroke of luck been removed from the house just days before the fire.

PARRINGTON PAYS

As well as supplying details of suspicious car accidents around Griffith, Jones told Wilkinson about the case known as the 'Lloyds of London fraud' in which a standard-bred two-year-old colt, Double Eclipse, had been found shot dead in a paddock at Lake Wyangan in November 1982. Insured for $350,000, Double Eclipse had never won a race and in June 1982 had been sold for just $1500. (The Australian record price for a yearling trotter in 1981 was $33,000.)

Griffith detectives had charged Antonio 'Tricky' Treccase, described as a pensioner; his wife, Elizabeth Bernadette Treccase, housewife, of Griffith; Antonio's brother, Saverio 'Sam' Treccase, of Yoogali; Antonio 'Young Tony' Sergi, of Tharbogang; and Edward John 'Johnny' Lee, of Griffith, with conspiring to cheat and defraud Lloyds of $350,000.

All five were eventually found guilty. The four men were sentenced to jail but sentence was deferred on Elizabeth Treccase, who was described as 'a traditionally loyal Italian wife'.

Many scams involved staged car accidents. In her *Four Corners* report Marian Wilkinson described a typical accident in which a 44-year-old Griffith man drove his dinner guest home. The driver's two sons and a cousin from Italy went along for the ride. The driver drove at 30 km/h down a familiar street towards a familiar intersection where another car with five local Calabrians was stopped at a 'give way' sign. It looked like just another rear-end collision, causing minimal damage and with no need for an ambulance. But everyone involved in the accident, except the driver at fault, lodged a claim with the Government Insurance Office (GIO) for whiplash, back strain and other soft-tissue injuries.

One of the passengers in the back seat was Francesco Barbaro, named by the Woodward Royal Commission as active in the Griffith drug trade. The driver at fault, Barbaro's dinner host, had been involved in four previous accidents; three had led to personal injury claims for which the GIO paid him more than $100,000.

The driver's two sons also made claims after this accident. Within two years, both had lodged other suspect claims with the GIO. The car had had four accidents by the time its registration finally expired.

The nine claimants in the 'Italian cousin' accident received around a quarter of a million dollars compensation for their alleged injuries. It had all the features of what the GIO came to regard as 'suspicious' accidents.

Wilkinson continued: 'If there is a case that tests the limits of coincidence in these accidents, it must be Antonio Sergi, known as "Young Tony". Sergi was also named by Woodward as a key player in the Griffith marijuana syndicate headed by the late crime boss Bob Trimbole. At best the following chain of events can only be described as bizarre: night . . . Sydney's west, a man is driving alone. Ahead another car is pulled up at a stop sign. Another rear-end accident. The driver at fault is not injured but all five men in the front car, four from Griffith, lodge claims with the GIO for whiplash and other soft-tissue injuries. They include a key player, Young Tony, later convicted of insurance fraud against Lloyds of London, and his cousin Domenico Sergi, named by Woodward as an influential member of the Griffith drug syndicate. The five victims received $465,000 from the GIO, but we have established that the mystery driver who hit them was in fact a drug courier for Bob Trimbole.'

These 'suspicious' car accidents, often involving multiple members of the same Calabrian families, were a standing joke in Griffith, but they cost the insurers millions of dollars.

It was the insurers, however, who had the last laugh when two drivers searching for a place to stage a fake accident were involved in a real accident. Police reported only minor damage in the real accident, yet one of the 'victims', Giuseppe Barbaro, nephew of Rocco, was initially awarded $142,000 for his 'injuries'. The NRMA appealed to the Federal Court, which ruled that because the accident victims were on the way to stage a criminal act, there was no 'duty of care' when a real accident happened.

To Terry Jones it looked like karma.

CHAPTER 18

Cops and crops

In the late 1980s the Australian Bureau of Criminal Intelligence examined 188 marijuana crops detected across Australia between 1974 and 1985. It found that of 250 people arrested on the plantations, 60 per cent were linked to just fifteen Calabrian mafia families, all but one of which 'were related by blood or marriage'. Of the other 40 per cent, many had secondary links to the fifteen named families and to other known Calabrian crime families. Overall, the bureau estimated that as much as 90 per cent of Australian marijuana was controlled by Calabrians, many of whom were based in Griffith.

In early 1987 Terry Jones began hearing 'weird rumours' about a cannabis crop grown near Bungendore, supposedly with police backing. Since the Mackay murder, Griffith's Calabrian citizens had been careful to keep their mouths shut, but even they could not help gossiping about police in Canberra growing cannabis. Inevitably, the gossip reached the ears of local reporters, but it was impossible to corroborate.

Jones was no longer editor at the *Area News*, having left Riverina Newspapers to write for Rural Press. As regional representative for *The Land*, based in Griffith, Jones gathered news from an area covering around 20 per cent of New South Wales, driving 100,000 kilometres each year in his Falcon, equipped with a fuel card, Flag motel card, camera and computer. At the same time his wife, Irene, was steadily climbing the career ladder from nurse-educator to director of nursing at Griffith Base Hospital, then manager of Griffith Base and a cluster of regional hospitals.

After quitting the *Area News* Jones continued to receive almost annual visits from the Australian Federal Police seeking updates on La Famiglia. The AFP was especially interested in Winery Tony's involvement with the new Casella winery and in the distribution network that was alleged to be shipping mafia drugs between South Australia, Victoria and New South Wales.

Jones was as curious as anyone to find out who was involved in the 'police crop'. Among the names being mentioned was that of Griffith's most notorious marijuana grower, Rocco Barbaro, who since growing his first crop at Tharbogang had moved just over 100 kilometres to Hillston. Barbaro was known to have Canberra connections.

Another name that kept cropping up was that of a man named 'Verduci', who had no apparent links to marijuana plantations in Griffith or the Riverina but was whispered to have recruited experienced crop growers on behalf of New South Wales and federal police. Luigi Pochi, who had been jailed for his part in the Coleambally crop, was another one named.

Born in Calabria in 1937, Giuseppe 'Joe' Verduci had approached the AFP in late 1980 with an offer to infiltrate

La Famiglia and its cannabis operations. With support from the New South Wales police, Colin Winchester, a superintendent in the AFP's criminal investigation branch, accepted Verduci's offer and approved a cannabis crop, which was to be allowed to proceed 'even to the harvesting and sale stage'—a fateful decision that would come to haunt those who made it. The 'controlled marijuana plantation', to be grown at Verduci's own property at Bungendore, north-east of Canberra, became known as Bungendore 1.

In August 1982 Verduci told Winchester and another AFP officer that Rocco Barbaro and Luigi Pochi had spoken to him about locations for a possible marijuana plantation. The pair had been keen to involve Verduci because they believed he had police protection. Verduci said he had not committed himself but was waiting on instructions from the AFP. In anticipation of a second crop, however, he had suggested various locations. At this meeting Winchester reminded Verduci that his job as an agent provocateur was not to incite people to commit crimes but merely to pass information to the police. He also warned Verduci not to become involved in any illegal activities—especially the cultivation of other marijuana crops—without the express permission or tacit approval of police.

The second crop, Bungendore 2, was grown in the Tallaganda State Forest. The joint New South Wales police/AFP operation, code-named Seville, was widely criticised because large amounts of the cannabis—worth as much as $2 million—were stolen, some allegedly by police. Bungendore 2 had to be shut down after a series of raids by gangs using furniture trucks.

While the police were preoccupied with Seville, Verduci used equipment from Bungendore to grow an unauthorised

50,000-plant crop on his wife's property at Guyra, near Armidale.

The purpose of Operation Seville had been to infiltrate La Famiglia cells in Canberra and Griffith. The AFP would later argue that one positive outcome from Seville had been the solving of Donald Mackay's murder. When Victoria Police first intercepted Gianfranco Tizzoni, on 31 March 1982, he was transporting marijuana from Bungendore, although Tizzoni waited another year before confessing to his role in the Mackay murder conspiracy.

As with most of the gossip in Griffith, the 'weird rumours' about police being involved in a marijuana crop at Bungendore would eventually be confirmed. During 1987–88 the National Crime Authority in Sydney prepared briefs of evidence against several people involved in the Bungendore crops, including Antonio Barbaro (born 25/3/44); his brother Rocco Barbaro (23/9/49); and Luigi Pochi (7/1/39). Verduci, who had been granted immunity in return for testifying against those involved in the Bungendore and Guyra plantations, refused to give evidence when the cases came to court. In the end, all charges were thrown out or dropped.

■ ■ ■

On 10 January 1989 Colin Winchester, by then assistant commissioner of the AFP, was shot in the back of the head as he got out of his car outside his home in Canberra. Winchester's feckless attempt to infiltrate La Famiglia by joining forces in the large-scale cultivation of cannabis made the Calabrians obvious suspects, although in fact they were not involved. All those charged over the Bungendore cannabis plantations were interviewed about their movements on

10 January. Background information provided by the ACT major crime squad on Antonio Barbaro described him as the 'production manager for both Bungendore 1 and 2', and Rocco Barbaro as 'one of the principal organisers in both Bungendore 1 and 2'. As the Independent MP John Hatton told the New South Wales Parliament, if the date of Don Mackay's disappearance, 15 July 1977, was notable for the alibis it produced, it was rivalled by the night of Colin Winchester's murder.

On the night Winchester was killed Rocco Barbaro was confirmed as visiting his daughter Elizabeth, who was then a patient at Griffith Base Hospital. Antonio Barbaro was given an alibi by his wife, who said that he was watching TV in their Canberra home.

Hatton was convinced that the deaths of Mackay and Winchester were 'inextricably linked' and that the events between those two murders formed a 'continuum'. He told the parliament, 'The key principals involved in marijuana growing in Griffith are the principals involved with Operation Seville in which Assistant Police Commissioner Winchester played a pivotal role. These people continue to flourish. The key figures are Antonio Barbaro and Luigi Pochi, but there are others.'

In April 1989, the Canberra drug boss Pasquale 'Il Principale' Barbaro was hit with two blasts from a shotgun at his home in Brisbane. A fortnight later, still recovering from the attempted assassination, Barbaro was interviewed by the ACT major crime squad about the Winchester killing. He told detectives he was at home with his wife on the night Winchester was shot.

Soon afterwards Barbaro was rumoured to have begun talking to the National Crime Authority about Winchester's murder and other matters. Less than a year later he was shot and stabbed to death on his front lawn by a 'long haired man with jeans and a heavy dark beard'. Another witness saw the same man—now clean-shaven with short hair—drive off in a cream-coloured 1970s Ford Falcon. Police suspected the killer was a hitman wearing a fake beard and wig.

Six years later David Eastman, a former public servant who claimed to be the victim of police harassment, was convicted of murdering Assistant Commissioner Winchester. Questions over the fairness of the trial eventually led to an inquiry and a recommendation by Justice Brian Martin that Eastman be pardoned, despite Martin being 'fairly certain' of his guilt. There were many in Griffith who had always suspected La Famiglia of committing the murder.

■ ■ ■

On 12 December 1989, three months before Pasquale Barbaro was killed by a mafia hitman in Brisbane, a police helicopter crew detected a huge cannabis plantation hidden among corn on a property near Moulamein, 260 kilometres from Griffith. One of the men arrested over the $40 million Moulamein crop—the biggest ever planned in Griffith—was Pasquale's namesake, Pasquale 'Pat' Barbaro, 29-year-old son of Frank 'Little Trees' Barbaro. Just a teenager when Justice Woodward branded his father and uncles as senior members of La Famiglia, Pat Barbaro was charged along with three other Calabrians. In order to convict Barbaro, prosecutors had to prove that he was the fictitious 'Tony Trimarchi' who had taken a lease on a property called 'Lenlin' near Moulamein.

All four pleaded not guilty (Barbaro listed 160 alibi witnesses, all male and many related) but they were all convicted. Barbaro had not only leased the property under a false name—his fingerprints were found on the lease document—but he was also identified as the buyer of farm equipment. The $80,000 paid to lease the farm was far above the market value. Describing him as the ringleader of the conspiracy, the trial judge sentenced Barbaro to ten and a half years' jail.

Appeals by Barbaro and another of the accused, Griffith real estate agent Carmelo 'Charlie' Rovere, resulted in retrials and yet more appeals. At Barbaro's 1999 retrial Judge Shadbolt said that great care had been taken to distance Barbaro from the crop, which had been grown in extreme secrecy. Rovere, he said, had been careful to discourage anyone from coming near the cannabis farm by telling tales of 'diseased sheep'.

Noting that the conspirators had exhibited 'improved life-styles' since their arrests, Judge Shadbolt said that none had shown the 'slightest contrition'. They had put the community through a long and expensive trial and 'once again they have failed'. However, he took into account submissions by Barbaro's lawyer, who played down his client's position in the hierarchy and said there was 'absolutely no proof' that Barbaro was to have been involved in the distribution of the cannabis.

Barbaro, he said, had suffered considerable expense and emotional trauma as a result of having the trial 'hanging over his head' for ten years. Although he had the 'same name and same body', Barbaro was 'not the same man he was at the time of his arrest aged 28'.

In an unusual move, Barbaro read a prepared statement to the judge saying he had been on bail since April 1990, never breaching his bail conditions despite being allowed to travel overseas four times. Despite his legal pressures he was establishing an olive oil production business which he planned to pass on to his two sons. '(This) has affected my wife and children very much,' Barbaro told the judge. 'At the age they are now, they need a father. Please don't let them suffer.'

It worked. Judge Shadbolt announced a reduction in the original sentence by 50 per cent, leaving Barbaro—after deducting time already served—just three and a half years to serve. Rovere, 46, would spend just another five months and 25 days in prison. Barbaro and Rovere were already thinking ahead to their next appeal, which would see both men released on bail in December 1999. Six months later, the two convictions were quashed. Rovere had already served the minimum jail term and was acquitted. The court of appeal ordered a retrial for Barbaro, noting that it was up to the Crown whether the retrial went ahead. It never did.

■ ■ ■

While Barbaro and Rovere got away nearly scot-free, another Griffith man paid a heavy price for his role in the $40 million Moulamein cannabis conspiracy.

Solicitor Simon Mackenzie had surprised reporters at the *Area News* by not just acting for Pat Barbaro in the Moulamein case, but also appearing as a defence witness. This put the usually astute lawyer in the sights of the New South Wales director of public prosecutions, Nicholas Cowdery.

In May 1995 Adrian Simon Mackenzie was tried for perjury in Sydney's Supreme Court. He was accused of lying during Barbaro's 1991 trial in an effort to have Barbaro acquitted. Rather than a Crown advocate or hired QC, it was Cowdery himself who led the prosecution. Barbaro's fingerprints, Cowdery said, were on the lease document signed by the fictitious 'Tony Tremarchi'. The document, he said, had been shown to Barbaro from a distance at the Griffith police station during a police interview in April 1990. At the 1991 trial, however, Mackenzie had claimed that Barbaro handled the lease during the interview. It was not difficult, Cowdery told the court, to see how Mackenzie's evidence could have saved his client.

After deliberating for two days, the 'youngish' jury found Mackenzie guilty of giving false evidence but not guilty of the more serious charge of giving false evidence with intent to procure an acquittal. Referees described Mackenzie as 'a good, kind and honourable man', although it did not escape notice in Griffith that the Riverina Law Society refrained from offering supportive character evidence in Mackenzie's trial. Cowdery argued that perjury from a lawyer was at the 'serious' end of the scale. Ignoring pleas from Mackenzie's counsel, Barry Toomey QC, not to send his client to jail, the judge sentenced Mackenzie to a minimum of nine months. He later appealed and was acquitted after serving nine months.

While Mackenzie's former client Pat Barbaro was back walking the streets of Griffith as a free man, his ten-year sentence quashed on appeal, the millionaire solicitor—reputed to be one of the wealthiest lawyers in New South Wales—was locked up in Sydney's maximum security Parramatta Jail, bail refused.

In the newsroom of the *Area News* the question being asked was, 'What made Cowdery go after Mackenzie?' There was no shortage of opinions. After lining his pockets over many years as a defender of the Griffith 'Mob', Mackenzie was a valuable scalp for the DPP. There was no doubt that the bush lawyer had personally profited from handling third-party insurance claims running to millions of dollars, many of which looked suspicious. (He was known to be the subject of 'Annexure A' of the AFP's 'Trojan' report.)

The real mystery was why Mackenzie had stuck his neck out by leaving the bar table and taking the witness stand. Everyone knew that in his work for La Famiglia Mackenzie had sometimes strayed close to the edge, but nobody seriously believed he was a crook. Barbaro, however, was a man to be feared. Someone close to the family told Terry Jones, 'Simon had to do everything he could to get Barbaro off. The evidence was stacked against him. The trial wasn't going well. Simon didn't have a choice.' Joe Sergi, who owned a takeaway fish 'n' chip shop in Griffith, was one of the few Calabrese not taken in by Mackenzie's courtroom guile. 'So they've got the monkey,' Sergi told Jones. 'The organ grinder's monkey.'

An appeal was inevitable. Mackenzie's lawyers argued that the jury's guilty verdict on perjury charges was 'perverse' given that they had found him not guilty of intent to procure Barbaro's acquittal. The Crown appealed against the leniency of the sentence. Both were dismissed by the Court of Appeal.

By the time Mackenzie was given leave to appeal to the High Court, his non-parole period was almost over. Mackenzie had been moved from Parramatta Jail and was serving out his final months at the minimum security Mannus Correctional Centre at Tumbarumba. After being quietly released in March 1996, Mackenzie went straight to Griffith Base Hospital for long-delayed surgery on a hernia. He was still recuperating when Terry Jones received an unexpected telephone call from Tori Salvestrin, a TV reporter who had started out as a cadet on the *Area News*.

Salvestrin said, 'There's someone who'd like to see you. It's Simon. He's in hospital at Griffith.'

Jones was surprised. He had heard that Mackenzie would be getting out, but had no idea he was already in Griffith. 'What does he want to see me about?' he asked.

'I don't know, TJ. He just asked me to ring you. Please . . . do it for me.'

Jones hesitated. 'I don't know if I've got anything to talk to Simon about, Tori. I'll have to think about it.'

A few hours later, Tori was back on the phone. 'It's me again, TJ. Simon's very disappointed. He's really keen to see you.'

Jones said, 'Tell Simon I'm still thinking about it.'

Over the years that he'd been working in Griffith, Jones had gathered a vast trove of documents—newspaper cuttings, letters, reports from inquests and inquiries, as well as personal reminiscences—that formed the basis of a manuscript he was calling 'The Griffith Diaries'. Jones had started writing after Don Mackay had gone missing. Since then it had grown to more than 100,000 words. He had shown the manuscript to a few people, including Chris Masters at *Four Corners*, and it seemed that someone had told Mackenzie about it. Not surprisingly, the solicitor was curious to know what Jones had written about him.

Tori called him again the next day. 'Come on, TJ. He just wants to have a chat. What harm can it do?'

Finally Jones relented. 'All right. Tell Simon I'll be there about 5 o'clock, after work.'

If Mackenzie was curious to talk to Jones, Jones was equally curious to talk to him. Despite bumping into each other regularly around town, the pair had never really talked in the twenty years they had both lived in Griffith. There was professional respect, but also suspicion on both sides.

When Jones arrived at Griffith Base Hospital he discovered

he was not the only one visiting Mackenzie. The crowds coming to pay their respects at the solicitor's bedside rivalled those Mackenzie was said to have entertained during his stay at Parramatta Jail and Mannus.

Jones immediately recognised Giuseppe 'Joe' Sergi and his wife, Caterina, sitting with Mackenzie. The last time Jones had seen the couple was in court, when 'Joe' Sergi, 'Young Tony' Sergi and Tony's wife, Jennifer, were facing charges of having criminally defamed Barbara and Paul Mackay and their solicitor, Ian Salmon. 'Joe' Sergi was a longtime friend of Al Grassby, who had miraculously escaped facing the same criminal defamation charge.

'Joe, Caterina,' said Mackenzie, 'this is Terry Jones.'

An awkward silence followed. It was clear to Jones that they had no wish to speak to him. Taking their leave of Mackenzie, the couple quickly left.

'I hope you haven't been catching all my trout in the mountains?' said Jones, shaking hands.

'Are there trout at Mannus?' said Mackenzie. 'Yes, I suppose there are. There's a little creek running through the camp.'

With his eye on a scoop, Jones asked, 'Are we on the record?'

'I'd prefer us to be off the record,' the lawyer answered.

The conversation soon turned to Jones's manuscript. Mackenzie wanted to know if it was true that Jones had offered a document entitled 'Griffith Crime & Justice—Life and Times of Simon Mackenzie' for publication to the *Daily Advertiser* in Wagga Wagga and the *Area News* in Griffith. Jones said it was, but that both papers had been frightened to publish while Mackenzie's case was being appealed because of the defamation risk.

'Very sensible,' said Mackenzie.

'The manuscript is privileged,' said Jones. 'It's entirely from protected sources: courts, commissions, inquests, extradition proceedings, *Hansard* parliamentary records.'

'I'm sure we'd all like to have a properly researched history of events in Griffith,' said Mackenzie. 'Perhaps I could help with a retainer . . . or copies of recent court proceedings . . . to make sure it's balanced.'

'Forget the retainer,' said Jones. 'You might not agree with all that's written. Anyway, the manuscript isn't finished yet.'

'I'd still like to read it,' said Mackenzie. 'Who else have you shown it to?'

Jones said he had mentioned it to Channel 9's *Sunday* program. 'I told them it was about colourful events in the life of a solicitor representing the Honoured Society. They were interested but they are biding their time. They told me Channel 9 will pay more than the ABC if they use any of my stuff.'

'My trial and appeal transcripts are essential reading,' Mackenzie said. 'You must get hold of them.'

'I followed the trial,' said Jones. 'I've spoken to Kate McClymont at the *Herald* and to Warren Owens at the *Sunday Tele*. They were there?'

'No. They didn't sit in.'

'Well, they told me how the trial was unfolding.'

'They got that from the DPP.'

'I've read the appeal finding, all 48 pages. I know what the judges said. They noted that you tried to change your story. That didn't impress them. They said you were trying to improve your position. Anyway, they were convinced the jury could have found you guilty on all four charges, not just two.'

Mackenzie shook his head. 'It wasn't true. In any case, the trial should properly have been before a judge without a jury—a lawyer judged by his peers. Justice Levine was to have heard the perjury charges, but then someone started whispering that Levine had been a guest at a social gathering with staff from Mackenzie & Vardanega [Mackenzie's law firm]. It tainted him and the case went instead to Justice James and a jury.'

Jones could see what Mackenzie was up to: he was blaming everyone but himself. 'But it was you who put your reputation on the line,' he said. 'You were baited by the prosecution to denounce the police evidence in Barbaro's trial. You took the bait, allowed yourself to take the witness stand. You played into their hands, didn't you? When Barbaro went down, you were left high and dry, facing perjury charges.'

Mackenzie frowned. 'The trial jury was not fully instructed by the judge. There was a serious lack of instruction on several points. The jury was out for two days . . . we sensed it was ominous. They were obviously confused. Toomey approached the judge to ask for the jury to be recalled for instructions, but the panel stayed locked away. We felt we were denied natural justice. The DPP had originally said it wouldn't ask for a custodial sentence. They were never confident of winning. Cowdery bloody well went and asked James for a prison sentence, saying that perjury by a solicitor was the most serious case of a person lying under oath.'

'You came through it all right,' Jones said, trying to ease the tension.

Mackenzie shrugged. 'I coped.'

Solicitors were not supposed to be streetwise, but Mackenzie had been a 'safe prisoner' among the hardened criminals in Parramatta Jail, largely by guaranteeing his own security. Voluntarily, Mackenzie had worked on the cases of fellow prisoners awaiting court appearances. Few if any city solicitors jumped to answer legal aid calls from prisons, but Mackenzie took instructions regardless of who he was dealing with, preparing meticulous briefs. 'I made legal aid redundant,' he boasted. 'The system inside Parramatta had never run so smoothly!'

After seven and a half months at Parramatta, Mackenzie was transferred to Mannus, a minimum security prison that felt like a country retreat after Parramatta. Mackenzie claimed to be the first prisoner to have been driven from Parramatta to Tumbarumba by the camp governor.

The inmates at Mannus had to give undertakings they would not escape. Having arrived at the 'farm' in spring, Mackenzie offered to work in the garden, growing flowers and vegetables and pruning the Mannus shrubbery. Trees and bushes that had not seen secateurs for 25 years were made neat and tidy. Other prisoners dubbed him 'The Governor', a title he accepted and answered to with pride. When the chairman of the Serious Offenders Review Council, Judge Torrington, visited Mannus, he recognised Mackenzie straight away, mistakenly believing him to be visiting a client. Mackenzie quickly put him right, telling the judge, 'I'm the new prison gardener!'

Early reports had filtered back to Griffith of Mackenzie discouraging visits to Parramatta, even though it was classed as 'medium' among the state's maximum security jails. It made Mackenzie shudder to think about the indignity of intimate body searches for illicit drugs after close contact visits. Professional friends from Griffith who were reluctant to visit him in Parramatta were happy to make the three-hour drive to scenic Tumbarumba for picnic outings at Mannus.

Mackenzie seemed to have fond memories of his time at Mannus, especially of the farewell barbecue arranged for

'The Governor' beneath a shady tree. A dozen inmates joined Mackenzie for smoked oysters and salmon, fresh salads and fat steaks cooked on an open fire. Four dozen cans of light ale were drunk. 'One muster passed with twelve prisoners absent,' Mackenzie recalled. 'But nobody sounded the alarm. They all answered the final muster that day.'

Dressed in polka-dot pyjamas, with a phone and recorder at his elbow and letters and legal documents piled on his fold-out table, Mackenzie looked completely at home. Jail seemed to have stripped him of his old self-consciousness, but Jones could see that the spark had dimmed. The age lines around his thin lips were more pronounced. There was none of the jaunty free spirit of nine months earlier.

A constant stream of southern Italian visitors turned up at Mackenzie's bedside. They arrived at precise 30-minute intervals, as if a roster had been drawn up. Among them Jones recognised various men whom Mackenzie had defended on drug, fraud and conspiracy charges and damages claims stretching back three decades. One was 'Young Tony' Sergi. Jones could not believe his luck, although Young Tony's arrival put an end to any thoughts of an 'off the record' talk with Mackenzie.

'Tony!' said Mackenzie. 'Good to see you! You know Terry Jones?'

'I know Tony,' said Jones. 'I've written stories about his lemons. How are things on the farm? You've got grapes now, haven't you?'

'No grapes. Just the same fruit trees. The lemons are really good, thanks to you.'

'So there's good money in lemons, is there?' asked Mackenzie.

'They're the best price of anything,' Sergi answered.

Sergi told Mackenzie how Jones had called at his Thar-bogang farm to write a story about lemons for the *Land* newspaper. His wife, Jennifer, answered the door, saw Jones, and would have shut the door in his face if Young Tony had not intervened, saying he was happy to talk to Jones about lemons. Sergi took Jones to the Scenic Hill slope where he had started to cut the tops off his lemon trees before pulling the stumps. After hearing Jones out, Sergi realised that other farmers had done the same. He was one of the few citrus growers in the district to have healthy lemon trees still standing. Jones predicted he would make a killing and he was right: the lemons sold for 50 cents to $1 each.

Mackenzie had given Sergi advice at least twice on serious criminal matters, but Jones reckoned his advice about lemons had been more valuable than anything Mackenzie had told him.

After Sergi was jailed over the Lloyds of London insur-ance fraud, he and three of his four co-conspirators spent Christmas 1985 at Mannus. Young Tony did not share Mackenzie's fond memories of the place. 'I found it very hard in maximum security waiting assessment,' he said. 'But at camp it was just as hard.'

'Everyone feels the loss of freedom,' Mackenzie agreed. 'It's something you have to adjust to. You have to adapt quickly, find some sort of work.'

'Tony and Johnny [Tony Treccase and Johnny Lee—two of Young Tony's co-conspirators] never came to grips with being in jail. Neither of them would do any work. They just moped about. They made it harder for me. I just went off and worked the garden, like Uncle Frank [Francesco Sergi, another of Mackenzie's clients, who served time in Mannus after being convicted for his part in the Coleambally crop].'

'The work ethic is disgraceful,' said Mackenzie. 'I'm writing to the prison authorities about it. Prisoners shouldn't be sent to farms unless they're willing to put in a hard day's work.'

As Sergi bid ciao, Mackenzie joked, 'The rock and water melons will be ready to pick. Those lucky bastards back there will get to eat them all!'

Jones felt sorry for 'Young Tony' Sergi, who had a lot on his mind. It was gossipped around Griffith that his wife, Jennifer, had become friendly with Rocco Barbaro while Young Tony was in jail. There were also rumours of a dalliance with Antonio 'Tony' Romeo (born 21 January 1956 in Platì), once regarded as the heir apparent to the Trimbole drug network. At Glebe Coroners' Court on 10 October 2008, Detective Sergeant Eugene Stek told Coroner Mary Jerram, 'Giovanni Sergi ostracised [Tony] Romeo after an affair with Jenny Sergi in 1994 ... When Romeo was released from prison eight years later [after serving time for conspiracy to import drugs] police alleged Giovanni was determined to seek revenge for the sexual indiscretion.' Stek also stated, 'In the early 1990s Ms Jolliffe [Jenny Sergi] had conducted an affair with Rocco Barbaro.' Jennifer now lived without the children in a unit in Griffith. The consequences for Rocco Barbaro had been a lot more serious. In October 1993 Rocco had had his kneecap blasted off with a shotgun—supposedly the result of an 'accident' at his Hillston farm. Griffith detectives had been forced to walk away in frustration after Barbaro refused to change his story of having shot himself in the back of the leg, with a long-barrelled gun, while stalking a fox. The leg had to be amputated. Having only one leg turned out to be no hindrance to Rocco Barbaro's drug activities. Some in Griffith thought that Barbaro had been lucky not to lose more.

Jail saved Tony Romeo—at least temporarily—from a fate as bad as Rocco Barbaro's, or worse. Together with Young Tony's father, Giovanni 'Johnny' Sergi, Romeo had been involved with the cultivation and supply of illegal drugs for a number of years before being convicted and jailed in 1994 for conspiracy to import cannabis. The plan had been to use a light plane to import 750 kilograms of cannabis (the maximum load the plane could carry) from Papua New Guinea. Unfortunately for Romeo, two of his fellow 'conspirators' were undercover police.

Romeo was sentenced to ten years in prison. There would be trouble waiting for him when he got out.

CHAPTER 19

Witness X

On 14 May 1996 the Supreme Court in Brisbane began hearing evidence about an 8500-plant marijuana bust in far western Queensland. One-legged playboy Rocco 'Roy' Barbaro, 47, had pleaded not guilty to cultivating cannabis between 1 May and 16 November 1993 at Yulebar, about 80 kilometres east of Roma. The seeds were reputed to have cost $80,000 and to have come from the Netherlands. The crop of 'skunk' cannabis, high in the chemical THC, was estimated to have a street value of $80 million.

There was no evidence of Rocco Barbaro having visited the Queensland plantation but the National Crime Authority had an abundance of secretly monitored phone conversations that put Barbaro at the heart of the enterprise. Many of these calls had been made from the public telephone at the Hillston Ex-Servicemen's & Citizens Club, where Barbaro had a habit of settling in for long conversations. It soon became obvious to club members that Barbaro was ringing long distance to

Queensland, switching from English to Calabrese to hide what he was saying from the club's predominantly Anglo-Saxon patrons.

Barbaro was careful, but not always careful enough. Occasionally he was overheard giving instructions about the cultivation of agricultural crops. The club's manager, Warren Scanlon, tipped off Hillston police, who passed the information to the NCA. The NCA installed a video camera and bugged the telephone in anticipation of Barbaro's visits. Scanlon operated the devices from his office. As well as capturing lively conversations between Barbaro and an unidentified woman who might have been Jennifer Sergi, they recorded him giving advice to crop sitters about culling male marijuana plants from female.

Interviewed by the NCA in January 1994, Scanlon said, 'If Roy wasn't there to answer [the public telephone], I would pick it up and the phone would go dead. I have often seen Roy Barbaro standing next to the phone. As soon as the public phone rang he would then pick it up. He would often have lengthy conversations . . . I have seen him talking on the phone for up to an hour and a half . . . I can say that I have seen Roy Barbaro using the public telephone in this club up until the time he got his leg blown off.'

When the NCA played some of the tapes to 'Young Tony' Sergi he was unable to identify the voices as belonging to either Rocco Barbaro or Jennifer Sergi. A linguistics expert from Melbourne identified Barbaro's voice for the Supreme Court jury.

At the trial Barbaro's wife, Catarina, told the court her husband suffered severe phantom pains from his amputated leg. She claimed Barbaro had trouble sleeping and kept others awake. He also needed help to shower. Barbaro tried to win the jury's sympathy by coming into court in a wheelchair. Barbaro's charade would have been laughed at in Griffith, where people often saw him walking with scarcely a limp on his way to the TAB in Banna Avenue. Fellow punters had also seen Barbaro half running and half hopping across the betting ring at Dalton Park to snap up generous odds of 2–1 on a 6–4 runner at Griffith races.

The NCA kept Barbaro under surveillance on the weekend before his conviction and during his sentencing. One afternoon, after being released early from court, they followed him to a motel near the Doomben racecourse. NCA video recordings showed Barbaro walking freely on a balcony, his walking stick resting over his forearm, speaking into a mobile telephone. Among the names on the guest register was 'Jennifer Jolliffe', the maiden name of Jennifer Sergi.

The Brisbane jury deliberated for a day and a half before finding him guilty. Barbaro was sentenced to eight years' jail, although Justice Moynihan recommended he be considered for parole in six months due to the ongoing health problems and complications he suffered from being an amputee.

■ ■ ■

It was nineteen years since the murder of Donald Mackay but despite all the trials and inquests and inquiries, nothing seemed to have changed. Mayors had come and gone, each one promising to change perceptions and restore the town's reputation for enterprise and honest toil, but the name 'Griffith' was still synonymous with marijuana, the mafia and murder. The town could not rewrite its history, although some tried.

Santa Portolesi never missed an opportunity to portray her father, Domenico Sergi, as a hero—to her, to his children, his grandchildren, nephews and nieces. In September 1996 Santa proposed her father as a subject for John Laws's annual 'Keeping the Dream Alive' calendar. Domenico's picture was included in the 1997 calendar, one of twelve chosen from 3000 entries. The *Area News* reported the news under the headline, 'Santa's dad part of Laws calendar'.

Jones wasn't the only reader who felt uncomfortable seeing the paper's adulatory story about 'Griffith peach farmer Domenico Sergi'. It was no secret that Sergi had been mentioned in Justice Woodward's report in connection with a 'laundering operation' involving Winery Tony. Like many other citizens, Jones wanted to look to the future, but not if it meant whitewashing the past.

■ ■ ■

On 29 January 1997 Jones was astonished to read a story on the front page of the *Area News* headlined 'High honours for father, son'. In recognition of his work for 'the sick, elderly and financially stricken', Griffith had made Domenico Sergi its Citizen of the Year. Sergi's son, Pat, had received an Order of Australia medal for his service to the Spastic Centre of New South Wales.

It struck Jones at once that the story carried no byline—often, in Jones's experience, the sign of a story that no journalist wanted to be seen to have written. He also noted the story's failure to make even a cursory reference to the Woodward Royal Commission, which in its final report had named Pat Sergi and his brother, Antonio (born 25 September 1944), as money-launderers for La Famiglia. Pat, a real estate agent, admitted to 'finding' properties that were bought with money supplied by Trimbole. Woodward found that Antonio had acted as a 'dummy' for Winery Tony in business transactions and that both brothers had 'acted in concert with Trimbole'.

Nor did the front-page story in the *Area News* mention John Hatton's address to the New South Wales Parliament in 1990, in which he denounced the mafia bosses. A series of photographs, passed by Hatton to the New South Wales police and the National Crime Authority, showed both Domenico and Pat Sergi in the company of the controversial judge John Foord and a number of prominent drug traffickers.

As Domenico Sergi accepted his award his daughter, Santa Portolesi, described him as 'Little Red Riding Hood'. She said her father 'always has a basket full of goodies, but instead of going to grandma's house, he goes to the homes of the needy, up to the hospital to visit the elderly and sick people ... my father would feed the whole world if he could—he is simply the best'.

There was no denying that Domenico and Pat Sergi had been energetic fundraisers for the Spastic Centre (now renamed the Cerebral Palsy Alliance) in Sydney. Congenital childhood birth defects were a subject close to the hearts of many of Griffith's Calabrian families. Regular intermarriage in Italy, and then among families migrating to Australia, had made the Calabrian community especially susceptible to genetic defects. Many Calabrian baby boys and girls had been born with birth defects that required specialist attention at the Spastic Centre. As young men and women, some had grown up with stunted limbs and visible growth deficiencies. In the largest Calabrian families, intermarriage between close blood relatives was also believed to have contributed to the early onset of psychiatric conditions.

Many of the citizens who attended Griffith's Australia Day awards ceremony in 1997 walked away in dismay.

In their eyes no amount of community work or visits to the elderly and sick could absolve Domenico Sergi and his son Pat of their links to the men named by Woodward as 'influential members' of the organisation that ordered Don Mackay's murder.

■ ■ ■

Not everyone was as willing to forgive and forget as the men and women who chose Domenico Sergi as Griffith's Citizen of the Year. In May 2002 Antonio 'Tony' Romeo was released from a prison work farm at Shepparton in Victoria after serving eight years on drug charges. Six weeks later he was shot dead as he pruned peach trees in his family's vineyard at Hanwood. Around 30 people had been working in the vineyard when Romeo was shot once in the back but none of them saw the assailant. Romeo was said to have 'collapsed with a groan'.

A white Toyota Prado that police suspected of being connected to the murder was stolen from a Griffith address on the day Romeo was released from prison, leading police to suspect that the hit had been planned well in advance. Five hours after Romeo was shot dead, the Prado was found dumped and set alight in a paddock 50 kilometres from Griffith.

The media had two theories about the shooting: it was payback for Romeo's alleged affair with Jennifer Sergi, or punishment for allowing undercover police to infiltrate the organisation's activities. The foiled cannabis importation had been a costly and humiliating setback for La Famiglia. Someone had to pay the price.

Six years passed before the coroner held an inquest into Tony Romeo's death. Many in Griffith were surprised that it took place not at the local courthouse but hundreds of kilometres away at the Glebe Coroner's Court in Sydney.

At the hearing before Coroner Mary Jerram, the officer in charge of the investigation, Detective Sergeant Egene Stek, cited Romeo's affair with Jennifer Sergi as a likely reason for his murder. Witnesses had told police that Giovanni 'Johnny' Sergi believed people in Italy would not talk to him until he 'saved face' by taking vengeance on Romeo. One witness, who could not be named for legal reasons, told police that Sergi had visited Romeo in mid-2002 to inform him he would have to take a 'scratch' to his leg 'the same as Roy [Rocco Barbaro]'. A scared Romeo was given a month to think about the proposal, the witness told police. Romeo was said to have told at least one person that he 'had to be shot to make someone happy'.

In his statement to the court, Detective Sergeant Eugene Stek said it was 'highly probable that Giovanni Sergi instructed persons unknown to kneecap the deceased and these persons murdered the deceased'.

Police alleged that on the night Romeo was shot, Giovanni Sergi and his son 'Young Tony' Sergi visited Romeo's mother, Elizabeth. A witness claimed to have heard Romeo's mother scream and Giovanni say in Italian: 'They said they were going to do one thing and they done another.' After this, Romeo's mother threw him out of her home.

But the police now had a more compelling theory: that Pasquale 'Pat' Barbaro—whose father, 'Little Trees', was the head of the organised crime family—had used the allegations of an affair with Young Tony's wife as a ruse to eliminate Romeo, who was establishing himself as a rival drug dealer.

The Barbaro family was reported to have put pressure on the Sergis to inflict more severe retribution on Romeo.

According to police intelligence a man nicknamed 'Bill the Blonde' was often used by members of the Barbaro and Sergi families for drug business and to carry out shootings. Police alleged that 'Bill the Blonde' had a long criminal history and was a regular visitor to Griffith. He was said to have links to Tyreworld in Griffith, the source of the stolen white Land-Cruiser that police believed was connected to the murder. Neither Giovanni Sergi nor Pasquale Barbaro had an opportunity to answer the allegations made at the inquest, and neither would ever be charged over the shooting.

In the absence of witnesses prepared to identify the killer, who was believed to have shot Romeo from a range of between 100 and 300 metres, the coroner, Mary Jerram, returned a verdict of homicide by a person or persons unknown. Asked by Romeo's widow, Maria, whether the inquest would be the end of the matter, Ms Jerram replied, 'unsolved homicide cases are never closed'.

The assassination of Antonio 'Tony' Romeo thus joined a list of unsolved killings linked to La Famiglia in Griffith that already included the murders of Romeo's brother-in-law Angelo Licastro; Rocco Medici; Frank Furina; Nunzio Greco (an alleged money launderer and marijuana grower); and Gordon Thompson (a suspected drug distributor who lived in Griffith and was murdered in Shepparton, Victoria).

■ ■ ■

As for Donald Mackay, the three men found guilty of conspiring to murder him had long since been released from jail; nobody had ever been charged with Mackay's murder and his body had never been found. All efforts to persuade the convicted hitman James Frederick Bazley, now in his eighties, to come clean and reveal the whereabouts of Mackay's body had failed.

On 13 July 2012, almost 35 years to the day since the murder, the New South Wales government announced a $200,000 reward for information leading to the discovery of Don Mackay's final resting place. The Griffith police commander, Superintendent Michael Rowan, said he was 'confident' a number of people still living in Griffith knew where Mackay's remains had been dumped and urged them to come forward 'anonymously if needed'. Community leaders, including the Member for Murrumbidgee, Adrian Piccoli, welcomed the news, as did members of the Mackay family, but it came too late for Barbara, who had died in 2001 still not knowing the truth about her husband's murder.

The reward was immediately denounced by John Jiggens, whose book *The Killer Cop and the Murder of Donald Mackay* put forward the implausible theory that Mackay had been killed by Fred Krahe and the Nugans. The main source for Jiggens's book was the Mackay family's solicitor, Ian Salmon. After the *Area News* published a story about Jiggens, three people contacted him to discuss his killer cop theory. One of them was Terry Jones. Retired from his job with *The Land* but still hard at work on 'The Griffith Diaries', Jones had never believed that Krahe was involved in the murder. Soon after speaking to Jiggens, Jones began receiving emails in which Jiggens mentioned a mysterious 'Witness X' who, he claimed, was about to blow the Mackay murder case wide open.

For nearly two years nothing happened. Jiggens continued to email Jones, telling him that 'Witness X' was his scoop 'just as you have your scoops'. Jones learnt that either Jiggens or Salmon had decided to write a sequel to *The Killer Cop*.

In early April 2014 Jiggens told the *Area News* about 'Witness X', without naming him. It seemed that Jiggens's prediction was about to come true. On 8 or 9 April 2014 Terry Jones received a phone call from his friend Bob Heffernan. Heffernan had been talking to a mutual friend, former constable Ian Fletcher, who had been stationed in Griffith at the time Mackay was murdered. (It was Fletcher who had warned Jones to watch his back before the staged 'random' breath test.) He told Jones that Fletcher was anxious to talk to him.

'He's in Bathurst now,' said Heffernan. 'I think you need to get in touch.'

'What about?' asked Jones.

'Fletch says there was an eye-witness to Mackay's murder—a young bloke who was in the car park at the Griff Hotel and saw what happened.'

'That's old news,' said Jones. 'It was a man named Peter Marcus. He gave a statement.'

A startled Heffernan replied: 'That's the name Fletch gave me—Peter Marcus, a kid in his twenties. He claims he saw it all.'

'No, Bob,' said Jones. 'Peter Marcus wasn't a kid. He was in his forties. I knew him. We've spoken about it.'

'You've got it wrong, Jonesy,' said Heffernan. 'This was definitely a young lad. He was in the bottle shop buying bottles of wine when Don Mackay came in for a cask. He witnessed what happened in the car park, told family and friends. There were a couple of old coppers in the car park, Fletch mentioned some names. Ring him, Jonesy. There could be something in it for that book you're writing.'

It dawned on Jones that the public record had been wrong: it wasn't 'Uncle Peter' Marcus who had spoken to

Don Mackay in the bottle shop; it was his nephew, 'Little Pete' Marcus.

Jones contacted another friend, Roy Goslett, a retired fruiterer and owner of Griffith's Central Butchery, who knew the Marcus family. It seemed that Little Pete had attended primary school in Griffith before being sent to a boarding school in Orange. After returning to Griffith, he had done odd jobs on the family farm. A keen athlete, Little Pete was often seen jogging around Scenic Hill—a pastime he shared with Don Mackay. But running was not his only interest. As a young man, Little Pete dabbled in marijuana and was familiar with the drug scene in Griffith—familiar enough to be terrified of being identified as a witness to Don Mackay's murder.

Through Goslett, Jones tracked down Little Pete's brother, Phil, and his wife, Penne, who were now living on the north coast. Penne had been following the Mackay case for 35 years and had kept old newspaper clippings, just like Jones. In 1977 she and Phil had lived in Griffith. They knew what Little Pete had seen but they always believed it was up to him whether he gave a statement to the police or not.

Gradually Jones pieced together the details of what Little Pete had seen and done on the night of 15 July 1977. Don Mackay bought a cask of wine, exchanged a few words with Little Pete in the bottle shop and then walked outside. After Pete had been served someone rushed up, pushed him back into the bottle shop and kept going. Pete heard three shots. He saw three or four men and a white car. They were close to Mackay's furniture van. A couple looked familiar. After the shots and a scuffle the men bundled Mackay's body into the white car, then jumped in and sped off.

Little Pete took off as fast as he could. He thought he'd been seen. He was sure the men in the car park knew who he was and would come after him. Pete went straight to the home of a family friend, a carpenter named Bruce Wilson, and hammered on the door, screaming to be let in. He told Wilson, 'they've just shot and killed Don Mackay in the "Griff" car park . . . I think they saw me.'

Wilson tried to calm him down. He suggested they call Fletcher but Pete was too scared. 'We can't go to the cops,' he said. 'They were there.'

Pete stayed at Wilson's place until daylight, then raced home to the family farm, locked the gates, let the dogs out and got a gun. He was convinced that the men who had killed Mackay would be looking for him.

The morning after the murder Griffith was a town in turmoil. Little Pete Marcus fled, as far and as fast as he could. Wilson told the whole story to Constable Fletcher, who urged him to tell Joe Parrington. Fletcher knew and liked the Marcus family. They drank with the local police at the Irrigana Hotel. If they needed someone to drive a wheat truck on the farm, there was always an off-duty cop happy to put his hand up. Fletcher heard that Little Pete plucked up courage to tell the police and went to the police station, but while he was standing outside he saw a man inside the station who had been at the Griffith Hotel when Mackay was killed. When Little Pete asked who the man was, he was told he was an 'undercover policeman'. Hearing that, Pete turned and ran—and hadn't stopped for the next 30 years.

According to Fletcher, the carpenter Bruce Wilson told Joe Parrington about Little Pete and Parrington had tracked him down to somewhere in Papua New Guinea. But there was no record of Wilson or Little Pete giving a statement to Parrington or giving evidence to Justice Woodward. Jones wondered whether it could be another case of Parrington withholding evidence, as he had in Pursehouse's case.

And what of 'Uncle Peter' Marcus? In order to protect Little Pete, Uncle Peter had put himself forward as the witness in the bottle shop, even though he wasn't there. Uncle Peter had given evidence at both the Woodward Royal Commission and the coroner's inquest. If Joe Parrington had spoken to Wilson, he would have known that it was Little Pete who was there and that Uncle Peter had given false statements and committed perjury.

Peter Marcus and Terry Jones had been good friends. Marcus was a hard-working farmer and a good horseman who used to act as ringmaster at the annual Griffith Show. After giving evidence at the coroner's inquest, Marcus had approached Jones outside the Griffith courthouse and asked him not to publish the fact that he was the 'last man to see Don Mackay alive'. When Jones asked why, Marcus had replied that he was frightened someone might put two and two together and think he'd seen who killed Don Mackay. Marcus had told Jones he'd feel safer if his evidence was not put into print. Jones had pictures of every witness who appeared at the inquest but he let Marcus have his photograph back.

Jones's view at the time was that Marcus's evidence was not very significant—he could not even remember whether the hotel car park lights were on or not. Now it all made sense: Uncle Peter's evidence had been vague because he was making it up.

All that remained was to contact Little Pete—something of a misnomer for a man now in his sixties. It was an awkward conversation. Pete was still worried that his phone might be bugged and that his life and those of his wife and children were in danger. But he confirmed that it was him, not his uncle, who was in the bottle shop on the night Don Mackay was killed. He sounded surprised, even horrified, to learn that Uncle Peter had spent all these years covering up. 'I can't believe it,' he told Jones. 'He wasn't even there!'

If Jones had been hoping for any more revelations, he was disappointed. After 37 years, Pete could no longer distinguish between what he had seen and what he had told people he'd seen. He admitted having spoken to Parrington and claimed to have given a statement to Fred Krahe, the rogue Sydney detective who had retired from the force and was working as a heavy for Ken Nugan. Jones wasn't sure whether to believe Marcus or not. It was the story of the Mackay case: solving one mystery only led to another.

If Jones felt betrayed, it was by Uncle Peter Marcus, not Little Pete. Uncle Peter's false evidence had stood in the way of police investigating what Little Pete had seen, especially the identities of the men in the car park. The Mackay investigation had been fatally compromised from the moment it began. Joe Parrington never really stood a chance.

CHAPTER 20

Blackmail

Arrests in Queensland, Victoria and South Australia involving the second and third generation sons of the original commercial cannabis growers of the 1970s proved that Griffith remained close to the epicentre of La Famiglia in Australia. Frank 'Little Trees' Barbaro's son Pasquale, who had been sentenced to ten and a half years' jail for his part in the $40 million marijuana crop at Moulamein, was convicted in 2015 of conspiring to traffic 4.4 tonnes of ecstasy, trafficking 1.2 million ecstasy tablets and attempting to possess 150 kilograms of cocaine. This time he was sentenced to life. Barbaro's cousin and co-conspirator, Saverio 'Baldy' Zirilli, also of Griffith, was sentenced to 26 years. Altogether more than 30 gang members were jailed for a total of nearly 300 years.

It seemed that Griffith could never break free of its criminal past. Those on the council who believed that the slate could be wiped clean by making a man like Domenico

Sergi 'Citizen of the Year' were deluding themselves. La Famiglia would never change, but future generations would grow smarter, greedier, more ambitious; the money trail would be harder to follow.

More than half a century earlier, in response to an outbreak of mob violence in Melbourne that became known as the Victoria Market murders, the Victorian government enlisted the help of an American anti-mafia expert, John T. Cusack, a district supervisor in the US Bureau of Narcotics. Cusack's 1964 report was the first detailed assessment of Italian organised crime in Australia. 'The Calabrian L'Onorata Societa is well entrenched in Australia,' he wrote, and was active in 'extortion, prostitution, counterfeiting, sly grog, breaking and entering, illegal gambling and the smuggling of aliens and small arms'. If unchecked, the society was 'capable of diversification into all facets of organised crime and legitimate business'.

In his report Justice Woodward noted that Antonio Sergi's winery, then called House of Sergi Winery, appeared 'to have been financed with cash funds from unknown sources' and commented that 'Aussie Bob' Trimbole had 'loaned' Sergi more than $350,000 cash that was 'used in the Winery operations and construction' and never repaid. The winery, since renamed Warburn Estate, sold a range of wines under the names 'Gossips' ('The wine on everyone's lips') and 'Rumours' ('A mix of truths and untruths that are happily shared')—names that were interpreted by some as a joke at Woodward's expense.

Afterword

Griffith is not a mafia town, although the mafia has been there for nearly a century. After the failure of many pioneer farms, it was hard-working Italian migrants who put Griffith on its feet. Rows of black marble headstones in the town's cemetery testify to the Italian labour and enterprise that helped make Griffith wealthy. Some of those headstones belong to members of L'Onorata Societa. As in its native Calabria, the organisation's power lies not in its size but in its ruthlessness. The mafia has never hesitated to use violence to protect its criminal interests.

Don Mackay was killed for his determination to take on the marijuana growers and change Australia's outdated drug laws. After Don's murder, the Concerned Citizens of Griffith took up the battle. Unrelenting pressure from the group led to inquests and royal commissions; forced the federal government to sign extradition treaties and revise deportation laws; and was instrumental in establishing the National Crime Authority and the Australian Crime Commission. Don's courage will not be forgotten. The Don Mackay monument, put up by the combined Rotary Clubs of Griffith, greets every visitor driving into the town along Banna Avenue.

A decade after Don's murder, on 19 March 1987, the Chief Commissioner of the New South Wales Police, John Avery, visited Griffith to launch the Donald Mackay Churchill

Fellowship. The aim of the fellowship was to enable researchers to study methods of investigating organised crime. Sitting beside Commissioner Avery was the mayor, John Dal Broi, who pledged a contribution from the Griffith Shire Council to fund the fellowship. Avery said it was 'an honour' to be launching what he called 'one of the most dynamically relevant memorials ever conceived to honour an individual'.

The commissioner went on, 'Although unaware of it, Donald Mackay, and the standards he represented, were the catalyst of an organisation called the Concerned Citizens of Griffith . . . Donald Mackay was not just an innocent victim tragically struck down by a criminal act. He was a casualty of the actual fight against organised crime . . . killed on active service, as it were . . . The man, as well as his wife and family through their consequent actions have become an ineradicable part of Australian history. His name should never be forgotten, his passing must not be allowed to be in vain. The story of Donald Bruce Mackay has focused national attention not only upon the loss of a decent and honest citizen, but also the sinister effect that organised crime is having on this country.'

The fellowship, Commissioner Avery said, would 'act as a perpetual tribute both to Donald Mackay and the Concerned Citizens of Griffith, who have decided to take positive steps to resist the intrusion of organised crime into their community'.

Emphasising the 'ethical and moral responsibility' of people of all professions to deter organised crime, Commissioner Avery drew special attention to the role of the media and, in particular, investigative journalists. 'In short,' Avery said, 'we, the community, must pursue every avenue available in our efforts against organised crime to complement the [police] activities ... We need information, we need knowledge, we need research to do battle with the vicious and rapacious criminals who are masterminds of organised crime in this country.'

Griffith has grown rich on its wineries and citrus orchards. The region now produces 90 per cent of Australia's rice. There is a tendency to play down the past, to forget the years when much of the money washing through Griffith was drug money. That is why I started writing 'The Griffith Diaries'. Those diaries now comprise numerous files of archival documents and photographs and more than 1.5 million words of commentary.

I always hoped others would share my vision of a museum of local history or an archive within the Griffith library. The archive would include bound volumes of the commissions of inquiry; Hansard records of torrid debates in the New South Wales Parliament that led to the long-awaited 'Mackay laws' against drug growers and traffickers; and hundreds of press photographs taken during my years as editor of the *Area News*. It would be an invaluable resource for historians and scholars, as well as for citizens of Griffith too young to know what it was like to live through the turbulent decades after the murder of Don Mackay.

On 16 May 2013 I rang my old friend John Dal Broi, the current mayor of Griffith, to ask for the council's support in finding a permanent home for 'The Griffith Diaries'. He made it clear that he was not keen on the idea. I continued writing 'The Griffith Diaries', hoping the council would change its mind.

In an official letter dated 9 February 2016, Dal Broi told me that Griffith would continue to honour citizens such as Don Mackay for their efforts to stamp out 'criminal activity in any form'. In case I had forgotten, he reminded me that a bust of Donald Mackay was 'proudly mounted' at the intersection of Banna Avenue and Jondaryan Avenue. (The Mackay statue notes that Don was 'callously murdered' but does not mention the mafia.) After listing a number of development works being planned for the town, Dal Broi informed me that 'your suggestion of the construction of a "Griffith Justice Museum" is not one of these works'.

My correspondence with Mayor Dal Broi and the Griffith City Council ended with an email in which Dal Broi said he had canvassed the idea of a justice museum with 'Griffith councillors, leading citizens and the general community' and found 'very little support for such a facility'. In his view the matter was now closed.

I was disappointed but not surprised. I'm sure the council wishes it could wipe the 'four Ms'—'mafia, murder, marijuana and Mackay'—from the story of Griffith's first hundred years. Whitewashing the past would also suit the mafia, whose members would surely like nothing better than to erase all public record of their crimes.

At the ceremony to unveil the Don Mackay monument in October 2008, Don's son Paul held up a copy of the front page of the *Area News* from 7 November 1979. It named the six men Justice Woodward identified as conspiring to murder his father. 'Recent drug busts suggest it is business as usual in the Griffith underworld,' said Paul Mackay. 'The town's reputation as a drug capital will unfortunately continue for another generation.'

In February 2017 three men were charged over a $5.5 million cannabis crop on a farm at Colinroobie, about 70 kilometres east of Griffith. Has Griffith's past become its future?

Terry Jones
June 2017